THE FEDERAL
GOVERNMENT SERVICE

 The American Assembly, *Columbia University*

THE FEDERAL
GOVERNMENT SERVICE

Prentice-Hall, Inc., *Englewood Cliffs, N. J.* A SPECTRUM BOOK

Preface

This second edition of *The Federal Government Service* was revised under the supervision of the original editor, Wallace S. Sayre of Columbia University. The first edition, published in 1954, served as source material for participants in the Sixth American Assembly at Arden House, Harriman, New York. Both editions were also intended for general readership.

The chapters in this volume reflect the individual opinions of the authors and not of The American Assembly, which takes no official position, or of the Ford Foundation, whose generosity helped make the Sixth American Assembly possible.

Clifford C. Nelson
President
The American Assembly

Table of Contents

THE FEDERAL
GOVERNMENT SERVICE

Wallace S. Sayre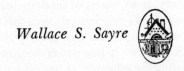

Introduction

Dilemmas and Prospects of the Federal Government Service

The years that have elapsed since the first edition of this volume was prepared in 1954 for the Sixth American Assembly have served to demonstrate how durable are the problems then discussed. Although the author of each of the five essays that follow has thoroughly revised his presentation to take into account all relevant changes, no major issue is found to have been fully resolved. Some of the contours have been modified, and the priorities of concern have been somewhat altered. But the eventful decade has in the main reconfirmed the continuing dilemmas.

The Power of the Bureaucracy

Americans in the 1960s are properly concerned with the size and power of the federal government service. This relatively new phe-

WALLACE S. SAYRE *is Eaton Professor of Public Administration and chairman of the Department of Public Law and Government at Columbia University. In addition to teaching posts held at New York University, City College of New York, Stanford, California (Berkeley), and Cornell University, he has also served as a public official in the capacities of New York City Civil Service Commissioner, Director of Personnel: Office of Price Administration, and a consultant to federal, state, and local governmental agencies. He is the author of several works on public administration and politics, including* Governing New York City *(with Herbert Kaufman).*

nomenon, accelerated in its development in the second quarter of this century, is an aspect of modern life in the United States not likely to be changed. We are indeed confronted with the hard fact that the federal government service has great power that will more probably increase than decline. It has power because of its size, which makes traditional controls less effective. It has power because of its variety and complexity, another factor which makes leadership and control more difficult, perhaps in geometric progression. But more fundamentally the federal government service has power because it is inescapably and influentially involved both in the making and in the execution of public policy.

The staffs of the executive branch agencies have come to exercise an important share of the initiative, the formulation, the bargaining, and the deciding in the process by which governmental decisions are taken. They are widely acknowledged to be leading "experts" as to the facts upon which issues are to be settled; they are often permitted to identify authoritatively the broad alternatives available as solutions; and they frequently are allowed to fix the vocabulary of the formal decision. These powers are shared and used by the career staffs in an environment of struggle and competition for influence, but the relatively new fact to be noted with emphasis is that the others who share the powers of decision —the President, Congress, the political executives, the congressional committees and staffs, the interest groups, the communication media—now rarely question the legitimacy of the career staff spokesmen as major participants in the competition.

Great power also belongs naturally to those who carry out decisions of public policy. In this stage, the career staffs have a paramount role. The choice of means, the pace and tone of governmental performance, reside largely in the hands of the federal government service. Constraints are present, and most of these uses of discretion by the career staffs are subject to bargaining with other participants, but the civil servants have a position of distinct advantage in determining how public policies are executed.

The System of Control

The civil service reformers have had a simple and attractive answer to the problem of democratic control over the burgeoning bureaucracy. A competent civil service, they have argued, once freed from bondage to the party leaders, would become a neutral instrument to carry out the policy directions of the elected officials. For a small nineteenth-century civil service engaged in routine performance, rather than the large and complex twentieth-century bureaucracies exercising great discretionary power in major policy matters, the reformers had an oversimplified but workable answer. But yesterday's solutions often become today's problems, and so it is in today's management of the federal government service. Accordingly, the root dilemma with which the essays in this volume deal is still the same as it was in 1954:

> How can we combine, in the federal government service, high competence and motivation with a system of control that insures the responsiveness and responsibility essential to a democratic society?

PRESIDENTIAL LEADERSHIP

Since the 1937 Report of the President's Committee on Administrative Management there has been a sustained emphasis upon the values of presidential leadership in the direction and control of the career staffs. These views were reaffirmed by the Hoover Commission Reports of 1949 and 1955, and have been underscored in an important series of Executive Orders issued by Presidents Roosevelt, Truman, Eisenhower, and Kennedy. But the problems represented by the autonomous inclinations of a skilled and self-confident bureaucracy have been relatively impervious to such diagnoses and remedies.

The new instruments and powers given to Presidents for their use in exercising leadership and control over the federal government service have at best enabled them no more than to hold their own as their task has expanded. In the personnel field there has been no invention of a presidential leadership instrument as effective as the executive budget established in 1921 by the Budget and Accounting Act, nor does any such presidential opportunity now seem imminent. Instead, the fundamental rearrangements of federal personnel management required for a presidential hegemony in the personnel process comparable to his resources in the budget process appear today to be as distant and as difficult to achieve as such proposals were more than twenty-five years ago.

CONGRESSIONAL OVERSIGHT

Congress has shared with Presidents in the twentieth century both the urge and the difficulty of supervising the expanding career bureaucracies. If, as some observers have asserted, Congress in recent decades has compensated for its loss of initiative in policy proposals by shifting its attention to the administrative oversight of the executive agencies, the experiment has not lacked considerable frustrations for Congress in personnel matters.

Congressional aspirations to influence the shape of the federal government service and to guide and constrain the uses of power by the career staffs are supported by a number of resources. Statutory detail in the personnel process greatly exceeds that in the budget process, for example; and congressional committees, subcommittees, and their staffs often achieve a satisfying intimacy with bureau career staffs that brings committee influence to a high level. But these accomplishments, whether in the detailed terms of personnel statutes or in the particularistic victories of committees, serve more often to weaken presidential discipline over the bureaus than to give Congress a system of comprehensive control over the bureaucracy. That is to say, the absence of a combined and mutually supporting plan between President and Congress to supervise the federal government service places the two in competition with each other, while the bureaucracies find in that competition increased opportunities for their own autonomy.

PARTIES AND PATRONAGE

Almost a century of civil service reform has reduced the political party role in the federal government service to anemia and ambiguity. In the earlier decades of reform the debate centered on the scope and uses of patronage to sustain and nurture the party system. In recent years a more sophisticated issue has been emphasized: the number and hierarchical location of the positions needed by the victorious party in a presidential election if it is to "govern" the executive branch. The reformers (supported today by their more powerful allies, the bureaucracies) hold to their implicit goal of an executive branch in which patronage would closely approach zero (a goal toward which we have now come more than nine-tenths of the way).

In this increasingly one-sided debate, the spokesmen for patronage to sustain the parties have failed to make their arguments in persuasive form. The actual functions of patronage remain clouded in dispute: does it strengthen state and local party organizations in their tendencies to resist national party organs? Whose party leadership is strengthened by patronage—that of members of Congress (mutually centered with local party leaders in the states and districts) or that of the President? The consequence of this ambiguity of function is that patronage has lost most of its legitimacy. Similarly, the claim for positions essential to governance by the administration which has won the Presidency has failed to achieve articulation in compelling form; the question is debated at each party transition in the White House (e.g., 1953, 1961), but soon recedes. No sharp resolution of these two issues appears likely to reverse or retard the secular decline of the party role in the federal government service.

INTEREST GROUP INFLUENCE

The competition between President and Congress for leadership of the federal government service, and the decline of the political party organization from its once important leadership role, have opened up opportunities for the interest groups to assert their influence in the system of control. They have not been slow to do so. In concert with whichever ally seems most generously disposed—whether presidential, congressional, or bureaucratic—interest group leaders seek to shape the composition and guide the behavior of career staffs dealing with their interests. These efforts and achievements are most visible in the regulatory agencies but are by no measure limited to them. The instruments of influence are numerous and diverse—e.g., advisory committees, reciprocal staffing, continuous consultation, strategic rewards of public support, or penalties of reprisal—and they are in the main effective devices for the interest groups.

SELF-DIRECTING CAREER SERVICES

The doctrine of the neutral, impartial, and competent civil service, selected and promoted by objective standards of merit and protected in its tenure, has largely determined the style and strategy of the federal government service but has not adversely affected its power in the governmental system. And although the American national bureaucracy lacks the centralization and cohesion of its British and some of its European counterparts, and although it must exercise its influence in a more pluralistic system of power than they, it has nevertheless long since arrived at a sufficient level of autonomy in the system of control to possess a considerable capacity for self-direction.

In support of this enviable status of equality with the other participants in the control system, the career bureaucracies offer an effectively argued justification: their acknowledged competence, their commitment to a public service career, their recruitment from widely representative sectors of American society, their formal deference to law and to the

directives of elected officials, their use of objective professional standards
in the gathering and appraisal of data, and their apparent self-restraint
in the exercise of power. They thus convert their most admired group
characteristics into a bid for autonomy and for the use of that autonomy
in the exercise of power, much as Presidents, senators and congressmen,
party leaders, and interest group leaders make their respective claims.
Particularly in matters that affect personnel management (that is, their
own internal self-government), the bureaucracies have succeeded in
achieving levels of self-direction satisfying even to their own aspirations.

Elected Officials and Bureaucrats

Within the system of control described here the confrontation
of most significance is the effort of elected officials to assert their leadership over the career bureaucracies. Numbers give some clue to the nature
of that struggle: 435 congressmen, 100 senators, a President and Vice-
President—a total of 537 elected officials—confront 2½ million civil servants and 2½ million military personnel. Even if to the 537 elected officials are added the less than 1000 officials the President may ordinarily
appoint to supervisory posts and the approximately equal number of
assistants that members of Congress and the congressional committees
have on their staffs, the leadership assignment of the elected and closely
related officialdom still appears as an enormous, if not insuperable, task.
Many other qualifications must of course be made in this equation to
make it a realistic one. But these modifications will in some instances
cut both ways, and in sum the intractable aspects of the elected officials'
dilemmas will not be much diminished. The future of the federal government service thus involves questions at the center of democratic government.

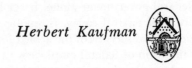

Herbert Kaufman

1

The Growth of the Federal Personnel System

A Profile of the Federal Civil Service

IT GREW IN SPURTS

When George Washington was inaugurated for his first term as President,* the population of the United States was about 3½ million—not

---

* While I have borrowed from many sources in the preparation of this paper, I have relied especially heavily on three: Carl Russell Fish, *The Civil Service and the Patronage* (Cambridge: Harvard University Press, 1920); United States Civil Service Commission, *History of the Federal Civil Service* (Washington, D.C.: U.S. Government Printing Office, 1941); and Paul P. Van Riper, *History of the United States Civil Service* (Evanston, Ill.: Row, Peterson and Co., 1958). Although the authors may not always agree with the use to which the data I borrowed so liberally have been put, I am nevertheless happy to confess the extent of my dependence upon them and to add my plaudits to those they have already received.

I should like to mention also my obligation to O. Glenn Stahl, especially for his *Public Personnel Administration* (New York: Harper and Brothers, 1963), Fifth Edition. I have consulted this encyclopedic work often and with great profit in the course of my writing, and have doubtless appropriated more of its contents than I know.

HERBERT KAUFMAN *is Professor and Chairman of the Department of Political Science at Yale University. He has worked in a number of federal, state, and municipal governmental agencies, and is co-author of* Personnel Administration in the Government of New York City *and of* Governing New York City. *He is the author of* The Forest Ranger: A Study in Administrative Behavior *and* Politics and Policies in State and Local Governments, *as well as several case studies in public administration.*

7

too much greater than the number of civilian workers now employed by
the federal government alone, fewer by far than all those on the federal
government payroll today, if among the latter are included the men in
the uniformed services of the armed forces.

If the ratio of federal employees to total population in those days had
been what it has been in recent times (in 1963, for example, 2½ million
civil servants constituted 1.3 per cent of our 190 million people), there
would have been about 45,000 on the payrolls. As a matter of fact, however, the federal government service then numbered in the hundreds
rather than in the thousands; there were about 350 people in it at the
start of Washington's administration, and only about 2,100 as late as
1801. The public service has increased in size far more rapidly than the
general population.

It was not a steady, orderly growth; it occurred in spasms of expansion
and contraction, in fits and starts. It started modestly enough. As late
as 1861, the year of the start of the Civil War, the total civil service consisted of 49,000 employees (less than two-tenths of one per cent of the
population, which had meanwhile risen to 31 million), and it comprised
only 208,000 at the turn of the century (while the population had reached
76 million, so that the ratio was still less than three-tenths of one per
cent). In the twentieth century, however, federal employment increased
more rapidly—it had reached 435,000 when World War I broke out;
515,000 in 1923; 572,000 in 1933; and 920,000 in 1939, when it constituted seven-tenths of one per cent of the population of 130 million.

Then the number of civil servants shot upwards under the impact of
World War II; by war's end in 1945, it stood at 3¾ million. The figure
declined with the cessation of combat, but government employment was
never again to fall back to the pre-World War II levels. Even in June
of 1950, the month of the North Korean invasion of South Korea, it
was almost two million. The Korean War brought it back up to more
than 2,600,000, but even after the end of that action the number of government personnel has never again dropped below 2,300,000. The figure
has risen gradually in more recent years and now exceeds 2½ million.

Perhaps the most striking fact in this brief historical sketch is that
three-quarters of the positions in the federal government service today
were established and filled in the last 30 years!

Why has this happened? Clearly, the increase in population, though a
factor, is by no means sufficient to explain it.

For the answer, merely consider some of the existing younger agencies of government. The Federal Communications Commission, for example. The Civil Aeronautics Board. The Federal Aviation Agency. The National Aeronautics and Space Administration. The Atomic Energy Commission. The National Science Foundation. The Office of Science and Technology. All of these—and the list is not exhaustive—were forced into existence by technological change.

Take the Department of Defense. The Veterans Administration. The Selective Service System. The Foreign Claims Settlement Commission. The Agency for International Development. The Central Intelligence Agency. The Office of Emergency Planning. The Peace Corps. The U.S. Information Agency. The Arms Control and Disarmament Agency. These were imposed by the conduct of war, the consequences of war, the threat of war, the "cold war."

Look at the Federal Deposit Insurance Corporation. The Department of Health, Education, and Welfare. The Housing and Home Finance Agency. The Securities and Exchange Commission. The National Labor Relations Board. The Farm Credit Administration. The Small Business Administration. These, and many other units in the old-line departments, were brought into being by economic crisis and hardship.

These are some of the reasons the civil service grew so large so suddenly.

ITS FUNCTIONS

The reasons for the recent increase in the civil service are even more apparent from the way government workers were divided among the agencies of the federal government. In 1964, 41 per cent of them worked for the Department of Defense. (This does not include uniformed personnel; it includes only civilians who man the shipyards of the Navy, the arsenals and ordnance plants and factories of the Army and Air Force, and who see that soldiers, sailors, airmen, and marines get their paychecks, that the proper allotments are sent to their dependents, that their records are kept up to date, and a thousand and one other things.) Another 23 per cent worked for the Post Office. An additional seven per cent were in the employ of the Veterans Administration. (They run hospitals for disabled veterans. They operate a huge insurance system. They help veterans get through school, get started in business, get established in homes.)

Pause here for a moment. Three agencies accounted for 71 per cent of all federal personnel and for most of the growth in recent years. Before World War II, the Veterans Administration was about one-sixth its post-war size (there were 13 million veterans of that war, millions more from the Korean War, thousands more completing their terms of military service every year, and a GI Bill of Rights that did not exist before 1944 to be administered). Even the Post Office's work force more than doubled (from 270,000 to over 580,000) between 1934 and 1964. In these three organizations—the Department of Defense, the Veterans Administration, and the Post Office—worked all but 29 per cent of the federal civil servants, and all three increased enormously in size almost overnight.

What did the other 29 per cent do? Everything else the United States Government does. There were 86,000 in the Treasury Department who printed its paper money and stamps, minted its coins, collected its taxes and customs, manned the Coast Guard, controlled narcotics, and handled the records on United States Government Bonds. About 116,000 worked in the Department of Agriculture, providing technical advice, service, and financial assistance to the nation's farmers; managing 180 million acres of national forests; operating crop insurance programs; promoting soil conservation; and conducting research. In the Commerce Department, 32,000 performed the work of the Civil Aeronautics Administration, the Coast and Geodetic Survey, the Census Bureau, the Bureau of Standards, the Weather Bureau, and the Patent Office. The Department of the Interior employed 72,000 to revitalize unproductive land, run a vast system of national parks, administer grazing permits on the public domain, and generally manage the remainder of the public domain. It took 81,000 in the Department of Health, Education, and Welfare to run the social security system, the Public Health Service, and the Food and Drug Administration, to name a few of its components. There were 32,000 in the Department of Justice enforcing federal law, including the famed FBI. That much-maligned child of scorn, the State Department, had 42,000 employees maintaining posts in every corner of the world. These seven departments, together, had about 464,000 civil servants— about 18 per cent of the total.

Ten agencies, in sum, employed almost 90 per cent of all those on the federal civilian payrolls in 1964. The remaining ten per cent staffed a total of 45 agencies—the Bureau of the Budget, the Department of Labor, the Panama Canal Zone Government, the Export-Import Bank, the General Services Administration, the Interstate Commerce Commission, the Federal Reserve System, the Securities and Exchange Commission, the

Panama Canal Company, the United States Information Agency, and three dozen others.

SOME COMMON MISCONCEPTIONS ABOUT THE CIVIL SERVICE

This review of the functions performed by civil servants suggests the inaccuracy of the common stereotype of "the bureaucrat." There is no "typical government employee," for the civil service is but little less diversified than society itself. Every sort of work, every type of skill, every level of technical and professional specialization is represented. Included, in 1964, for example, were not only the tens of thousands of lawyers, accountants, and administrative specialists of whom everyone knows, but literally thousands of engineers, doctors, dentists, nurses, biological and physical and social scientists, mathematicians, statisticians, librarians, archivists, veterinaries, and many others. And some 900,000 employees were blue-collar workers—in shipyards, arsenals, ordnance plants, and other industrial installations maintained by the armed forces, and in crafts, custodial, and protective positions to operate, maintain, and guard the physical properties of the vast federal establishment.

Nor is the civil service concentrated in Washington. After World War II, only about ten per cent could be found in the capital in any average year. The vast majority (about 84 per cent) were dispersed throughout the fifty states, another five per cent or so in duty stations all over the world, and the remainder in territories and possessions of the United States.

It is also untrue that once people enter the federal service, they never leave it. On the contrary, the rate of turnover has almost always been a major source of concern to federal personnel managers, even though the separation and quit rates are lower for the federal government than for industry. Separations have varied considerably over the years, but rarely have dropped below 400,000 in any year after World War II, or from one-sixth to as high as one-fourth of the total work force. Many of the separations were voluntary, and many more were from temporary positions. But discharges for cause invariably exceeded 10,000 a year, and reductions in force and other involuntary departures accounted for up to four times this number in addition. This does not mean there are huge opportunities for patronage, it will be seen later, but it does explode the myth that the civil service is a single, vast, unchanging, permanent group.

In short, heterogeneity, dispersion, and change have always been the essence of the federal government service. Indeed, only in the loosest sense is it a single civil service at all; in another sense, it becomes a collection of civil services, divided by loyalties to occupation, to area, to agency, to program. But whatever feature may mark any of its subdivisions, they all have one element in common: they are part of the government, and therefore fated to serve from the start as battlegrounds for the partisans of different parties, different branches of the government, different ideologies, different political programs, and different concepts of administration. The federal personnel system never escapes this destiny; in this context it was born, grew, and acquired the characteristics that became its distinctive traits.

The Stable Years (*1789-1829*)

Many an executive, private as well as public, in small organizations as well as large, has probably wished at one time or another that he were in a position to build his organization from scratch, to wipe the slate clean and start again from the very beginning.

At such moments, these executives might envy George Washington's situation when he became Chief Executive of the newly formed federal union in 1789. For Washington had an opportunity that has come to none of his successors in office: he could construct a public service from the ground up; there was no going organization to hamper him. The civil service of the Confederate Government under the Articles of Confederation had been small, and what there was of it was automatically returned to private life as soon as the new government was established. The first President had no holdovers in a legal sense. As a matter of fact, not only *could* Washington build a new executive structure; he *had* to.

However, if Washington began with a clean slate as far as the federal government service is concerned, he also had a great many people telling him what to write on it; from the very beginning, men seeking office for themselves or their friends pressed their requests with the greatest vigor and persistence.

THE RULE OF FITNESS

Washington was wise in the ways of politics, and he perceived quickly that appointments would constitute "one of the most difficult and delicate parts of the duty of my Office." He therefore took pains to avoid any suggestion of nomination to office on any grounds except "fitness of character," and he adhered so firmly to these principles that, in the words of an authority, his "rules of selection shone in statesmanlike splendor." Qualification for the post to be filled was a *sine qua non* for appointment, and he turned aside even many veterans of the Revolutionary War, whose sufferings he knew so well, on the grounds that such service by itself could not be permitted to outweigh the greater efficiency of other applicants. He also made it perfectly clear that kinship would not become a basis for preference in appointment. Washington wanted able men; he was concerned primarily with the competence of his civil service; he made competence the central factor in selection.

Of course, his standards of fitness, his measures of ability and criteria of competence, were not precisely what ours are today. He was interested more in the honor and esteem in which his appointees were held by their neighbors than in sheer technical expertise. Respect and reputation counted heavily; he sought men of standing, not merely of skill. There is doubtless much to be said for these principles under any circumstances, but they were especially well adapted to the unspecialized and largely clerical bureaucracy of that day. Washington stood firmly by them, resisting the heavy pressures that sought to penetrate his resolve. The result was a group of civil servants selected more from the gentry than from other elements of the population, distinguished by their capabilities and integrity.

EXPEDIENCY OBSERVED

As an able politician, however, Washington knew when and where to compromise. He was careful to see that every region of the country was represented among the principal officers, and that field stations were staffed almost entirely from the populations of the localities served. He did give some civil appointments to officers of the Revolutionary Army in preference to other candidates. He did seek some assurance that appointees were supporters of the new system of government ("that is," commented Carl Russell Fish in his famous volume on *The Civil Service and the Patronage*, "political orthodoxy was considered as one of the elements of fitness for office"), and while, for most of his term of office, he gave some recognition in terms of appointments to Antifederalists, he did begin to make appointments along more strictly partisan lines as the Republican and Federalist parties took more definite shape.

Washington gave special weight to the opinion of members of Congress in making local appointments because of their special knowledge of local

people and situations; however, it was for their unusual opportunities
to furnish first-hand information that he consulted them, as he did many
other informed citizens whose views he respected, rather than in recognition of any legal right on their part to participate in this fashion in
nomination and appointment. Even the influence of senators derived
from their personal prestige at least as much as from their official positions, despite the Senate's power to confirm presidential nominations to
many offices (which had been conferred on the upper house to prevent
the Chief Executive from using his appointing power to build a personal
machine that would enable him to overwhelm the legislative branch of
the government). But the Senate remained aware and protective of its
role, and Washington's nominations were now and then rejected. In
fact, when the question arose as to whether the Senate's power to confirm appointments extended also to approval of removals from office,
the House of Representatives voted heavily to support the President,
but, in the Senate, which was jealous of its place in the control of personnel, the Vice-President's vote was needed to break a tie. Thus, although the President won this fight to establish his full control of removals, the Senate served notice that it was not withdrawing from personnel administration.

Civil service reformers of a later generation, looking back on Washington's terms of office, tended to depict him as a man untouched by the
forces of politics in his management of the public service. It is beyond
question that his unreserved dedication to the welfare of the recently
created nation and his exceptional integrity combined to make his administrations worthy of the greatest admiration. But the tendencies that
were to become sources of great controversy many years later were already in evidence. The partisan considerations, the preferments for veterans, the maintenance of territorial representativeness (overriding questions of merit), the battles between the legislative and executive branches
of the government—all these made their appearance at the very beginning. They were not abused, as some of them one day would be, but they
were not absent by any means.

THE STRENGTHENING OF EARLY TENDENCIES

John Adams was of the same political persuasion as his predecessor; he
therefore had little reason to fear that the civil service might not be
loyal to him. Washington had been, as we have seen, extraordinarily
scrupulous in the appointments he made, so there was no question about

the general level of competence of the bureaucrats. The civil service was a going organization, so Adams had only to fill vacancies as they occurred, and he extended his freedom from the need to select government employees by delegating the responsibility for minor appointments to his department heads. One would expect little change in the circumstances of the civil service under these conditions.

But some changes did occur. Political opponents were more consistently denied appointment. Adams did on occasion let his own personal prejudices rather than the qualifications of candidates for office govern selection. He was, on two occasions, charged with nepotism—in the heat of political battle, it is true, but on the basis of actions of the kind that Washington had deliberately avoided. A few civil servants, admittedly partisan but not unfaithful in the performance of their official duties, were removed for purely political reasons. There was no general dismissal of government employees, but the tendencies apparent even under Washington were a little more prominent under Adams. Furthermore, in its assertion of power in the selection of the civil service, Congress gained ground vis-à-vis the President; Adams lacked the wide personal acquaintance of Washington, and was therefore forced to rely more heavily on the judgments and recommendations of the legislators.

It was under Jefferson that the subsidiary tendencies, which had been subordinated by Washington and Adams to competence, became more important and frequently invoked standards of appointment. For Jefferson found virtually every government post filled by members of the party he had just defeated at the polls. It seemed to him this negated the mandate of the electorate, and he set about to "redress the balance." His objective he declared to be the achievement of a balance between Republicans and Federalists in the civil service corresponding to their proportionate shares in the general population, which, once achieved, would allow him to make appointments purely on the basis of honesty, ability, and loyalty to the Constitution. He went about this task with some discretion, for he did not want to arouse the Federalist voters who had helped put him in office. But he moved with firmness, appointing only Republicans to vacancies resulting from death and resignation, and, when this proved to be too small a stream to fulfill his goals or the demands of the party faithful, he resorted to removal of incumbents. At first, he acted against those the validity of whose appointment he questioned. However, this source, too, was soon exhausted. Then he found some positions of such a critical nature that it was essential, to carry out the dictates of the electorate, to fill them with Republicans. Only when it was clear that these measures were not costing him the support of the voters he had won away from the Federalists did he proceed to remove civil servants for what were clearly political reasons. The extent of the changes thus worked was considerable: 109 out of a total of 433 officers of the presidential class were removed, several hundred were let out of lesser posts, and elements of the population hitherto unrepresented on government payrolls, in addition to the gentry, appeared there for the first time, broadening the basis of politics.

However, Jefferson was not indiscriminate in his appointments, and he did not by any means surrender his discretion to party leaders. In spite of his conviction that efficiency was not the sole consideration in the administration of the civil service, he did regard fitness for the posts to be filled as an essential qualification for candidates, and he succeeded in keeping the quality of the service at the same high level established by his predecessors. If he was less vulnerable to charges of nepotism than Adams, he was exceptionally willing to do a favor for a friend; he continued to observe the unwritten rule that appointments should be geographically distributed in proper proportions; he installed some individuals in office so that they could live out their remaining years in economic security. Yet the level of performance did not decline. Jefferson managed to satisfy the competing claims of the voters, his party, and his conscience in a remarkable display of political navigational skill.

Like Washington and Adams, Jefferson gave special weight to the information on candidates supplied by members of Congress, and he solicited the comments of the state delegations when names were submitted to him from other sources. Influence was exerted also by men of such political strength in various areas that Fish, in the book previously mentioned, referred to them as "incipient political bosses"; they, too, were consulted on appointments. Thus, in the control of the civil service, Congress and the party wielded increasing influence. But the President remained firmly in control, just the same; he did not become a puppet. He felt free to reject their suggestions and advice, and did. And, in the exercise of his discretion, he continued to consider other values in addition to the technical competence of the appointees.

TWO DECADES OF STABILITY—AND WARFARE

Neither Madison nor Monroe found any reason to embark on a program of replacing the members of the civil service, for they were of the same party as Jefferson and he had accomplished, before he completed his terms of office, the task of redressing the balance. John Quincy Adams, although of a different party, did not disturb the service as a matter of principle. For 20 years, therefore, there was little change in personnel.

It was not that Adams lacked the opportunity to effect changes; under Monroe, the Tenure of Office Act had been passed, automatically terminating the tenure of many government officers and employees at the end of four years, thus giving incoming Presidents an opportunity to make a great number of new appointments without the embarrassing need to remove incumbents. Nor was there a dearth of pressure; his party and his supporters in the Senate demanded patronage. It was just that Adams was a man of principle with the courage of his convictions. He removed only 12 presidential officers in his entire four years, in spite of the fact that the civil service had been staffed almost entirely by predecessors of a different party, and he dismissed abruptly a group of Senators who visited him to urge that he exercise the powers vested in him by the Constitution and the statutes.

This stability was not without its drawbacks. From about 1803 on, after Jefferson had found the balance he sought, there had been little turnover in the federal government service. Employees were growing old and feeble after long years of work. It would have been less than humane to turn them out when they could no longer fend for themselves. Carried on the payrolls, therefore, were what was probably an inordinate number of persons who had lost their vigor and efficiency. The criterion of fitness for office was thus tempered by the humaneness of a generous people.

If things were quiet with the personnel of the civil service, they were less harmonious in the realm of congressional-presidential relations with respect to the patronage. This was a period in which the Senate began to assert its authority energetically, and the balance of power shifted in favor of Congress. Madison did not have the personal force to master the factions within his own party, and, operating through the Senate, they were able to block a number of his nominees for high positions. Even when the War of 1812 expanded the patronage, Madison left military nominations almost entirely to the congressional delegations of the states. Monroe delegated much of his appointing power to his department heads. Since three of his cabinet officers were leaders of powerful factions in their own right, the net result was to transfer control of the patronage to party cliques, which determined appointments in a process of bargaining that gave state political organizations a pronounced influence. Adams was more independent, but, as a result, the Senate was cool to him and reflected its coolness in action, as we shall see in a moment.

In 1811, Congress revealed its increasingly aggressive attitude toward the President's patronage power in its action on a proposed constitutional amendment to prohibit any President from appointing to governmental employment during the term of that President anyone who was serving or had served in either house of Congress during that President's term. The purpose was to prevent the President from subordinating Congress by rewarding submissive members with government jobs; members of Congress apparently prized such appointments, for Jefferson placed 20, Madison employed 29, and Adams complained that half the legislators were seeking office for their relatives, the other half for themselves. The amendment did not get the necessary two-thirds vote, but it won the support of 71 Congressmen; only 40 voted against it. It was a note of warning to the Chief Executive that his use of the appointing power was under constant surveillance. "This attack," Fish observed, "tended to make the executive a little cautious."

In 1826, under Adams, a second attack on the appointing power was launched in Congress. A series of bills defining and limiting the President's authority, both as regards appointment and removal, were introduced on recommendation of a select committee of the Senate. While the bills were eventually tabled because of the illness of their principal sponsor, "they remained," said Fish, "a tangible threat held over the head of any president who should fail to recognize the prerogatives of the Senate." Fish called them "the first distinctly aggressive act on the part of the Senate in the great struggle between that body and the president for the control of the patronage." Congress was on the offensive now; it was seeking a division of the patronage between the two branches.

The score of years between the completion of Jefferson's administration and the inauguration of Jackson were indeed comparatively quiet as far as government workers were concerned. But they were eventful for the development of personnel management practices in the federal government.

A MYTH EXPLODED

"The common belief," Fish observed, "that the administration of the government before 1828 attained a level of efficiency which it has since sought in vain to recover, seems to be unfounded." The tendency of later generations to deify our first Presidents, whose achievements were indisputably remarkable, operates to obscure their brilliance as political leaders and practical administrators. When they built up the civil service of the country, they did, beyond the slightest shadow of a doubt, try to get the best men they could under the circumstances. But they also made concessions to veterans' status. And they made concessions to regional demands. They made concessions to the requirements of the emerging political system. They used civil service posts for honorific purposes, and as sinecures for old and ailing employees. The public service very early became a battleground in the relations of the President and Congress, with Congress seeking to lay its hands on the patronage and the President acceding to its wishes in return for a consideration—support of his programs and policies. Appointments of friends, and even of relatives, were not unknown. Had the early Presidents been the sort of men who never tempered idealism with acceptance of reality, had they ignored all considerations other than ability to perform jobs well, the story might well have been different—though probably worse rather than better. As it was, their heads were not in the clouds, and the civil service of their day was probably not the paragon of virtue and talent that it is sometimes represented to be.

One interesting fact worth noting at this point is that not one of the first five Presidents ever expressed any concern about the dangers of sabotage of their policies by a hostile public service—an anxiety not all of their successors escaped. They sometimes removed men who had worked for their opponents in elections, but they did so to provide a reward for their own followers rather than to ensure obedience in the discharge of public office; the latter was taken for granted. The reason is not far to seek. The civil service was smaller, relatively as well as actually, than it would be later on. Its work consisted almost entirely of clerical routine. Much less discretion was vested in the ranks below the cabinet level, and much less authority over people and property than would be the case in the twentieth century. Its influence on Congress was slight compared with what it was destined to become. Such a body did not occasion fears about its independence or power.

Among the *people* of the pre-Jackson period, however, a deep dissatisfaction was developing. There was resentment over the tendency of the rule of fitness to mean appointment of members of the "best" and wealthiest families, giving the government service an aristocratic complexion. There was alarm over the number of sons appointed to succeed fathers in civil posts, making the service seem more and more like a caste. As long as politics was confined to an elite, these and other anxieties were not reflected in government policy. But a storm was building up even during these years; when the common people found a champion in Andrew Jackson, the storm burst upon Washington, washing away many of the old policies and practices, and the civil service came out of it a thoroughly altered institution.

The Rhythm of the Spoils System (1829-1883)

In the books of the more zealous civil service reformers, the spoils system is portrayed as Hell and Andrew Jackson is often represented as its chief architect.

Not that Jackson invented the spoils system; far from it. It was already well established in several states before he came to office, and change of party or faction in these states was accompanied by extensive changes in state and local government posts. The senators from these states (who were then elected by the state legislatures) and the delegations to the House of Representatives were especially anxious to gain control of the federal patronage in their areas in order to strengthen their own positions; indeed, it was the legislators who often brought the heaviest pressure on Presidents to remove incumbents and make room for new appointments. The practice was not confined to either party exclusively; both engaged in it. The spoils system did not begin with Jackson.

Neither was he guilty of the most sweeping exercise of the patronage power among the Presidents; as we shall see, his successors, of both parties, not only followed his example but outdid him. He was not the first practitioner, nor was he by any means the most unrestrained.

It is not for originating the system nor for egregiously immoderate use of it that Jackson is condemned to eternal shame by some well-intentioned reformers. It is for *introducing* it to the national government on a wider scale than any of his predecessors, and for carrying it out *openly* —indeed, proudly—rather than apologetically and quietly as had been the fashion earlier. By this behavior, he set loose forces that for more than half a century dominated the American national political scene.

Let it also be noted, however, that he won as much praise from posterity for his accomplishments as censure from the reformers. For he achieved a bloodless revolution, opening the way to democratization of the political process by making that process accessible to great segments of the population previously excluded. The revolution was not confined to the federal government alone, nor to the executive branch exclusively. At the state and local levels, as well, and in the legislative and judicial branches, and in the political parties (except, perhaps, in the South), the gentry was displaced or at least demoted as government was transferred from the hands of a self-appointed elite to a more representative sample of the population. In this profound social metamorphosis, the administration of the civil service played an important part.

THE SWINGS OF THE PENDULUM

Jackson's broom swept exceedingly clean compared to those of previous administrations. Compared to later Presidents, however, he was far from extreme. He dismissed 252 out of 612 presidentially appointed officers; in the lower ranks, departmental and local appointing officials were vested with wide discretion, and if there were some localities in which they were painstakingly thorough in their purge of incumbents, there were also many areas where there were only the barest evidences of the change of administrations in Washington. To John Quincy Adams, the scope and boldness of the dismissals must have been astonishing and shocking; James Buchanan, in 1857, might well have been impressed with its moderation, so did the amplitude of the swings of the pendulum increase with the passing years. Moreover, Jackson, even as he manipulated the patronage to build the strength of his party and to secure congressional support for his programs, never lost sight of capability as a value to be realized. More than many of his successors, he tried to secure able as well as faithful men.

The Whigs professed great indignation over extensive presidential use of the power of appointment and removal during Jackson's administration and that of Martin Van Buren, Jackson's handpicked successor. But when the Whigs won office in 1841 under the banner of William Henry Harrison, they resorted to exactly the same tactics. Whig party workers were as eager for patronage as were the Jacksonian Democrats, and the Whig senators and representatives were no less anxious than their counterparts to satisfy the claims of the state political organizations that returned them to office. The pressure was enormous; 30 to 40 thousand office-seekers descended on the capital to press their demands, and the congressional delegations also pressured the President. So a new sweep began. The methods were not significantly different from those of the Democrats; the appointments followed closely the recommendations of members of Congress and other party functionaries. The only distinction between this administration and the previous two was that the Whigs drew more heavily on the wealthier elements of the population while the Democrats relied on a broader base. The new sweep was a little less extensive than Jackson's, but it was clear that the spoils system had arrived to stay for a while and that neither party had a monopoly on it.

And so it went. In 1845, under James K. Polk, the Democrats returned to power and there was another wholesale replacement of civil servants. But the Whigs came back in 1849 under Zachary Taylor, and a new wave of dismissals followed. Millard Fillmore, who succeeded to the Presidency when Taylor died in office, carried spoils practice to a new extreme when he removed members of his own party who were not of his particular *faction* within the party, but his followers were driven out in 1853 when Franklin Pierce, a Democrat, became President. James Buchanan, another Democrat, succeeded Pierce in 1857, and he followed the precedent set by Fillmore in the opposing party; he removed large numbers of Democrats appointed by his predecessor, appointing those who had supported him personally, and he argued that appointive offices should be rotated every four years whether there was a change in parties or not. Abraham Lincoln, in 1861, made the most thoroughgoing sweep of the government service that had ever been seen up to his time. In the higher ranks, the presidential posts, it was virtually total; he used the patronage deftly to win cooperation from a jealous Congress in the conduct of a life-and-death war, and he used it freely. Thus, every four years, with the regularity of the tides, the civil service was swept nearly bare and restaffed.

By 1865, however, the spoils system had passed its peak and was beginning slowly to decline. The first sign of the ebb was Lincoln's refusal, in spite of the continuing pressure on him, to undertake a new change of personnel as a result of his re-election. He made it clear that the service would remain undisturbed. Andrew Johnson apparently intended to follow suit, but when he realized that he was involved in an all-out contest with Congress over the control of Reconstruction, he resorted to the patronage to bolster his position. However, he had to move more cautiously than any of his predecessors because he needed every friend he could find in his struggle with Congress, and he could not afford to alienate supporters by ill-considered removals. Consequently, though there was a sweep, it was not proportionately as great as Lincoln's in 1861. When Ulysses S. Grant came to power, the spoils system was falling into public disfavor. The reformers, who had begun to agitate for improvements much earlier, were at least being listened to now, and their influence was gradually making itself felt. The parties began to mention civil service reform in their platforms, and Grant, in the course of his administration, established a Civil Service Commission to advise on stabilizing government employment and introducing a system of examinations for employment. The effort was unsuccessful. Rutherford B. Hayes also tried to promote merit appointments, but he, too, made little progress. And both Presidents, despite their interest in improving the civil service, continued to use government jobs as political currency.

Then, in 1881, President James A. Garfield was murdered by a deluded assassin who believed the President had failed to give him an appointment he had earned. The reform movement was thus given an impetus that helped push through the Civil Service Act of 1883. It would be a gross misconception to imagine that the spoils system came abruptly to an end with this statute; the practice continued with only slightly abated vigor for many years. But it was on the defensive from that day on, and, in the course of time, it would recede gradually until it was only a pale reflection of its former self. To that story, we shall return shortly.

SPOILS IN PRESIDENTIAL-CONGRESSIONAL RELATIONS

Even if the Consitution did not require the advice and consent of the Senate for all "officers of the United States," it is quite likely that Presidents would have consulted legislative leaders on many of the most important appointments. In the first place, senators and representatives, at least in the early days, knew more than anyone else in the capital about candidates for office who came from their home areas. Furthermore, the Chief Executive must have congressional support—principally in the form of legislation and appropriations—in order to discharge his executive functions, and he can never afford to arouse the hostile opposition of the members of Congress by arbitrarily ignoring their preferences. The strongest Presidents have learned this, often to their sorrow.

Senators and representatives are concerned about appointments, and can easily be provoked about them, in part because they know that the type of man who holds high office often determines the type of policy the government pursues. Of equal, if not greater, importance, however, is the fact that the American party system has always been highly decentralized, with its center of gravity at the state level and even in local party units, and the members of the national legislature owe their election to the state and local political organizations rather than to the national party headquarters. State and local party workers, whose efforts or lack of effort generally determine whether or not a man even has a chance of winning office, contribute their labor for many reasons. One of the main reasons for many of them has unquestionably been the hope of getting a job in the government. If the available jobs in the Federal Government were not given to the supporters of incumbent members of Congress, the seats of these legislators would be jeopardized at the next election, for few supporters would work for them in that case. Their political lives depend on the way patronage is distributed. It was especially true of senators prior to 1917, who were elected by the legislatures of their respective states rather than by the people. In those days, without federal patronage, the ability of a candidate for the Senate to influence the action of the state legislators would have been seriously curtailed. No wonder, then, they put in a strong bid for control of the federal government service.

Under these circumstances it is not surprising that every President, including Washington, who had the freest hand of all, had to be constantly on guard to protect the power conferred on his office. The intensity of the struggle increased as the spoils system burgeoned out and the stakes rose higher and higher.

As it worked out, the spoils system augmented the President's leadership in the formulation of governmental policy and in the functioning of his party, but, at the same time, it weakened his control of the composition of the civil service. In legal terms, he had the power to name the members of the civil service; only he could submit names to the Senate for confirmation, and only his signature (or that of his department heads in some cases) could validate appointments to lower-ranking positions. But by surrendering the *substance* of this power to Congress and to other party officials—by naming the people *they* recommended—he was able to get from them many things he wanted. So instead of using the patronage powers to *select* governmental personnel, Presidents used it instead only to determine who *could* actually make the selections. By judiciously parceling out their power over personnel, Presidents became stronger in other and broader respects. By the same token, while congressmen bowed to the desires of the President in those respects, they developed, as a consequence of the spoils system, a stronger voice in the management of government personnel than they had ever had. The makeup of the government service was largely their work in the period of unrestrained spoils.

This pattern of relationships was as true for strong Presidents in this period as for weak. Strong Presidents bargained their patronage away for legislative victories and party unity; the weak Presidents are so designated because they gave it away and received nothing in return—neither legislation, nor, very often, unity. Pierce, for example, showed much greater interest in trying to patch together the elements of his party in order to win a second term than in taking the lead in policy. He was not even renominated. Polk, on the other hand, used the patronage to push his own policy; he dismissed many of those appointed by his predecessor, but he used the resulting vacancies to get things done rather than to pull his party together. Lincoln used Pierce's method for Polk's purpose; he had to have unity to prosecute the war, and he went so far as allowing Republicans in a few districts to elect the men they wanted as postmasters and then appointing those men in order to minimize antagonism. It was by such concessions, in part, that he built the strength for which he is noted. He offered positions, for example, to win some doubtful congressmen over to voting for admission of Nevada as a state, a move he considered important to ensure adoption of the Thirteenth Amendment. Thus, he cajoled and threatened the factions of his party into going along with him—and thus he gave up much of his power to shape the composition of the federal service. Under Johnson, Grant, Hayes, Garfield, and Arthur, Congress—especially the Senate—made even greater advances in its influence on government personnel, and this without losing control of policy.

Let it not be thought that the Presidents selected government jobs as a medium of exchange entirely on their own initiative. Congress served notice very early that it meant to participate in the distribution of public offices, and from time to time these notices were renewed emphatically. Usually, the form of the warning was a move to restrict the appointing and removal power of the President. In 1811, as we have seen, there was strong support for a constitutional amendment to prohibit him from appointing to civil office anyone who had served in Congress during his term. In 1826, a Senate committee proposed that the requirement of Senate confirmation be widely extended, and that removals by the President be accompanied by a statement of reasons. In 1834, the proposals of 1826 were revived, and Daniel Webster urged vigorously that the Senate had the right under the Constitution to advise and consent to all removals as well as appointments. None of these measures actually became law, but no President could fail to observe that Congress would try, and might, if sufficiently provoked, succeed in the attempt, to cut down his power if Congress were ignored or threatened in the exercise of that power.

The severest lesson to American Chief Executives was the impeachment of Andrew Johnson in 1868. The impeachment, it is clear, was an outgrowth of the friction between the President (who was not distinguished by his tact and diplomacy) and Congress (in which an extreme wing had won dominance) for control of Reconstruction. It was this general background rather than any specific action that set off the chain of events. But the issue on which it turned was the removal power of the President—the familiar focal point. Under both Johnson and Lincoln a number of acts had been passed requiring concurrence of the Senate for removals previously accomplished by the President alone. Then, in 1867, over Johnson's veto, this requirement was extended even to Cabinet officers. Johnson considered it unconstitutional and removed his Secretary of War in defiance of it. It was then that he was impeached, and came within one vote of conviction. Congress had made its intentions known in no uncertain tones.

The Tenure-of-Office Act, as the legislation of 1867 was called, remained in force until its repeal in 1887. It was amended at one point, and the House sought to repeal it entirely, but the Senate resisted. Practice in effecting removals under it was more or less impromptu and varied greatly. But one thing was constant: the Senate was more vigorous in the challenge of nominations after this than it had ever been before. Even against Grant and Hayes, who were of the same party as the majority of the Senate, senatorial power was asserted. And when Garfield sought to use the patronage to reward some of his own supporters in New York at the expense of the friends of a senator from that state, both senators resigned in indignation, declaring in effect that senators were to have control over appointments in their respective states. The doctrine that either senator from any state should have a veto over federal appointments in his own state had been advanced as early as 1820, but nothing had then come of it. Now, in 1881, it was rejected again, both by the legislature of New York, which did not re-elect the two senators in question, and by the Senate itself, which confirmed the nominee to whom they had objected. Despite these initial repudiations of "senatorial courtesy," however, it became established practice by the time the Tenure-of-Office Act was repealed. With the repeal in 1887, commented Fish, "while the Senate resumed the legal position it had held previous to 1867, the history of the intervening years could not be forgotten; its prestige was too firmly fixed to depend on a single act, and the senators unofficially and by 'courtesy' have continued to this day [this passage was written in 1904] the main dispensers of the patronage:" * The heyday of the spoils system was the era in which congressional power over personnel administration in the federal ·government reached its height.

DEMOCRATIZATION THROUGH SPOILS

Not only did the relationships between the internal organs of government undergo change concurrently with, and as a result of, the spoils system; also, the extent of popular participation in the art of government broadened to such a degree in this period, partly as a consequence of the spoils system, that the old Federalists would have been astounded had they returned to Earth to view the transformation.

For, at the outset, politics was an occupation confined to the well-to-do. This is partially attributable to the early restrictions on voting and holding office—to property qualifications, religious standards, taxpaying minima imposed by the various states (which did and, within the limitations of Constitutional provisions, still do determine voting qualifications in federal as well as state elections). Many of these had disappeared in the western states, but even where they persisted in the conservative strongholds of the East, the barriers crumbled rapidly under the impact of the Jacksonian Revolution. This in itself tended to open at least the minimum possibilities of political participation to the multitudes.

However, it may be surmised that popular participation would have been limited even in the absence of restrictions on the suffrage because politics is an activity that takes time and energy, resources available only to those who were not compelled to invest them in the earthy business

---

* In 1876, Congress enacted a statute requiring Senate concurrence in the removal of presidential postmasters. This act was never repealed, and remained in effect until 1926, when it was ruled unconstitutional by the Supreme Court in an opinion which also declared the former act of 1867 in conflict with the Constitution.

of making a living. It was no accident that the men who were the first to govern the United States came from fairly wealthy families. The political system tended to be self-selecting in this respect.

The spoils system changed that by providing a source of income in the form of government jobs for men who made politics their career. Either because they hoped to get such a job, or because they had already earned one and were anxious to hold it, they worked for the candidates for elective offices to whom they were beholden. They spent part of their official time in these purely partisan pursuits. They paid assessments to the party in proportion to the salaries they drew. They moved to higher posts, and spent still more of their time and money on the political machines. Now the "cruder" elements of the population were drawn into the process of government; it was no longer the private preserve of the "better people," for the spoils system made it possible for all to participate. In truth, the American practice of government tended to be aristocratic in form prior to Jackson; it became much more democratic after he came to power. Said Fish:

> The armor in which democracy won its early victories in this country, and to which it still clings in great part, may now seem crude and heavy and inapt to the wearer; but we should not forget that at the time of its introduction it was the very best that had been devised; that by it, for the first time in history, a numerous and widely scattered people was enabled itself to direct its whole force to its own advancement; and present appreciation of the evils of the spoils system should not blind us to the fact that in the period of its establishment it served a purpose that could probably have been performed in no other way, and that was fully worth the cost.

In judging the spoils system, one should bear in mind an additional point: the specialization of function, which we have noted as perhaps the outstanding characteristic of the modern bureaucracy, had still not made its appearance. As America became more highly industrialized in the closing decades of the nineteenth century, the beginnings of intense division of labor with its consequent demand for greater skill, training, and knowledge could be discerned; but the bulk of the work of the civil service continued to be clerical for many years, and the discretion delegated to administrative officials below the very top levels remained circumscribed. The governmental budget was small compared to today's. The degree of governmental intervention in the economy was limited. It was an era of isolationism in foreign policy. Under those circumstances, there was at least some justice in Jackson's belief that anyone with a modest education and a little common sense could do the work of the public service. In his first annual message, he told Congress:

> The duties of all public officers are, or at least admit of being made, so plain and simple that men of intelligence may readily qualify themselves for their performance; and I cannot but believe that more is lost by the long continuance of men in office than is generally gained by their experience.

No one today contends that this simple philosophy would apply now. But it is less than just to project today's standards into the past. We who know to what levels the spoils system ultimately degenerated might, if we were in the same situation as our forebears, seek different means of achieving the same worthy ends. At the same time, it is clear that those who originated the spoils system were not necessarily unreasonable, shortsighted, or wicked in choosing the path they did.

THE VIRTUES OF IMPERFECTION

As a matter of fact, there were a number of conditions that meliorated the alleged inexperience of civil service personnel under the spoils system:

1. Many of the men removed from office when the opposing party was in power would be returned to their positions when their own party won again; this may have been the first trial of the two-platoon system.

2. There were large numbers of employees who continued under both parties. Their functions were already regarded as too technical to allow of casual replacement, and they maintained at least a minimum of continuity.

3. Some civil servants of long experience were not only retained in the service, but were moved up to key positions because their accumulations of knowledge transcended the demands of the parties.

The spoils system certainly disrupted the functioning of the civil service, but it did not by any means wipe the slate *perfectly* clean each time the government changed hands. There was considerable carry-over from one administration to the next.

A MATTER OF EMPHASIS

While the era of unmitigated spoils is certainly distinguishable from the periods that preceded and followed it, the distinctions are mainly differences in degree rather than in kind. In every period, we have expected the public service to realize multiple values; and what sets the periods apart, essentially, is the stress placed on one value relative to the others. Practically all values, however, have been recognized in some measure all of the time.

Thus, under the spoils system, Presidents were no less aware than their predecessors of the importance of procuring competent personnel. They did not worry too much about it because of their assumption that most government jobs were simple. Their attitudes implied that competence would take care of itself, leaving them free to concentrate on the political potentialities of the government service. And the truth is that the quality of governmental performance was *not* invariably worse under the spoils system than it had been before. "Efficiency depends more on the characteristics of the man appointing and appointed to office than on the method of selection."

There were still other purposes the civil service continued to fulfill in this period. It remained a means of pensioning off disabled soldiers,* defeated politicians, and even prominent citizens with no other claim than their prominence and need. The Senate kept a sharp eye on it to make sure that each state was adequately represented, although there was no need for concern because the influence of the Senate in appointments automatically operated to maintain the balance. It was occasionally used as a haven for relatives and friends, even by Lincoln himself.

The civil service, in short, did not suddenly become a totally transformed institution as a consequence of the spoils system. It still was required to live up to many standards familiar both before it appeared and after it almost disappeared. All that changed were the priorities placed on each standard. Just as most of these priorities had been modified when the spoils system grew to full flower, so they were to be altered again in the ensuing decades.

Neutralizing the Civil Service (1883-1964)

THE ATTACK ON SPOILS

A great many things were blamed on the spoils system during the fight to overthrow it. Every evidence of dishonesty. Every display of incompetence. Every suggestion of inefficiency. Everything low and mean and

---

* Legislation providing special preference in appointment to veterans with service-incurred disabilities was enacted in 1865, thus giving legal recognition to a practice begun even before the adoption of the Constitution. In 1876, this preference was extended to include the widows and orphans of veterans and was specifically applied to special preferment in the event of reductions in force.

degrading that ever occurred in the government service was blamed on the spoils system. Indeed, one merit system enthusiast, looking back to the days of spoils, even charged that the spoils system encouraged prostitution:

> Some young women in despair, losing hope at the loss of their jobs, went wrong on the town, for Washington like other cities big and little had its red light district. . . .

It is said that young women suddenly deprived of their positions under the spoils system were sometimes driven by extremity to those notorious resorts.

> Oh! the pity of it. Strangers in a strange city unexpectedly turned out of office, their salary then too small to permit of savings, without funds or friends, the amiable madam's [sic] of the oldest trade in the world hospitally [sic] extended a welcome to these unfortunate recruits, and the folks back home unknowingly continued to enjoy the wages of sin of an erring daughter whom of course they still thought a Government employee.

It was not really necessary to resort to near-hysterical accusations to discredit spoils. The disadvantages of this means of staffing government agencies were profound and obvious enough not to require artistic heightening. In the long run, the government service tended to deteriorate under these conditions. Spoils may have democratized politics; it threatened to degenerate administration as it continued completely unchecked. The government, it is true, continued to do its job under spoils —but at what cost? For how long could it have continued to do so after the rise of specialization? How well was it working?

The spoils system put a premium on the creation of extra jobs—both to provide additional political currency and also to lighten the workload so that loyal political partisans would have time for their assigned political tasks.

It resulted in the employment of many individuals who were not qualified to perform the duties for which they were hired.

It tempted government officials to use their official positions for personal gain, for they had generally only four years in which to reap the harvest for which they had labored long and hard in the political vineyards.

It meant that a good deal of energy went into the orientation and basic training of a new work force every four years.

It reduced the President to the level of petty job broker, and diverted his strength and attention from important matters of state to the dispensation of hundreds of posts under the greatest pressure. The President gained bargaining leverage, but at the price of his health and vigor, his peace of mind, and the dignity and decorum of his high office. The Executive Mansion was besieged. The Chief Executive could not escape to protect either the nation's welfare or his own sanity.

All these concomitants of spoils were clearly visible even to the most dispassionate observer. They moved men of conscience and goodwill to strive for reform.

THE BEGINNINGS OF REFORM

The reformers adopted a simple but drastic formula to correct the defects of the civil service system. Since they ascribed the defects almost entirely to politically motivated appointments and removals, they proposed to take these powers out of the hands of the politicians. They planned to vest the control of these personnel actions in a relatively independent non-political body that would administer examinations to screen applicants for vacancies, and that would act to prevent dismissal for purely political reasons. The politicians were accused of corrupting the public service; the reformers' remedy was to isolate the public service from their machinations.

Reform agitation began rather early. The first concrete evidence that reformers were making any progress toward their goal was the enactment, in 1853, of a statute requiring the major departments to establish examining boards to hold "pass" examinations for applicants for clerical posts in Washington. (A "pass" examination is a qualifying test in which an appointee merely has to demonstrate that he possesses certain minimum qualifications for his job. It is usually given to only one person; it is not competitive.) The examining boards, if they gave the examinations at all, made them so ridiculously easy that nobody was likely to fail, and it soon became apparent that even the form of the examination system was frequently omitted. But here was official recognition by the government that the spoils system was far from generally satisfactory.

The issue was raised more frequently and insistently in the next decade. A report submitted by the American Consul General at Paris at the request of the Secretary of State in 1863 described the French customs service and recommended that the United States adopt the system of appointment on the basis of competitive examination. In 1864, an act calling for the revival of a system of examinations for the appointment of a number of "consular pupils," a practice authorized but quickly repeated seven years earlier, was passed. In 1864, too, Senator Charles Sumner introduced a bill requiring appointment by competitive examination, promotion primarily on the basis of seniority, and removal only for cause, but this was tabled. Representative Thomas Jenckes introduced a bill in Congress, in 1865, providing for competitive examinations and nonpolitical appointments, but it, like Sumner's, was dropped. In 1866, a Joint Select Committee on Retrenchment was established, and among its responsibilities was the obligation to inquire into the "expediency of so amending the laws under which appointments to the public service are now made as to provide for the selection of subordinate officers after due examination by proper boards; their continuance in office during specified terms, unless dismissed upon charges preferred and sustained before tribunals designated for that purpose; and for withdrawing the public service from being used as an instrument of political or party patronage." During the same year, the Senate instructed its own Committee on the Judiciary to investigate the possibility of legislation establishing examination by proper boards as a prerequisite to appointment. The Joint Committee on Retrenchment was enlarged in 1867, and Jenckes, who was a member of it, presented a bill from it, but the bill was tabled. In 1868, he introduced another bill, which was referred back to the Joint Committee. Finally, in 1868, the Committee issued its final report, accompanied by a bill, which stands as a landmark in the history of civil service reform.

The report contained extensive analyses of the civil service systems of China, England, France, and Prussia, and summaries of the opinions of almost 450 American supervisory officials. On the basis of this evidence, it reiterated earlier recommendations for introduction of examinations, suggesting that they be extended to presidential appointments as well as inferior officers. However, it contained a revolutionary proposal for making the Vice-President the head of a new Department of Civil Service, and was defeated. Jenckes tried again in 1869, and again his measure was voted down. But his study contained a great deal of useful material, and it helped strengthen the hand of such leaders as George William Curtis and Carl Schurz in their indefatigable efforts to secure improvement of the civil service.

THE REFORMERS SCORE

During the 1870s, the reformers moved still closer to their goal. President Grant's Secretary of the Interior in 1870 ordered appointments in

the Patent Office, the Census Bureau, and the Indian Office to be made
on the basis of competitive examinations, but he found political pressures on him so heavy that he resigned before the year was over. The
Secretary of the Treasury, George S. Boutwell, put into effect in the
same year competitive examinations for appointments to lower-grade positions in his agency. It was also in 1870 that Grant, in his second annual
message, called for a reform of the system of making appointments as
part of a general reform of the civil service. Several bills designed to
comply with his request were introduced, but none was enacted. Not
until the following year, 1871, was any relevant legislation passed, and
that in the form of a rider to an appropriation bill.

That rider is still on the statute books and even today constitutes part
of the underpinning sustaining the President's authority to issue civil
service rules and executive orders on personnel administration. It authorized the President to prescribe regulations governing admission into
the civil service, to establish rules of conduct for civil servants, and to
employ a staff to put the regulations into effect. Grant set up an Advisory
Board of seven members headed by Curtis, but the demands of politics
could not be ignored, and, when the President yielded to those demands,
Curtis resigned in protest in 1873. Congress, which had passed the rider
only because it was then too late in the session to jeopardize the entire
appropriation bill to which it was attached, later refused to make available any new funds for continuation of the system, and the whole system of examinations, just getting under way, hung in the balance.

Grant presented Congress with a ukase in 1874. If it failed to give
positive support to the experimental program, he said, the whole thing
would be abandoned. Nevertheless, Congress adjourned without appro-
priating any money for it, and, in 1875, the President formally dropped
the conduct of competitive examinations. The Civil Service Commission
(the name finally adopted by the Advisory Board) continued legally in
existence, but, even with so outstanding a reformer as Dorman B. Eaton
heading it, it had little influence.

President Rutherford B. Hayes had pledged himself in the course of
the campaign of 1876 to advance civil service improvement, and he
asked Congress for money to administer the act of 1871, which was still
in effect although the Commission was inactive for lack of funds. But
Congress turned a deaf ear on his requests, and any progress to be made
had to be accomplished by executive action alone. Hayes did actually
achieve a few gains in this way. He made Carl Schurz Secretary of the

Interior, and Schurz, in turn, revived the system of competitive examinations in his department. At Hayes' direction, competitive examinations were instituted in the New York City customs house in 1879, from which they spread to other federal offices in the city and to post offices and customs houses in several other cities. The President also forbade political activity by government employees, and attempted to enforce a ban on political assessments on civil servants, but he made little headway against these practices. His actions, however, heartened the reformers, and their efforts became still more energetic and enlisted increasingly widespread support as they organized themselves into Civil Service Reform Associations. And it was at Hayes' request that Dorman B. Eaton, at his own expense, prepared two reports that were to serve as ammunition for the reformers—one on the civil service in Great Britain, where, in 1870, a system of competitive examinations had been introduced on a service-wide basis, and one on the improvements effected in the New York customs house as a result of the introduction of competition. The reformers were moving ahead.

As a congressman, James A. Garfield had been a supporter of civil service reform. While his inaugural address disappointed the reformers because it was silent on competitive examinations, the latter nevertheless had reason to hope that they would make new gains under his administration. Within four months, however, he was slain, and his death was laid at the door of the spoils system.

This tragic event accomplished overnight what the reformers had been striving for two decades to do: it aroused the country against the spoils system. Political appointments and removals were denounced in press and pulpit, and, in the congressional elections of 1882, in the voting booths. Congress had at first dawdled over legislation drafted by Curtis and Eaton and others in the reform movement, but, when it reconvened in the last months of 1882, it had been forewarned by the defeat of some congressmen in the fall elections, largely on the basis of their stands on civil service revision, that action was necessary. Hesitation ended: on January 16, 1883, President Chester A. Arthur signed into law the Civil Service Act. The reformers won their first major victory after twenty years of struggling.

But this was only one battle in a long and hard war. As we shall see, the spoils system would be a long time dying, and even the Presidents who supported the Civil Service Act could not resist the pressures and temptations to use the government service for political bargaining.

NEUTRALITY THROUGH ISOLATION

The provisions of the Civil Service Act of 1883 reflect the reformer's conviction that power to make appointments had to be transferred in large part, if not entirely, from political officers to a nonpolitical agency as they believed it had been in England. It is worthwhile to quote at length from the law itself:

. . . the President is authorized to appoint, by and with the advice and consent of the Senate, three persons, not more than two of whom shall be adherents of the same party, as Civil Service Commissioners, and said three commissioners shall constitute the United States Civil Service Commission. Said Commissioners shall hold no other official place under the United States.

The President may remove any commissioner; and any vacancy in the position of commissioner shall be so filled by the President, by and with the consent of the Senate, as to conform to said conditions for the first selection of commissioners. . . .

SEC. 2. . . . it shall be the duty of said commissioners:

First. To aid the President, as he may request, in preparing suitable rules for carrying this act into effect, and when said rules shall have been promulgated it shall be the duty of all officers of the United States in the departments and offices to which any such rules may relate to aid, in all proper ways, in carrying said rules, and any modifications thereof, into effect.

Second. And, among other things, said rules shall provide and declare, as nearly as the conditions of good administration will warrant, as follows:

First, for open, competitive examinations for testing the fitness of applicants for the public service now classified or to be classified hereunder. Such examinations shall be practical in their character, and so far as may be shall relate to those matters which will fairly test the relative capacity and fitness of the persons examined to discharge the duties of the service into which they seek to be appointed.

Second, that all the officers, places, and employments so arranged or to be arranged in classes shall be filled by selections according to grade from among those graded highest as the results of such competitive examinations. . . .

Fourth, that there shall be a period of probation before any absolute appointment or employment aforesaid.

Fifth, that no person in the public service is for that reason under any obligation to contribute to any political fund, or to render any political service, and that he will not be removed or otherwise prejudiced for refusing to do so.

Sixth, that no person in said service has any right to use his official authority or influence to coerce the political action of any person or body. . . . .

Seventh, there shall be noncompetitive examinations in all proper cases before the Commission, when competent persons do not compete, after notice has been given of the existence of the vacancy, under such rules as may be prescribed by the commissioners as to the manner of giving notice.

Eighth, that notice shall be given in writing by the appointing power to said Commission of the persons selected for appointment or employment from among those who have been examined, of the place of residence of such persons, of the rejection of any such persons after probation, of transfers, resignations, and removals, and of the date thereof, and a record of the same shall be kept by said Commission. And any necessary exceptions from said eight fundamental provisions of the rules shall be set forth in connection with such rules, and the reasons therefor shall be stated in the annual reports of the Commission. . . .

Third. Said Commission shall, subject to the rules that may be made by the President, make such regulations for, and have control of, such examinations and, through its members of the examiners, it shall supervise and preserve the records of the same; and said Commission shall keep minutes of its own proceedings.

Fourth. Said Commission may make investigations concerning the facts, and may report upon all matters touching the enforcement and effects of said rules and regulations, and concerning the action of any examiner or board of examiners hereinafter provided for, and its own subordinates, and those in the public service, in respect to the execution of this act.

Fifth. Said Commission shall make an annual report to the President for transmission to Congress, showing its own action, the rules and regulations and the exceptions thereto in force, the practical effects thereof, and any suggestions it may approve for the more effectual accomplishment of the purposes of this act. . . .

SEC. 7. . . . no officer or clerk shall be appointed, and no person shall be employed to enter or be promoted in . . . the classes now existing, or that may be arranged hereunder pursuant to said rules, until he has passed an examination, or is shown to be specially exempted from such examination in conformity herewith. . . .

SEC. 10. . . . no recommendation of any person who shall apply for office or place under the provisions of this act which may be given by any Senator or Member of the House of Representatives, except as to the character or residence of the applicant, shall be received or considered by any person concerned in making any examination or appointment under this act.

The law, it will be observed, was almost silent about removals; the reformers did not get themselves entangled in the fight between the

President and the Senate. The logic of this omission was apparently two-fold. In the first place, it was strategic in that it did not alienate the President by restricting a power all previous Presidents had defended vigorously, and President Arthur, though not enthusiastic about the legislation, went along with it. Secondly, the Civil Service Commission was well enough armed if it controlled appointments, for there would be little reason for politicians to remove employees if they could not fill the vacancies thus created with hand-picked members of their own clique.

What the law did, in effect, was to substitute the Commission for congressional and party officials in providing appointment advice to the President and his department heads.* The politicians had determined who would be in the public service on the basis of the political contributions made by the applicants; the Commission would now make the same determination, but on the basis of fitness for office evaluated by examinations.

It was still true that the President could exert considerable influence on the policies of the Commission by virtue of his power to remove its members. The reformers, however, apparently counted on the desire of the Chief Executive to maintain an effective administrative organization once the pressures on him to dispense patronage were eliminated. In any event, the Commission was not powerless, for the members could raise a sufficient cry—if they thought the merit system was being subverted—to embarrass the President; and that alone, in an era when the civil service had become a national issue, was enough to give him pause, if not to deter him entirely. Moreover, one of the commissioners had to be of a different party from the other two; the reformers clearly hoped they were thus providing a suspicious watchdog who would not cooperate with any move to evade the provisions of the act. To be sure, they had not developed a foolproof system, but the odds seemed to be with them. Nor were they merely guessing; England had installed a

---

* The Attorney General, in 1871, ruled that a provision of the act of 1871 requiring appointment of the person who scored highest on the examination for the position for which he was applying was unconstitutional; it conflicted, he said, with the Constitutional provision that appointments be made by the President, the courts, and the heads of departments because it made the examining agency the appointing power. In order to comply with the Constitution, the Attorney General concluded, a range of latitude for choice and judgment must be left the appointing officer. Civil service rules of 1883 met this standard by allowing the appointing officer to select one of the top four on any eligible register; this was changed to "the rule of three" in 1888, which is still in effect today.

Civil Service Commission, purely as a recruiting body, in its Treasury in 1870, and the architects of civil service improvement in the United States were satisfied with the way the competitive examination system was working there. Their judgment was justified by the course of events even though the merit system still had an uphill fight ahead of it. The civil service was being taken "out of politics."

THE BALANCE OF VALUES

The assumption imbedded in the Civil Service Act—indeed, in the philosophy of civil service reform—is that the civil service is a "neutral instrument," without policy preferences of its own (taken as a body) and without any inclination to attempt to impose any policy on the country. For the civil service reformers, the civil service was like a hammer or a saw; it would do nothing at all by itself, but it would serve any purpose, wise or unwise, good or bad, to which any user put it. That is why the reformers concentrated all their efforts on the ability of government personnel to do their jobs; they were anxious to make the best tool possible available to whoever occupied the highest seats in the American governmental system. They conceived of policy and administration as distinct and separate, though related, activities, and they wanted to restrict partisanship to the policy-makers in order to provide a superlative mechanism by which the voters' mandates could be carried out. They perfected the instrument; let the people put it to what use they would.

Eventually, this assumption would be questioned. At a time when specialization in the public service had still not gone very far, when clerical duties still constituted a great part of its work, however, the premise that government employees would serve either party with equal faithfulness was not easily challenged.

Willingness to execute the program of the administration in power, even if the administration reversed its predecessors, was thus treated only tacitly in the reform act; other values, on the other hand, were explicitly recognized. The special claim of veterans of the armed forces, for example, a claim acknowledged from the days of the Revolutionary War, was specifically mentioned:

. . . nothing herein contained shall be construed to take from those honorably discharged from the military or naval service any preference conferred [by the acts of 1865 and 1876 mentioned earlier].

In like manner, the principle that the civil service shall be representative of all sections of the country, a principle that we have seen Washington was careful to observe, was also included:

. . . appointments to the public service . . . in the departments at Washington shall be apportioned among the several States and Territories and the District of Columbia upon the basis of population as ascertained at the last preceding census.*

The obligation of the government to keep on its payrolls as a humane gesture those employees who had grown old in its service also remained a value balanced against the rule of fitness. The silence of the Civil Service Act left this practice untouched, and not until years later did pension plans become general.

The act did not apply to laborers or to employees confirmed by the Senate (which protected the senatorial role in the appointment of postmasters and others). Practice here, too, remained unchanged.

But not all the old practices were continued. Although the requirement of examinations by itself was probably sufficient to prevent, for all practical purposes, the use of classified jobs for the employment of friends and relatives, a specific ban against the employment of more than two members of the same family in any of the classified services was included in the act. Drunkards were specifically excluded from these jobs. But these provisions, while important, were minor; in its main outlines, personnel practice under the Civil Service Act went on fulfilling many of the values familiar to our Chief Executives from the very beginning. The demands on the civil service remained, as they always had been, multiple.

THE MERIT SYSTEM GROWS IN BREADTH

Only about ten per cent of all the employees on the federal payroll were brought under the requirement of examination for appointment at the outset. The remaining nine-tenths were still selected on a spoils basis. From this point on, the reformers carried on a two-front offensive: First, they tried to bring an ever-greater number of employees under the jurisdiction of the Civil Service Commission. Second, they sought to expand the rules and regulations governing selection and promotion, and

---

* It was not necessary to include a stipulation of this kind for field stations outside of Washington because these were, by custom and convenience, almost always staffed by personnel drawn from the state or territory in which they were located.

to secure legislation enabling them to systematize other aspects of the personnel process.

EXTENSION OF COMPETITIVE CIVIL SERVICE*

[1884-1963]

Year ending June 30	Total number of employees	Number under classified civil service	Per cent under classified civil service
1884	131,208	13,780	10.5
1885		15,590	
1886		17,273	
1887		19,345	
1888		22,577	
1889		29,650	
1890		30,626	
1891	166,000	33,873	20.4
1892	171,000	37,523	21.9
1893	176,000	43,915	25.0
1894	180,000	45,821	25.5
1895	189,000	54,222	28.7
1896		87,044	
1897	192,000	85,886	44.7
1898		89,306	
1899	208,000	93,144	44.8
1900		94,893	
1901	256,000	106,205	41.5
1902		107,990	
1903	301,000	135,453	45.0
1904	290,858	154,093	53.0
1905	300,615	171,807	57.2
1906	326,855	184,178	56.4
1907	337,751	194,323	57.5
1908	352,104	206,637	58.7
1909	376,794	234,940	63.9

* *No figures are available for the years that are blank.*
Sources: Commission on Organization of the Executive Branch of the Government, *Report on Personnel and Civil Service* (February, 1955) pp. 97-98; U. S. Civil Service Commission, *Annual Report* (1955-63).

EXTENSION OF COMPETITIVE CIVIL SERVICE—*Continued*

Year ending June 30	Total number of employees	Number under classified civil service	Per cent under classified civil service
1910	384,088	222,278	57.9
1911	391,350	222,657	58.2
1912	395,460	217,392	55.0
1913	469,879	282,597	60.1
1914	482,721	292,460	60.6
1915	476,363	292,291	61.3
1916	480,327	296,926	61.8
1917	517,805	326,899	63.1
1918	917,760	642,432	70.0
1919	842,214	592,961	70.4
1920 (as of July 31)	691,116	497,603	73.0
1921 (as of July 31)	562,252	448,112	79.7
1922	527,517	420,688	79.7
1923	515,772	411,398	79.7
1924	521,641	415,593	79.7
1925	532,798	423,538	79.5
1926	528,542	422,300	79.9
1927	527,228	422,998	80.2
1928	540,867	431,763	79.8
1929	559,579	445,957	79.7
1930	580,494	462,083	79.6
1931	588,206	468,050	79.6
1932	583,196	467,161	80.1
1933	572,091	456,096	79.7
1934	673,095	450,592	66.9
1935	719,440	455,229	63.3
1936	824,259	498,725	60.5
1937	841,664	532,073	63.2
1938	851,926	562,909	66.1
1939	920,310	622,832	67.7
1940	1,014,117	726,827	72.5
1941	1,370,110	990,233	72.9
1942	2,206,970	....	
1943	3,157,113	....	
1944	3,312,256	....	
1945	3,769,646	....	
1946	2,722,031	....	
1947	2,128,648	1,733,019	81.4

EXTENSION OF COMPETITIVE CIVIL SERVICE—*Continued*

Year ending June 30	Total number of employees	Number under classified civil service	Per cent under classified civil service
1948	2,090,732	1,750,823	83.7
1949	2,109,642	1,802,708	85.4
1950	1,966,448	1,687,594	85.8
1951	2,486,491	2,175,668	87.5
1952	2,603,267	2,246,446	86.3
1953	2,470,963	2,137,705	86.5
1954	2,346,718	1,991,261	84.9
1955	2,397,268	2,004,814	83.6
1956	2,398,470	2,042,007	85.1
1957	2,416,083	2,067,285	85.6
1958	2,382,237	2,032,944	85.3
1959	2,382,807	2,042,034	85.7
1960	2,398,705	2,050,939	85.5
1961	2,435,808	2,096,638	86.1
1962	2,514,196	2,159,049	85.9
1963	2,527,960	2,164,163	85.6

It was not easy to include a greater portion of the civil service within the competitive system. Under President Arthur, some of the first rules were promulgated, and the system of classification originally introduced in 1853 was extended; this defined the "classified civil service," that is, the positions subject to entrance by competitive examination. But when Grover Cleveland took office in 1885, even the civil service reformers agreed that there was justice in his argument that he was obliged to "redress the balance" (as Jefferson had done) in a public service staffed by the opposing party for a quarter-century. He did not violate the classified positions, but, in the other 90 per cent that were unclassified, he executed a thorough sweep, completely in the tradition of the spoils system. On the other hand, before he left office, he had extended competitive requirements to a number of agencies to which they had not previously applied.

This presented a dilemma to Benjamin Harrison when he became President in 1889. While he was eventually to display a good deal of interest in the merit system, and to make moves that strengthened it, it seemed to him unfair that his predecessor Cleveland should "blanket in" to the competitive category whole agencies staffed with Democrats. ("Blanketing in" meant that incumbents were automatically in the classified posts and that not the incumbents, but their *successors*, would have to take examinations.) Some of the orders extending classification were therefore postponed, and, meanwhile, the Republican administration proceeded to outdo Cleveland in a proscription that dismissed over 35,000 employees in the course of the first year. But it redeemed itself, at least partially, in the eyes of the reformers by appointing Theodore Roosevelt to the chairmanship of the Civil Service Commission, introducing individual efficiency records for employees to be considered in making promotions, systematizing the hiring of laborers in Navy yards, and extending the competitive system to the scandal-ridden Indian Service and other offices.

Cleveland returned in 1893, and, while seizing all the ample opportunities for partisan manipulation, extended classified protection to agency after agency. In a single order unifying the rules governing the classified service, he increased its size by more than one-third; this order, issued in 1896, put over 85,000 positions out of almost 200,000 in the entire civil service on a competitive footing.

William McKinley was therefore under greater pressure than any other President had been since the adoption of the Civil Service Act, for the office-seekers of his party were clamoring for their rewards, descending on Washington as in the old days. Never before had such a large percentage of the patronage been withheld as was now the case under the merit system. It was even proposed that all the orders issued by Cleveland be revoked. This desperate step was not taken; the pressure was relieved by a rule going back to Harrison's day that veterans who had been in the classified service could be reinstated at any time, by partisan appointments in the unclassified service, and by the opportunity to fill temporary posts created as a result of the Spanish-American War. Moreover, a Senate investigation, growing out of McKinley's suggestion that classification had gone a bit too far, recommended that it be cut back substantially, and eventually the President issued Executive Orders exempting over 5,000 classified jobs from the requirements of competitive examination. But in spite of the pressures and this setback, the merit system made gains. One major advance was an order by the President providing that classified employees were not to be removed unless they had been given a written statement of the charges against them and an opportunity to reply to the charges in writing. Another was an increase in jobs in the classified service. A third was the extension of the merit system to the newly acquired territories. In the contest between spoils and merit, merit pushed steadily ahead.

Theodore Roosevelt had been a Civil Service commissioner for six years, and the merit system had a friend in the White House when he became President. He not only classified thousands of formerly unclassified jobs, raising to almost 64 per cent the proportion of classified to total jobs, but he clarified the rules on removals by defining the causes for which an employee might be dismissed and he sharpened the definition of political activity and required stricter compliance on the part of classified employees than had been imposed earlier. Moreover, there was no need for him to tarnish the splendor of his accomplishments with widespread removals; taking over the reins of government after four years of Republican rule, he found many of the demands of patronage already fairly well satisfied, and he was able to build up an impressive record of civil service improvement with relatively little interference.

William Howard Taft, succeeding to 12 years of Republican rule, showed equal enthusiasm for the merit system. He not only beat back an assault by the spoilsmen by vetoing a bill they succeeded in getting through both houses of Congress to limit tenure in the civil service to seven years (his party colleagues in the legislative branch were growing restless for patronage); he also added many thousands of positions to the classified service. Somewhat reluctantly, he also reinstated the McKinley limitations on the power of removal, which had been dropped after McKinley left office, and it was in his administration (though not with his support) that the Lloyd-La Follette Act of 1912 gave statutory approval to those limitations and, in effect, to unionization of federal employees.

Woodrow Wilson, succeeding Taft, found himself in a difficult situation. It had been 16 years since a Democrat occupied the White House, and the party was pressing for rewards; once again, Washington swarmed with office seekers. Wilson yielded to some extent by signing a statute exempting 8,000 deputy collectors of internal revenue from all competitive requirements. But he was a reformer at heart; in fact, at the time of his election, he was a vice-president of the National Civil Service Reform Association. So he introduced, by Executive Order, a system of examinations for many postmasterships (although these were not brought into the classified service). And when the size of the civil service more

than doubled as a result of World War 1, he was able to hold his followers in check to some degree and place most of the new positions in
the classified service almost as fast as they were created; in spite of the
explosive increase, 70 per cent of all civil service positions was classified
at the end of the war.

President Warren G. Harding found himself in the unpleasant situation that was by now a familiar one for Chief Executives taking up the
duties of their office after the opposing party had been in power; the
Republicans were as hungry for spoils after eight years of Wilson as the
Democrats had been after 16 Republican years, and the familiar pressures were once again exerted on the White House. But Harding was in
an even more difficult position because the civil service was contracting
following the end of the war, and he was more hard pressed than ever
to find some way to placate his followers. In the end, he modified the
orders on postmasters, thus creating some patronage, and he dismissed
employees elsewhere in the government's employ—"sometimes," a Civil
Service Commission history was later to comment dryly, "for rather unusual reasons." The merit system did well to hold its own ground in
this period.

Under Presidents Calvin Coolidge and Herbert Hoover, by act of
Congress or Executive Order, additional unclassified positions were
transferred to the classified service. The postwar reduction in the size
of the civil service was not accompanied by a corresponding decline in
the number of positions classified, with the result that the percentage
of classified jobs relative to the total reached almost 80 per cent by 1924.
Although the civil service began to increase during the latter '20s, the
increase in the number of classified positions was sufficient to maintain
the same ratio; at the end of Hoover's term, 80 per cent of the somewhat larger civil service was still under competitive regulations.

THE CRISES OF DEPRESSION AND WAR

Franklin D. Roosevelt faced the same old problem when he was inaugurated in 1933. After 12 years of Republican rule, the Democrats
were hungry, and the clamor for patronage, spurred by the depression,
became a deafening chorus. Jobs everywhere were at a premium, and
government positions were regarded as unusually attractive because of
their stability under the merit system (how times had changed from the
pre-Civil War days!), because their pay scales had not dropped as rapidly
as those in business and industry, and because of what were then re-

garded as unusually favorable collateral benefits, such as annual leave with pay, sick leave, and retirement plans (an important factor in the days before social security). Those must have been tense days for the civil service reformers, for while the system they had built so painfully over the years had withstood many a severe shock by that time, it was then under a greater strain—as, indeed, was the whole country—than ever before.

But the system survived. More than that; eventually, it advanced. For Roosevelt had other problems, too; the national economy, caught in a deflationary cycle, was still spiraling downward at a catastrophic rate. By 1933, the national income had fallen to about 40 billion dollars (it had been over 87 billion in 1929), and threatened to drop still further. In order to reverse the trend, and also to relieve the suffering of the millions of unemployed and their families, many of whom were literally starving, to aid the bankrupt and desperate farmers, to assist homeowners on the verge of losing their property, and to encourage business generally, the administration undertook a series of governmental programs on a scale hitherto unknown in peacetime. Agencies were established to administer public relief, render agricultural aid, extend financial assistance, regulate a host of economic activities where abuses had produced inequities and unsound economic conditions, build public works, undertake conservation, and a host of other projects. All these agencies had to be staffed!

Roosevelt was thus able to kill two birds with one stone. He put into effect all the programs and projects he considered vital for the welfare of the country. And he excepted the positions in these agencies from the classified service,* thus enabling him to fill many of the patronage demands threatening the merit system. Under enormous pressure, with no other outlet, the President might otherwise have been compelled to strip competitive examination protection from a great many jobs previously covered. As it was, he was able to forestall an attack on the established classified service by manning the emergency organizations with a new, parallel bureaucracy.

As a result, the size of the whole civil service leaped, but the number of competitive jobs did not, and the proportion included in the classified service declined; by 1936, it was under 61 per cent. But it began to

---

* Not *all* the new agencies were excepted, however. The Social Security Board, for example, was staffed on a competitive basis from its very beginning, the largest agency ever to have been so treated.

rise again in 1937—first to 63.2 per cent; then in 1938, to 66.1 per cent; then, in 1940 to 72.5 per cent. The Ramspeck-O'Mahoney Act of 1938 had brought almost 15,000 first-, second-, and third-class postmasterships into the classified service, and, under the Ramspeck Act of 1940, the President was not only authorized to eliminate practically every exemption granted since the passage of the Civil Service Act, but even to classify laborers who had originally been excepted by the Civil Service Act itself. The merit system was climbing to new triumphs. During World War II, to be sure, the system was virtually suspended by emergency regulations, but by 1948, as the civil service was approaching a somewhat more normal state of affairs under the vigorous leadership of the Civil Service Commission and President Truman, 83.7 per cent of all government positions were in the classified service despite the fact that the total number of government employees still exceeded two million. The Republicans watched with something less than glee, for they were well aware that many of the positions being blanketed in had been filled by Democrats on a patronage basis, but they were not in a position to complain too loud or long lest they expose themselves to charges of opposing the merit system and because Republican Presidents had done the same thing in their day. The Republicans had to bide their time.

The patronage was not a grave problem for Harry S. Truman after the election of 1948, although the civil service was still declining in number from its war-time high. For one thing, part of his party had deserted him and had no claim. For another, his victory was as much a personal triumph as the fruit of party efforts, and the demands on him lost some of their force. In any event, the Democrats had been in office since 1933. So things progressed quietly; the size of the civil service dropped below two million; there were no new exceptions made; many excepted jobs were blanketed in between 1946 and 1951; the percentage in the classified service consequently rose to 84 per cent in 1948, and then to 87 per cent in 1951. It went down slightly as a result of the emergency agencies and appointments necessitated by the Korean War, but even before the hostilities ended, the percentage rose again to the 1951 figure as additional excepted positions were blanketed in.

CRISES UNDER EISENHOWER

But the merit system was to undergo another severe trial in the first year of Dwight D. Eisenhower's administration. Like several of his predecessors, he assumed office after long rule by the opposite party. The workers of his own party were naturally eager for rewards. But President Eisenhower lacked the opportunities other Presidents had had. Never had so many positions enjoyed merit system protection; even in the unclassified service, there were many jobs under independent merit systems operated by individual agencies. There was no need for the kind of new emergency agencies that President Franklin Roosevelt had instituted. The military phase of the Korean War was over. The civil service was contracting, and the Republicans were pledged to reduce it still further. How was Eisenhower to satisfy his supporters? Where was he to find the jobs to give them? Even full employment and a high level of economic activity, though they reduced the critical necessity of supplying jobs far below what it had been when the Democrats took office two decades earlier, did not relieve the pressure on him.

So, a few months after assuming office, the administration resorted to one of the standard techniques—protection against removal was withdrawn from thousands of positions to which President Truman had granted such protection in 1947. There was doubtless more than a little justice in the Republican complaint that a desire to give tenure to Democrats rather than an interest in extending the merit system had motivated some of President Truman's moves. And the new administration had real reason to protest that the blanketing in of newcomers sometimes tended to dilute the status of many civil servants who had been in the government's employ for many years. Moreover, much of the hue and cry against the Republicans undoubtedly came from Democrats rather than nonpartisan civil service reformers. But the action of President Eisenhower did arouse alarm among many defenders of the civil service.

They were further aroused by the creation at the same time of a special category ("Schedule C") of positions of a policy-making character (but including the confidential aides and assistants and personal help required by the incumbents in such positions) whose occupants would serve at the pleasure of the President. The Republicans found that posts almost as high as cabinet level had been surrounded with merit system protections, and they objected on the grounds that they could not get control of the governmental machinery if the top officials of every agency were holdover appointees (of the Democrats) who could not be dislodged. Critics, on the other hand, complained that the new category and the justifications offered for it were merely screens for a raid on the competitive service. Even though the category was used sparingly by President

Eisenhower (it contained an average of fewer than a thousand posts during his administration—fewer than it was to have under his successor), and even though only about one-quarter of the positions in it were transferred from the competitive service, the importance of the positions, added to the number of positions stripped of removal protection by other actions, induced the Task Force on Personnel and Civil Service of the second Hoover Commission in 1955 to describe the actions as "the most significant cut-back of the competitive service in its history."

These impressions had been reinforced in the second year of the Eisenhower regime by the disclosure of the "Willis Directive" to the heads of departments and agencies, which originated in the office of an assistant to Sherman Adams, the chief of the President's White House staff. It instructed the agency chiefs to report vacancies in higher competitive and political positions to the Republican National Committee, and not to fill the openings until the Committee had had time to nominate candidates acceptable to the party leadership. Political clearance was not a novel practice, but a written White House issuance formally requiring National Committee recommendations startled even seasoned Washingtonians, especially since the story came to public attention only after the procedure had been in effect for several months and gave the entire practice a conspiratorial overtone.

Additional uncertainties about the status of the merit system were engendered by the turmoil over loyalty and security during the period when Senator Joseph McCarthy of Wisconsin served as chairman of the Senate Committee on Government Operations and of its Subcommittee on Investigations. These problems had also afflicted the Truman Administration, and it was under President Truman that the Summary Dismissal Statute of 1950, giving a number of agency heads authority to fire employees summarily in the interests of national security, was enacted. But the authority was widely extended early in President Eisenhower's first term as the head of every agency was made fully responsible for security in his own organization. It is doubtful that the number of dismissals under this program was very large (but the number of resignations under threat of loyalty proceedings may never be known); the program was not employed by the administration as a vehicle for patronage raids. But it did alter drastically the traditional safeguards against removal enjoyed by most federal civil servants, and it permitted Senator McCarthy, from his powerful committee position, to increase the influence of those who shared his views on policy, and to reduce the influence of those who had different views, in several important agencies. The prestige and morale of the federal service were apparently severely depressed as faith in the merit system was shaken badly.

Yet by the time the Eisenhower years in the White House came to an end, it had become fairly clear that the administration would be identified as restrained (compared to many of its predecessors) in the use of patronage and would even appear as a champion of the merit system. The positions from which removal protections were lifted were largely outside the competitive service. Although a substantial number of high-ranking posts were placed in Schedule C, it did not by any means become a massive repository of patronage appointments. The Willis Directive articulated and institutionalized practices normal under every President; it was not a break with tradition. And the senator from Wisconsin lost much of his influence as a result of a Senate vote of censure; even before his death, many of the worst abuses of the loyalty-security program were being gradually corrected. In the end, competitive employment lost no ground; although the total federal service increased only slightly in size during the Eisenhower years, many thousands of excepted positions were brought into the competitive ranks, so that the percentage of federal civilian jobs in the competitive classes was just about the same when the general left office as it was when he came in (between 86 and 87 per cent of the total). And significant advances in improving personnel management were made in many directions: Increased fringe benefits and pay adjustments put the government in a better position to compete with industry for talent than it had enjoyed for many years. The number of employees on temporary status was reduced from 670,000 to less than one-sixth that number. Executive development and training were greatly improved. Recruitment, examination, and placement procedures were strengthened. Consultation with employees and employee organizations was encouraged. Antidiscrimination measures were adopted and put into effect. And many other lesser reforms were instituted as well.

In short, the merit system survived a major test. Professor Paul P. Van Riper, in his *History of the U.S. Civil Service,* estimated that "the number of civil offices easily available to the party in power at any one point in time had probably diminished to less than 15,000 by the end of 1952. . . . The pickings for the [Republican] National Committee have thus been the leanest in history. Congress, too, continually complained of a paucity of political posts. . . ." In spite of the pressures for rolling back the merit system produced by such conditions, and in spite of some lapses in the early years of the administration, the neutralization of the civil service was not reversed.

THE COMPETITIVE SYSTEM TRIUMPHANT

Nor was it disturbed by the change of administrations when John F. Kennedy ascended to the Presidency, or by the accession of Lyndon B. Johnson. To be sure, the Democrats seized the opportunities open to them. Schedule C, for example, included only 900 employees in June, 1960; two years later, the figure stood at 1,400. Moreover, the size of the federal civil service also increased from slightly under 2,400,000 in 1960 to over 2,525,000 three years later. But Schedule C jobs under the Democrats were no more a substantial rollback of the merit system than they had been under the Republicans, and the overwhelming majority of new positions were in the competitive service. Under President Kennedy, all three members of the Civil Service Commission were career men in the executive branch for the first time in the Commission's history. With active support from the White House, the Commission continued energetically to improve the personnel and management practices of the federal service, to expand services to the line agencies, and to promote new personnel legislation. The discretion of the Commission was increased in many ways, particularly under the Federal Salary Reform Act of 1962. For the first time, an Executive Order required agencies to establish systems for employee appeals from adverse personnel actions, and another provided for the government's recognition of and obligation to negotiate with employee organizations, for advisory arbitration of grievances, and for equalization of appeal rights of veterans and non-veterans. And as the first term of the Kennedy-Johnson administration drew to a close, the percentage of civil positions in the competitive service remained where it has been for over a decade, at about 86 per cent.

This level—86 per cent—is probably as far as the victories of the merit system can extend in the federal service as long as there are no sweeping changes in our system of government and politics. In 1963, the 14 per cent of the federal employees not in the competitive service numbered slightly fewer than 364,000. But over 116,000 of these were excepted by the Civil Service Commission itself—some because examinations were not customary or practical for their jobs, many because they occupied temporary or part-time openings at a low level for which examinations were unnecessary or unwarranted. Nearly 82,000 foreign nationals serving outside the United States were also excepted by the Commission. Thousands of additional jobs—in such agencies, for example, as the Tennessee Valley Authority, the commissioned corps of the Public Health Service, the FBI, and the Atomic Energy Commission—were excepted by statute, but were in separate and independent merit systems even though not under Civil Service Commission jurisdiction. The area of excepted positions was thus not a preserve for party patronage from which party pressures excluded the Civil Service Commission; rather, it was an aggregate of relatively small pockets of employment where ordinary civil service procedures were not required or appropriate, and in which the leaders of the political parties also found few plums. In its scope, the system of competitive admission to the federal government service reached as far, and achieved as high a degree of durability and compliance, as the original civil service reformers could have hoped.

ADDED DIMENSIONS OF NEUTRALITY AND MERIT

But the merit system grew not only in scope; it gained also in depth. At first, the Civil Service Commission had concentrated exclusively on screening applicants for vacancies in the government service, on admitting only those who demonstrated their qualifications for the jobs they were to fill. Appointing officers retained virtually unlimited legal authority to remove employees from their positions. President McKinley, it will be recalled, added a new dimension to the system when he ordered that reasons be given for removals and that employees be granted opportunities to reply. While Theodore Roosevelt returned to the original practice, President Taft, under pressure, reintroduced the McKinley order, and Congress, over the President's opposition, enacted the restrictions on removal powers into law, the Lloyd-La Follette Act of 1912. In 1944, the Veterans Preference Act directed the Civil Service Commission to review the adequacy of the reasons given by officials removing veterans from employment, and a 1947 addition ordered administrative officers to take corrective action in such cases as the Commission recommended. In 1962, by executive order, President Kennedy extended these protections to non-veterans as well. Thus, the jurisdiction of the Commission was expanded from guardianship of the *entrances* to the public service to surveillance of the *exits* also. As the appointing authority of administrators had been restricted in 1883, so too their removal powers were eventually to be circumscribed.

Other wedges were also driven between the parties and the government service. The Civil Service Act prohibited political assessments upon civil servants; these contributions to the political parties, calculated in proportion to salary and exacted as a condition of continued employment, were commonplace prior to 1883, in spite of a law of 1876 that forbade them. But the Civil Service Act provided substantial penalties for violators, and the practice was well under control within a couple of decades thereafter.

Other Civil Service Act prohibitions against political activity by civil servants were less effective. The Commission developed policies on this question, but it was limited by the terms of the legislation and by lack of enforcement authority. When, however, in 1938, President Roosevelt attempted to "purge" Congress of his opponents, in his own party as well as in the opposition, Congress struck back by imposing stringent limitations on the extent to which those on the public payroll (who were, with reason, presumed to comprise many active supporters of the President) could take part in partisan politics. Drawing in large measure on the policies worked out over the years by the Commission, the Hatch Act of 1939 proscribed a wide variety of activities, including:

(1) candidacy or service as a delegate to any political convention; (2) service on any political party committee or as a party officer; (3) organization or conduct of political rallies; (4) delivery of political speeches; (5) solicitation of campaign contributions or getting out votes; (6) publication of any statement for or against any candidate, party, or faction; (7) organization of or leading participation in political parades; (8) distribution of political campaign literature; and (9) partisan candidacy for public office.

In 1940, the second Hatch Act extended these prohibitions to state and municipal employees whose salaries are derived from programs financed in part with federal funds.

There can be little doubt that curbing the power of President Roosevelt was a primary intent of this legislation. It was to limit the political effectiveness of those who "owed" their public jobs to his programs, whether at the federal, state, or local level; since nine out of ten federal employees are distributed through the country, and since state and local employees paid in part out of federal funds are also at the grass roots, restricting their partisan activities was a way of preventing the White House from damaging congressmen in their own home grounds. But, more generally, it further insulated the civil service from patronage considerations by reducing the incentive of any President to build a personal political following through the appointment process; if appointees could not perform political chores on behalf of the chief executive, he would be less inclined to devote his energies to influencing their selection. Thus, while the Civil Service Act sought to keep political workers out of the government service, the Hatch Acts operated to keep government workers out of the parties. Neutralization of the public service was thereby made more complete.

Yet another dimension of neutrality and merit was added to the system by the Civil Service Commission itself. As it made rapid strides in extending its jurisdiction, and as it made more and more headway in its efforts to separate politics from the public service, it began to turn its attention from the negative to the positive aspects of personnel management: gradually, it transformed itself into a modern personnel agency. Armed with powers added by new legislation and by presidential orders, many of them recommended by the Commission itself, it set out actively to promote high quality in the government service instead of merely preventing the admission of incompetents. So it embarked on a program of establishing and managing for position-classification—that is, the systematic grouping of jobs according to duties and responsibilities in such a way as to facilitate effective and economical recruitment, provision of equal pay for equal work, and development of orderly promotion ladders for a career service. It undertook to administer pay scales. It helped develop and operate pension systems, thus relieving the government of the need to maintain superannuated employees on the payrolls. It instituted programs of aggressive recruitment, deliberately seeking to attract the best qualified people to the civil service instead of passively testing those who applied on their own. New methods of examining and scoring, especially adapted to the needs of the public service, were worked out. Policies and procedures for probation, transfers, promotions, attendance, leave, discipline, separation, relations with employee organizations, and handling of grievances were developed and supervised. The Commission assumed primary responsibility for serving as a link between the civil service and the community at large through the medium of public reporting and public relations program. It paved the way for improvements in supervision, employee suggestion plans, promotion of health and safety, performance evaluation, and employee recreation programs. Training—pre-service and in-service, on the job and outside—was encouraged and assisted, and some programs were actually conducted by the Commission itself. Personnel research became a regular function.

The expansion of the range of its activities as well as the number of federal employees subject to its authority made the Civil Service Commission the kingpin of federal personnel administration. Formally, the personnel function was widely scattered. The basic framework was provided by legislation and by executive orders of the President issued under authority conferred on him both by statute and by the Constitution directly. More detailed regulations were issued by the Civil Service Commission, whose staff then either executed the provisions of the regulations or exercised surveillance over the line agencies to ensure compliance. The bulk of the personnel actions in the federal government were taken by the dozens of departments and independent agencies that make up the executive branch, operating within the laws, rules, and regulations, and under the watchful eye of the Civil Service Commission as well as with its advice, assistance, and stimulation. It was the administrators who actually appointed, assigned, promoted, transferred, trained, disciplined, and discharged government employees. After 1938, by presidential order, each major agency had a personnel office, headed by an agency personnel officer, to assist with these functions at the agency level and to serve as liaison with the Commission. In practice, however, the Commission played a key role in initiating most of the legislation and Executive Orders under which it operates, its views were invariably solicited when any other source initiated proposals, it was consulted by the heads of other agencies who did not want to run afoul of its enforcement powers, and it enjoyed strong support among civic organizations and among unions and associations of federal workers. From 1958 on, its members have had six-year, overlapping terms instead of serving at the pleasure of the President. In the partitioned world of federal personnel management, there was probably no single dominant force, but the Civil Service Commission was unquestionably the central figure.

THE RISE OF A "NEW POLITICS"

In but 80 years, despite great political swings, enormous governmental growth, deep depressions, and global wars, the process of neutralizing the civil service and promoting the merit system thus progressed from hesitant, uncertain beginnings to almost total victory in the federal government.

To be sure, it did not completely isolate the civil service from politics, a condition a democratic polity could not tolerate even if the condition were attainable. In point of fact, however, it is not attainable. Administrative agencies get their appropriations from Congress. Their enabling legislation comes from Congress. They are subject to investigation by Congress, and many have felt the fury of a member of the legislature embarked on a vendetta against them. They therefore do not ignore an applicant who is referred to them by someone on Capitol Hill. They do not casually send away an applicant with an introduction from a powerful party official. This does not mean the law is violated; rather, it means that there are ways of accommodating pressures within the letter of the law, which federal administrators, in order to protect their agencies and their programs, soon learn. The vigilance of the Civil Service Commission and the increasing professionalization of the federal government service tend to keep these practices at a minimum. But they are often there.

These practices are not initiated by politicians exclusively. Organization survival in the constantly shifting governmental environment often calls for the greatest managerial skill, expertness not only at yielding to pressure regarding personnel administration but also at building systems of defensive alliances to stabilize the environment. For federal administrators, this has come to mean collaboration with congressional committees and with interest groups, both of which can have a profound impact on the fate of an agency, either for better or for worse. In this situation, adept use of discretion in wielding the power of appointment can be an important instrument, and it is no doubt used in this way from time to time. So it is not merely a matter of politicians assaulting the purity of the classified service; the "victim" is frequently willing, frequently the instigator. The classified service is party to a new kind of political cooperation.

It is important to distinguish between the politics played by the civil service prior to the Civil Service Act and the kind practiced after the merit system was firmly established. Originally, civil servants engaged in political activity to further the cause of a particular candidate or group of candidates. After the installation of the merit system and the growth of agency consciousness and professionalization, the end of political collaboration was defense of the agency and its program, and was practiced by both parties. This was politics of a different kind.

So the neutralization of the civil service did not entirely stamp out all vestiges of the "old" politics, and it intensified new elements on the political scene. Nevertheless, the efforts to isolate administration from party politics through personnel management, in a span of 80 years, attained a level of completeness that its originators would doubtless regard as fulfilling their fondest hopes were they alive to see the fruit born of their labors.

New Dilemmas

THE LINE ADMINISTRATORS COMPLAIN

As the merit system began to push toward its upper limits, words of criticism were heard from the very people the system was designed to assist and protect—the line administrators. Top management personnel of the line agencies, their organizations now protected against the raids of the spoilsmen, began to pray for deliverance from their guardians. They did not deny that it would be impossible to conduct effective administrative operations if their staffs were inexpert because of the influence of politics, but they contended that good administration is difficult also if personnel management is taken partly out of their hands.

No adequate explanation of this seeming paradox is possible unless two closely related facts are taken into account. One is that the federal government moved into areas calling for increasingly intensive specialization on the part of its work force described earlier. The other is that the component elements of the civil service, developing a continuity (as a result of the merit system) and a sense of the importance and difficulty of their work (as a result of specialization), began to display an awareness of themselves as identifiable bodies in society and a deep interest in expanding and perfecting the programs they administered; in a word, they gradually came to exhibit the characteristics of a series of sizable bureaucracies. Party loyalty of the patronage days gave way to program and professional loyalty.

As a result, the leaders of the line agencies grew more intolerant of incompetence than even the reformers; they developed a greater interest than the reformers in the ability of their own membership. In the first place, dedicated as they were to the welfare of their agencies and their programs, they were unwilling to see these jeopardized by lack of proficiency; they had an ideological stake to preserve. In the second place, the *esprit de corps* of the organizations and their prestige in the community engendered insistence by members of line organizations upon capable personnel; identification with, and pride in, his group constituted another stake for each civil servant. In the third place, as government workers became more and more skilled and professional, they tended to grow resentful of newcomers who received the same rewards without the same qualifications; this was another investment for them to keep safe. All in all, then, the forces at work among government employees thrust in the direction of higher attainment. To be sure, there were tendencies in the *other* direction, too, generated by the new conditions of government work. Members of tightly-knit organizations become emotionally attached to each other and to the old ways of doing things, and when it became necessary to make any changes in either or both, strong currents of resistance appeared; hardening of administrative arteries is another facet of bureaucratization. But the fact remains that federal government employment, considered over-all, had become almost a profession, and federal officials were as concerned about professional standards for their membership as anyone else.

Yet, when the officers of the line agencies tried to take personnel actions considered routine in the business world, they were on occasion prevented from doing what they wished by the interpretations placed on laws, rules, and regulations by the staff of the Civil Service Commission. Often, therefore, before even making a move, agencies checked with the Commission staff to see if the proposal would meet with disapproval. And even if they secured approval, it was sometimes slow in coming. Let them try to fill a vacancy, to transfer a man, to promote someone, to increase an employee's pay by changing the position-class to which his job is allocated, to take any of a host of such ordinary steps, and they encountered the Commission.

To a line officer, this hardly made sense. He was not less anxious than the Commission to protect the merit system. Moreover, he was apt to feel he knew the employment situation in his technical field a good deal better than anyone on the Commission. Yet he felt hemmed in from every side. The labyrinthine procedures developed to keep politics out of administration were alleged to have grown into prisons for administrators, and many administrators charged that they, like the spoilsmen, were treated by the Commission as the enemy. Their every move was suspect; the very machinery constructed to promote energetic, creative, imaginative administration, they bewailed, now obstructed it. This complaint was common in Washington, an oft-repeated story in administrative circles.

THE CHIEF ADMINISTRATOR HAMPERED

At the same time that the professionalization of the civil service was producing dissatisfaction with the Civil Service Commission among line administrators, a kind of uneasiness sprang up among other students and practitioners of American government.

The great, sprawling complex of organizations that constitutes the executive branch was something of a patchwork, put together by bits and pieces, each added as the need for it was felt, piled on the rest without any real effort at system or order. As one outstanding administrative committee once put it, it grew like a farm—a wing added to the house now, a new barn put up later, a shed built some other time, a silo at one stage, a corn crib at another, until it was spread over the landscape in a haphazard and thoroughly confusing way. America's pragmatic genius assembled this crazy quilt because problems were attacked as they arose; it might have been done more tidily had we been functioning on a smaller scale, but we were conquering a vast and rich continent, and the rough edges of the structures we built in the process could be smoothed off whenever there was time. Besides, through the spoils system, the parties exerted substantial influence on the shape of American public administration; the parties are highly decentralized, and they therefore helped to produce a fragmented pattern of administrative organization.

Each fragment, despite its formal subordinancy to the President, became a local center of power. Congress, not out of preference but out of necessity, delegated to them authority to "sub-legislate"—that is, to issue, within the framework provided by statute, rules and regulations binding upon the people to whom they applied—and to make administrative adjudications—that is, to decide cases involving individual citizens in a quasi-judicial fashion. At first, the courts attacked this blurring of what had traditionally been considered the boundaries of the separate legislative, executive, and judicial branches, but eventually, they reluctantly admitted the inevitability of the new phenomenon in view of the needs of an industrial civilization, and administrative law took its place beside the common law, the law of equity, and statutory law. For a long time, each agency secured its own appropriations directly from Congress; there was no central review. Each agency became influential with respect to the formulation of legislation in its own sphere of expertness, and much of the legislation enacted by Congress originated with the agencies themselves. Every segment of the executive branch thus became a decision-making center, and if not every decision, considered individually, was of great significance, all of them taken in the aggregate were of tremendous importance.

Congress, too, is fragmented; the real work of Congress is done in its numerous committees, and it is in the committees that much of the real legislative power resides. With a decentralized party system, a diffused legislature, a splintered executive, and a plethora of interest groups exerting pressure at all these points, there was for a long time no place at all in the government where a coordinated policy could be worked out and a unified set of plans devised for accomplishing the ends selected. The operation of the government in each policy area devolved upon clusters of administrative agencies, congressional committees, and interest groups.

One consequence of this arrangement—or non-arrangement—with its lack of central control and direction, was the rise of familiar administrative defects in a most acute form. Agencies not only duplicated each other's work; one would sometimes unwittingly undo what others had carefully done. They not only pursued contradictory ends; they sometimes became involved in administrative wars of incredible bitterness and long duration over the shaping of policy and its execution.

A second consequence was the appearance of "self-directing bureaucracies," the agencies that began to function almost autonomously, behaving less like parts of a large team than as individual, independent establishments. With the end of the spoils system, the civil service grew steadily into a corps of specialists outlasting political officers. The politicians come and go; the civil servants remain. The transients are amateurs, laymen; the permanent body is expert. In the relations between the two groups, it was often the political officers who felt themselves at a disadvantage, psychologically, factually, technically.

If there had not been the rise of this autonomy, the defects of unplanned administrative growth might have been easier to remedy; if it were easier to control all the executive agencies, it might have been simpler to do away with the clashes and contradictions and other inefficiencies that characterize the executive branch. It is not surprising, therefore, that insulation of the civil service from political influence came under questioning. Is it possible, asked some political scientists, that insulation from political influence contributes to insulation from political control (a problem that never occurred under the spoils system)? Is it possible, inquired some administrative experts, that the way our system of personnel administration operates deprives the President, as Chief Administrator of the nation, of an important tool of management? Neither political scientists nor administrative experts advocated return to the spoils system, nor did they ascribe to one cause a complex phenomenon that was obviously the product of a large number of things. All that their questions implied is that the triumph of the merit system may have brought its own administrative difficulties.

PROBLEMS OF PARTY AND POLICY LEADERSHIP

But administrative problems were not the only ones intensified by the rise of the isolated personnel system. Jobs in the government service had long been used as political currency by Presidents, enabling them to establish their authority as leader of their parties and to provide leadership in the formulation and execution of policy; a fragmented legislative body is far less able to perform these functions. Every President has found patronage a device to provide himself with the necessary currency. But once the merit system had been pushed almost to its limit, and the likelihood of the rise of new parallel bureaucracies comparable to those built under President Franklin D. Roosevelt declined, the supply of currency of this kind was almost at an end—as long as Chief Executives continued to respect the practices that have now become personnel traditions.

There is perhaps insufficient evidence to reach any hard and fast conclusions about the impact of this state of affairs on presidential-congressional relations, but there is enough to warrant some concern about the attenuation of leadership in the federal government and the tendency of the government to become paralyzed as a result of conflict among its component political (as well as administrative) units, or as a consequence of the simultaneous pursuit of mutually contradictory ends by its political (as well as administrative) constituent elements. It appears to be more than a coincidence that these symptoms were to grow most acute just at the time the patronage was reduced to a very low point. That is not to say the decline of patronage is the only cause or that restoring patronage the most advisable remedy. But the decline of patronage brought in its train many consequences besides those advertised by the reformers, and some of them were almost as vexing as the conditions the reformers sought to relieve.

New Trends and New Battles

ANTI-ISOLATIONISM

If the isolation of the civil service from politics produced these new dilemmas, then it was almost inevitable that the political scientists and administrative experts concerned with these problems should begin to wonder whether the process of neutralization had possibly gone too far. While recognizing the worst evils of the spoils system, they also concluded that the neutralization of federal employment had done its work; the quarantine had almost obliterated spoils while permitting new standards, and new forces defending those standards, to take root and flourish. If so, the time had come to return authority and discretion over personnel matters to the executive and administrative officers charged with the conduct of the government's business. The risks of revival of the spoils system seemed low; the promise of gains, in terms of solutions of the new problems, seemed great. As the new critics of "excessive" isolation saw things, the major need of government in the twentieth century was to strengthen leadership—in the departments and agencies, in the executive branch, in the processes of policy formation.

Much of the effort to strengthen leadership had little to do with the wall between politicians and the civil service. It was directed at other targets—the provision of staff assistance to Chief Executives, for example; the improvement of financial management; the rationalization of administrative structure; and delegation to executives of broader powers to reorganize the units and agencies under their command. At the presidential level, in pursuit of these goals, the movement produced the executive budget, an expanded Executive Office of the President, Reorganization Acts conferring on the President authorization (subject to congressional veto) to shift and regroup administrative agencies. At the departmental level, too, administrative management was strengthened by provision of expert staff aides, addition of undersecretaries and assistant secretaries to help top officials, and by employment of special assistants.* The advocates of better management achieved many notable successes in many areas.

* See Commission on Organization of the Executive Branch of the Government, *Task Force Report on Personnel and Civil Service* (February 1955), pp. 204-209.

But while they recommended sweeping changes in personnel organization, designed in large part to increase managerial discretion in this field as well, their accomplishments were more modest. For their proposals would have reduced the isolation of the civil service from managerial direction, and this ran counter to what had become a deeply entrenched, widely accepted tradition. So when the President's Committee on Administrative Management recommended in 1937 that the Civil Service Commission be abolished, that the responsibility for personnel management be assigned to a personnel director serving in the President's immediate official family, and that the guardianship of the merit system be charged to a Civil Service Board with advisory and investigatory powers but no administrative authority, the recommendations were rejected by Congress. The intent of the proposals was to return to the Chief Executive the personnel powers that were his in form, but in substance were actually wielded by a Civil Service Commission functioning, like other specialized agencies, with remarkable independence. A single officer, close to the President and the problems of the line agencies, would be more apt to interpret his mission in terms of program accomplishments, it was contended, than in terms of technical compliance with detailed regulations regardless of the effect on program. Many reformers, the bureaucracies, and the federal employees' unions and associations resisted vigorously, and with telling effect.

Nevertheless, the pressure of the anti-isolationists continued, and the first Hoover Commission, which reported in 1949, accepted a modified version of their recommendations. The Commission advised that the administrative functions of the Civil Service Commission (examinations, position-classifications, enforcement, internal operation, etc.) be separated from its rule-making and appellate duties, the former to be assigned to the chairman alone (assisted by an executive director), the latter to be discharged by the three commissioners sitting together. President Truman offered a Reorganization Plan to put these provisions into force, and Congress did not veto the Plan; in 1949, this major change took effect.

The Hoover Commission also recommended that personnel responsibilities be decentralized to the departments and agencies. The majority, however, adopted such modest proposals in this direction that one of the commissioners, James K. Pollock, filed a minority opinion taking the majority to task, urging a full and complete decentralization, and contending that such a course of action would make it possible and reasonable to follow the advice of the Committee on Administrative Management a decade earlier regarding the dissolution of the Civil Service Commission. His presentation is still one of the most vigorous and uncompromising statements of the anti-isolationist viewpoint ever issued by a responsible and authoritative public figure, but its effect on practice at the time was negligible. It is true, however, that anti-isolationist sentiment did find its way into practice on a limited basis. The Classification Act of 1949 authorized allocation of positions to position-classes by agencies without prior reference to the Civil Service Commission (though subject to post-audit and revision by the Commission, and even to revocation of the allocation authority). The Commission granted agencies a larger role in the examining process, and in other personnel management procedures, subject to its supervision. It also strengthened its field organization to speed service to the nine-tenths of the federal bureaucracy located outside Washington. If the strides toward anti-isolation of the government service were not momentous, they were nevertheless steps in the anti-isolationist direction. And further measures of this limited kind were taken from time to time in the years that followed.

A more dramatic stride in the same direction occurred in 1953, when President Eisenhower, having named the new chairman of the Civil Service Commission, also named him Presidential Adviser on Personnel Management, invited him to attend cabinet meetings, and relied on him as his personal lieutenant in connection with all federal personnel matters. In many respects, this came closer to the suggestions of the 1937 Committee on Administrative Management than any change in structure and relationships ever made. The tide seemed to be turning.

THE MOVEMENT STALLED

But there were tides running in the opposite direction, too. The report on personnel and civil service of the Second Hoover Commission in 1955, in the long tradition of neutralization, tried to draw a precise line between political posts and permanent positions, so that "career administrators . . . should be relieved by the noncareer executives of responsibility for advocacy or defense of policies and programs and should be kept out of direct participation in political controversies." The wall of separation, originally erected to remove civil servants from the pressures and temptations of political parties, was thus to be raised another notch to keep them from the presentation or justification of their agency programs and functions. To assist department and agency heads, a large number of new political executive positions were introduced in the federal government, and the incumbents did take on many of the responsibilities urged by the Hoover Commission. While the insulation of the permanent service was something less than total, for Congress always guards jealously its access to administrative agencies, the philosophy of isolation thus continued to advance.

In the same vein was another—and, as it turned out, far more controversial—proposal of the Hoover Commission: the establishment of a Senior Civil Service. A logical product of the emphasis on separating political from career executives, it was a plan to meet the need for a reservoir of executive talent experienced in the ways of the government service, available for flexible assignment, capable of furnishing essential administrative counsel to the noncareer officials, yet easily replaceable at the discretion of agency chiefs. To this end, the plan proposed putting rank in the men (an elite corps) rather than in the jobs they would occupy, and called for them to be completely neutral politically, even to the extent "that they must avoid such emotional attachment to the policies of any administration that they cannot accept change and work in harmony with new leaders." Thus, the requirements of the government for high-level managers was to be met without blurring the line between politics and administration. The plan was never put into effect, partly because high civil servants themselves were uneasy about it, and partly because the idea of an elite group was not easy to reconcile with American governmental traditions. But the fact that it was not immediately adopted did not mean it was dead; the idea would be actively, and heatedly, discussed for many years, yet another manifestation of the deep commitment to the belief in neutralization that moved the civil service reformers for generations.

There were still other indications that the anti-isolationists would have heavy going. In 1958, as noted earlier, the Civil Service commissioners were given fixed terms instead of serving at the pleasure of the President, thus carrying the concept of civil service autonomy even further than the original reformers ever intended. In 1957, the relations between the President and the chairman of the Civil Service Commission (tightened in 1953 when President Eisenhower brought his chairman into the White House circle) were loosened again and restored to pre-1953 separatism when a new post of Special (presidential) Assistant for Personnel Management, divorced from the Commission, was created. (This was applauded by the advocates of total neutralization, who feared that the guardian functions of the Commission would be impaired by close association of the chairman and the President.) Furthermore, in 1961, the Commission's report would proclaim with pride that "for the first time in the Commission's 78-year history, all three Commissioners are career men in the executive branch of the Government," so that the self-directing tendencies of the civil service were further reinforced. And the "decentralization" announced in 1949 ended up essentially as a delegation of detail, but not of control, to the line administrators: "Decentralization," wrote Professor Van Riper, "deteriorated into a type of workload decentralization which discouraged initiative and permitted little time for any imaginative contemplation of personnel management. . . . Greater return of the personnel staff function into the main stream of line management would have to await major modification of a myriad of restrictive federal statutes." More than 15 years after the 1949 decentralization, the "rigid net of procedural controls" had not been significantly relaxed.

On balance, the efforts to return personnel management from its position of splendid isolation to a role as an instrument of administration in the hands of the government's executives must be regarded as having made little headway even after more than a quarter-century. The 1937 report of the President's Committee on Administrative Management remained the landmark of this philosophy of the role of the personnel function in government, but the goal it set was not much closer in 1964 than it was when the report was first issued.

A NEW FIELD OF BATTLE

It is most unlikely that the slow progress of the anti-isolationists will end in the demise of their movement. The lesson of American political history is that the proponents of any significant change win their points only if they have patience and persistence; civil service reform itself is an outstanding illustration of this principle. Moreover, the factors that produce the anti-isolation movement are likely to grow in intensity rather than to diminish; the demands for government service in a rapidly increasing population and an expanding economy will ineluctably lead to a larger federal establishment, and the pressure for executive discretion in managing this vast enterprise will rise correspondingly. The battle will not end in this century.

The outcome in the twentieth century is by no means beyond doubt. The advocates of managerial discretion in personnel matters, who correspond in background and objectives to the civil service reformers of the nineteenth century, have demonstrated that they will not let the issue drop. They are informed and articulate. The conditions they seek to correct will in all probability grow more pressing with the passage of time. And they will have the oblique support of those who support Presidents in policy matters. The resources behind critics who think neutralization of the government service has been carried to excessive lengths are thus substantial.

But the defenders of the isolation of the civil service have impressive sources of support, too. Working for them is the long history of glorification of traditional civil service reform, which has produced an atmosphere in which any who question the system on any grounds are suspect. The specter of the spoils system is a powerful ally that is easily evoked. A large coalition of groups with vested ideological, emotional, or material interests in the traditional system has developed: large numbers of federal employees, their unions, and their associations, for example, are concerned about the job rights and security built up slowly and painfully over the years under the traditional system. The Civil Service Commission and departmental experts in the intricacies of civil service procedures are unfriendly to changes that might erode the basis of their expertise. Many civil service reform organizations and civic groups find it difficult to abandon or substantially modify the time-honored premises on which they have operated, and with which they have scored so many victories. Congressmen fear loss of control over the executive agencies through the lines of access and influence established over time, and congressional committees as expert as any personnel specialists in the complexities of the old arrangements are hostile to modifications that would reduce their power. Interest groups enjoying stable relationships with the federal officials and employees who serve or regulate them are uneasy about the possibilities that greater presidential discretion over personnel might disrupt those relationships. The array of forces supporting the *status quo* is formidable.

Thus do the outlines of controversy over the federal government service shape up for the last third of the twentieth century. Some observers see in the approaching struggles a setting back of the clock of history. Others see only the correction of an imbalance brought on by excessive reforming zeal. Still others view emerging events as the swinging of the pendulum of time, the continuation of an inescapable cycle in the political affairs of men. One thing, however, is certain: the fights will be vigorous and unremitting. When values clash in the political arena, as in this case the fear of spoils conflicts with the hope for managerial effectiveness, an enduring settlement is seldom easy to find. What kind of settlement is reached in the case of the federal government service, if one is reached at all, will affect not only the service itself, but, in various ways, all the institutions of government and politics at the national level (and perhaps other levels) in the United States.

Herman Miles Somers

2

The President, the Congress, and the Federal Government Service

Introduction: How, and by Whom, Should the Bureaucracy Be Governed?

Effective administration of the federal government has become a major political problem of our time. This is not only because a $100 billion annual business has vast room for waste and corruption. Even more vital is the fact that federal activities now have a marked effect upon the total economic life of the community, the conduct of individual business enterprises and the cost of living, upon the nature of international relations, the furtherance of war or peace, and the moral tone of society.

Administration is not only the execution of policy formulated in law. Inescapably, the latitude for judgment, interpretation, initiative, and rule-making is broad. As the range and complexity of government functions increase, a substantial part of the expanded authority of government is expressed through administrative policy-making.

In part, such policy-making comes from deliberate delegation; to a

HERMAN MILES SOMERS *is Professor of Politics and Public Affairs at Princeton University. A regular consultant to federal, state, and international agencies as well as private organizations, he has served with four presidential commissions and task forces. Among his books are* Presidential Agency, *and* Doctors, Patients and Health Insurance *(with Mrs. Somers). His articles on politics, administration, and social welfare have appeared in numerous journals.*

greater extent it is an inescapable element of the decision-making process in effective administration. Not only is policy made in the course of administrative activity, but the practices followed will have a vital influence upon later legislative determinations.

With greater public appreciation of such facts, recent years have seen a more lively public concern with the basic issue: How, and by whom, will the administrative personnel of government be controlled?

It is now clear that these are not merely "technical questions," but are basic to democratic control of public policy. More specifically, the following issues call for resolution:

How is the bureaucracy to be kept responsive and accountable to political authority without forsaking the essential advantages of experience, specialized knowledge, and the capacity to attract the quality of personnel which demands adequate provision for tenure? The problem is not the attitude of particular individuals but the direction of a large and complex apparatus, and the development of a tradition.

Who should be responsible for personnel policy and personnel management? Recruitment, selection, promotion, transfer, tenure and other elements of personnel management are now known to be far more than procedural matters. They are at the heart of administrative control.

How is the widespread and specialized administrative personnel to be kept acting in reasonably coordinated fashion? How are the activities of the men and women of government to be organized and controlled for an overall common purpose?

How can the necessary security of tenure for federal employees be prevented from becoming a source of stultification or sluggishness? Studies have shown that security alone does not interfere with incentive, as is sometimes supposed, but guaranteed tenure without direction or without clear sense of purpose may have such injurious effects.

It may come as some surprise that such basic questions remain yet unresolved. This is not a source of discredit. Primarily it is an index of the baffling complexity of modern government and its continuously changing character. Partially it is a mark of our own growing maturity as a society that issues once overlooked or appraised in over-simplified terms are now receiving more sophisticated recognition.

Competing Sources of Accountability and Supervision

Control of federal personnel involves at least three major elements: 1) assurance of ultimate accountability to elected officials, those who must periodically present themselves directly to the electorate for approval; 2) over-all leadership and general direction; and 3) clear location of responsibility for supervision at the departmental and agency level.

There are many forces which undertake to influence or control the whole or portions of the bureaucracy. They include the President, the Congress, the courts, political parties, organized special interests, professional group standards, internal bureaucratic self-discipline, and unions of government employees. As the executive and legislative authorities and the only elected officials, the President and the Members of Congress are obviously not only the foremost formal sources of authority, but the nature of their supervision will in substantial degree condition the kind and amount of influence the other forces may have.

PRESIDENT VERSUS CONGRESS: A BUILT-IN CONFLICT

The issue of personnel management, like all other aspects of federal administrative management, is profoundly enmeshed in the labyrinthine complexities of executive-legislative relations. In the built-in struggle for control, the administrative employee may sometimes have difficulty getting a clear answer to his question, "Whom am I supposed to be working for?" He who isn't nimble may get "caught in the middle."

The attraction of easy slogans has perpetuated the hoary fiction that the United States operates under a system of separation of powers. Yet everybody who has observed American government in action knows that much of the tumult and the shouting derives from the fact that virtually all *power is shared* between rival units of government driven by different interests. What the founding fathers designed was a system of relatively discrete areas of responsibility—the President as the executive and the Congress as the legislature, each politically independent of the other. But there is in reality no completely clean division between execution and legislation and the so-called "checks" furnished by the Constitution are, in fact, forms of shared power.

The purpose of such checks is to establish some means of surveillance and even veto (and, perhaps, as some people insist, to provide ultimate accountability to Congress, although the Constitution is certainly not clear on this). But such checking powers can be used to effect a virtual transfer of function without responsibility. Congress not only has sufficient power to prevent the President from exercising virtually any aspect of executive authority that it wishes but, if it is so minded, it may also take unto itself executive functions.

THE DIVISIVE FACTORS

Sources of conflict abound. The President may be of a different party affiliation from the majority of either or both houses of Congress, as was true during six of President Eisenhower's eight years in office. This possibility is encouraged by the institution of mid-term elections, when all the House of Representatives and a third of the Senate may conduct campaigns without relation to the President's program, and when people are not obliged to consider whether their vote will influence a change in the administration. Two-thirds of the upper chamber are not subject to election at the time a President is elected.

The President is chosen by the total electorate of the nation. But neither the Congress as a whole nor individual congressmen are voted upon by the whole people. Congressmen are elected by and consider themselves obligated to local constituencies frequently dominated by special interests. The viewpoints derived from representation of a national constituency and a local and specialized constituency are frequently quite diverse. Furthermore, the American electoral system grants considerable over-representation to rural interests in Congress. In contrast, the nation to which the President is accountable is now dominantly urban. The bonds of party organization are not virile enough effectively to tie together what all these counter forces pull apart.

The government was deliberately not unified, structurally or politically, at the top. This was part of the checks and balances theory. It therefore should be no surprise that harmonious tandem action by President and Congress is so difficult to obtain.

THE PRESIDENT'S ROLE IN ADMINISTRATION

The Constitution provides that "the executive Power shall be vested in a President of the United States," although the scope of such power is not defined. Americans learned under the Articles of Confederation that a legislature could not govern. They tried to provide a unified executive which would derive enduring strength from political props independent of the legislative assembly. The independently elected Chief Executive is one of the most significant American contributions to the art of government. The design of "unity of the executive" was confirmed in *The Fed-*

eralist Papers and reaffirmed by "the decision of 1789" on the manner in which Washington's administration was to be organized and operated.

During the nineteenth century it was for the most part possible to neglect this constitutional prescription without courting disaster. However, President Jackson demonstrated the dynamism and the potential leadership inherent in the executive powers, and President Lincoln showed us that in times of national crisis survival may depend upon an undivided and vigorously employed executive authority. On the other hand, periods like the Johnson-Grant era illustrated the chaos and the perils which could ensue from violation or attrition of the executive role.

Technological advance, economic growth and complexity, and increased world interdependence have rapidly expanded the volume, the importance, the speed and the complexity of government activities. Everywhere they have tended to make the executive the core of modern government. Everywhere it is being recognized that the viability and stability of modern government are in large measure a question of the effectiveness of the executive. Action, performance and initiative are inescapably in the domain of administrative authority.

As the American executive is clearly focused in the President, and as he is now in effect the product of national popular election, the Presidency has become the center of responsibility. Americans look to the legislature to see that the President does not get out of hand, but they hold the President accountable for the success or failure of an administration and for the entire governmental program, notwithstanding the great constitutional and practical limitations upon his authority. The President is expected to formulate a legislative program and policy, and he will not be considered successful unless he can persuade Congress to adopt that program. He is held to account for the effectiveness and the integrity of administration and the decisions within the bureaucracy. As one wag put it, the President is expected "to make a mesh of the government."

But the President's formal authority is in no way commensurate with such expectations. To the extent that Presidents can satisfy such expectations it is due to the degree of public support they are able to muster through personal popularity or public interest in a particular issue. As Chief of State, as a sort of symbolic embodiment of government itself, the President has informal sources of power that are greater than his formal ones.

But it is in the realm of the organization and personnel of the government and internal coordination that the power and influence of the

President have been weakest and least adequate to fulfill his executive responsibilities or to satisfy the criteria of public accountability. He lacks adequate authority to determine the internal organization and structure of the executive branch. Large portions of the executive functions of the government have been removed from his reach on the theory that they are quasi-judicial or quasi-legislative. Direct statutory authority to conduct programs is sometimes vested in subordinate officials, and appropriations are often legislated in such detailed form as to deny the executive the discretion for intelligent administration. The discharge of his principal subordinates is the sole important constitutional power which he can exercise in complete independence, at least legally. These and similar circumstances alone sharply restrict the control and effectiveness of personnel management.

THE ROLE OF CONGRESS

Congress' role in administration is theoretically as overseer. Through its powers of investigation, control of the purse strings, its creation of the laws under which the executive must perform, including if it pleases, detailed procedures of administration as well as agency structure, and its ability to determine which of the appointed officials shall be subject to senatorial confirmation, the Congress has an arsenal of controls adequate for authoritative surveillance over every aspect of executive life.

Members of Congress are, however, becoming painfully aware that in many respects they are losing the practical capacity to do so intelligently. As the size of government increases, as functions become more technical and specialized, the tendency is for the executive to acquire a monopoly of knowledge and Congress, like legislatures at all levels, feels the frustration of a declining ability to comprehend and weigh the range of executive activities. The classic illustration is its frenetic futility in attempting to cope with the military budget, especially in an environment where failure to accept military judgments may result in accusations of injury to the national security. The frustrations sometimes express themselves in ways which can paralyze the executive. It is insufficiently realized that a more effective and comprehensive supervision of the executive branch by the President is one of the most realistic channels for strengthening the Congress in its overseer role. For example, when Secretary of Defense McNamara managed to establish greater central unity in his department and strengthened its control of the budgetary process he not only augmented presidential control but greatly enhanced Congress' capacity to comprehend and oversee the department's operations.

The reason for powers of congressional surveillance are sometimes misunderstood. The Congress is often pictured as the representative of the people whose job it is to control the executive so that the people's liberties are protected, much as if the Congress were an elected board of directors and the President a hired manager. The design of American government is quite different. The American President is elected by the people and is as much their representative and accountable to them as is the Congress. The President's powers are granted directly under the Constitution in the same way as the Congress receives its powers. The President is not a creature of the Congress. The constitutional spirit is one of checks and balances as between governmental authorities with separate responsibilities.

However, as already indicated, powers granted for check and balance can be used not only to stop or negate administration, they may destroy responsibility, as the founders so well understood and feared. And, as the founders also understood, while Congress can readily prevent executive management and control, it cannot undertake the task itself. It can divide up the executive branch and parcel out the pieces for the delectation of individual committee chairmen, but it cannot organize itself into an administrative hierarchy for integrated management. Few would maintain that Congress could or should undertake active supervision of the day-to-day activities of the bureaucracy. Thus, when central management authority is denied to the President, it goes by default. There is no other place in the government structure where it can be located, quite aside from the inhibitions of constitutionality.

Congress' tendency to fragment the executive branch arises from its own inherent fragmentation. It starts by being two independent houses of virtually equal power. We have already talked about the local character of the accountability of the individual congressman; if he has a boss, it is some local interest or the city or state machine, not the national party. The individual congressman is not regarded as a representative of the national interest but as a delegate from a particular community to defend its special interests. The tradition of insistence that a congressman reside in the community he represents is significant.

The theory is that the parties will furnish the mucilage to bind the individuals into responsible units, and thus permit the Congress to take on a collective character, so one could speak realistically of "Congress as a whole" instead of a disarray of relatively autonomous individuals and committees. Never entirely effective, it seems clear that party discipline in Congress has weakened almost to the point of invisibility and that no substitute form of organizational responsibility has replaced it.

In large measure this is what has made Congress mainly negative and obstructive. The committees are virtually independent forces, which Congress as a whole rarely undertakes to control or coordinate. Chairmen and members are not selected on the basis of adherence to a party's policies but by seniority. As the committees are permanent they develop characteristics of private power domains. Agriculture committees wish to maintain full control over agricultural activities; the Subcommittee on Veterans Affairs does not wish to permit the Veterans Administration to get into other hands.

The composition of the committees tends to be unrepresentative of either public or Congress; their interests are narrow. However wise they may attempt to be within the compass of their own domain, objectives of different committees frequently overlap. Desirable means to attain one end may not prove compatible with the means to attain another objective. But coordination is not the responsibility of individual committees. Said Woodrow Wilson before he ascended to the Presidency, "I know not how better to describe our form of government in a single phrase than by calling it a government by the chairmen of the Standing Committees of Congress."

Were there an organized Congress as a whole it should have a positive interest in seeing a higher degree of government coordination and central management. But this would jeopardize the direct control of the committees, each with its separate fief within the executive domain. Don K. Price, one of our most acute students of American government, has observed that it is hard to get reasonable unity in the United States less because congressmen are against the President than because they are against each other. The great barrier to cooperation lies in Congress' inability to so organize itself to prevent the yielding of its powers to autonomous committees.

The great problem is how to obtain sufficient unity within each of the branches so they may find themselves in a posture to permit cooperation. Unless this goal is accomplished, the task of achieving responsible management of the government's personnel is at best limited in its possible degree of success.

THE MAJORITY PARTY

There is an important school of thought which holds, with considerable theoretical merit, that the victorious party must take full responsibility for the conduct of government during its term in office. The characteristics and the role of the American party system are discussed elsewhere in this volume. Here it is sufficient to indicate summarily that the concept of a disciplined entity in the form of a party taking responsibility for the conduct of government does not bear much relevance to the contemporary American scene.

Some of the time there may not be a party in control of "the government" in the sense that the same label covers majorities of both houses as well as the President. To the extent that the party of the President has organizational cohesion or a real spokesman it is through the President. Except through the Presidency the party has no avenue for achieving meaningful responsibility for the federal services.

SPECIAL CLIENTELES OR PRESSURE GROUPS

American political arrangements encourage the organization and activity of private persons to influence, on a continuous basis, the conduct of government. The popular view is that such interest groups center their activities mainly upon legislation. But most important interest groups are more sophisticated than this. They are aware that the accumulated actions or omissions of the administrative agencies may be as, or more, important than legislative action. They have come to recognize the interaction of agencies and congressional committees and that neither end of the axis should be neglected.

Not only does the diffusion of formal political control magnify the influence of organized private groups, but the increasing need for specialized technical information in the conduct of most governmental functions has necessitated a considerable reliance by agencies upon the knowledge of specialized private groups regarding their own areas of activities in our complex economy.

For such reasons, recent years have seen a vast expansion of private-citizen participation in policy formation at the administrative level or, as it is often put, the participation of the regulated in the process of regulation. This may be stated in terms of a desirable principle or as an unavoidable necessity. There is considerable belief in the desirability of "functional representation" in a pluralistic society. In any event it is now a substantial reality. It has often been demonstrated that an agency which fails to mobilize group support may find itself impotent to carry out its mandate, regardless of statutory authority. It is clear that legal authority to set price controls or fix wages, for example, will not prove adequate if the organized interests affected are not conciliated.

For such reasons, administrative agencies not only find themselves in a continuous state of negotiation with affected interest groups, whose Washington representatives keep a suspicious eye cocked to the details of agency activity, but there has developed a variety of ways for building the private groups into the government's formal structure itself.

Advisory bodies, characteristically including representatives of labor, management, agriculture, and the "general public," are now attached to virtually every administrative agency. If the agency is more specialized, like the Department of Agriculture, advisory bodies may be more specialized. Large agencies may have separate advisory boards for several bureaus. Even a technical bureau, like the U. S. Bureau of Labor Statistics, has advisory committees of statisticians representing major labor and employer groups. These bodies behave not only as general watchdogs over administrative behavior, but Congress often looks to them for guidance on legislation.

The official staffs of "clientele" government agencies—those which behave as functional representatives of special segments of the population: business, veterans, farmers, Indians, and so on—often include designated representatives of private organizations. The American Federation of Labor and Congress of Industrial Organizations usually designates, from its own members, at least one of the Assistant Secretaries of Labor. Moreover, in special situations there has been a tendency to place actual administrative authority in boards composed of representatives of specified private groups. During the Korean conflict the Wage Stabilization Board was made up of six representatives of labor, six of management, and six of the public. They were in charge of the agency's program and administration.

The men directly and indirectly appointed to government posts by special interest groups do not often regard themselves as primarily responsible to the administration. They continue to be responsible to those whom they represent. In some cases where such an appointee confuses his role and transfers his primary loyalty to the agency, he may find himself cut off from his interest group roots. ("He decided to be a 'statesman!'" is the contemptuous epithet of the interest groups for such a fellow.) Ironically, as a result, he loses much of his value to the agency. The interests of the special group may sometimes be compatible with the goals of the administration; frequently they are not.

What, then, does this do to the problem of controlling personnel by the responsible officials in the government? The ordinary civil servant must work side by side with, or report to, other workers accountable to outside groups. He can work out his solution in a variety of informal arrangements, but he cannot easily take the formal lines of authority too literally even if he were originally so disposed.

PROFESSIONAL STANDARDS

A substantial and increasing portion of the federal service is engaged in pursuits of a specialized or technical character which have recognized professional status. The professional group establishes standards of conduct to which the individual, wherever employed, is committed. The group's hold upon him is partially moral, partially a matter of prestige and self-respect, partially a retaining professional standing.

The meteorologist in the Weather Bureau, the chemist in the Bureau of Standards, the medical doctor in the Public Health Service, the statistician in the Bureau of Labor Statistics have definite outer limits beyond which they cannot go in response to orders from above or from Congress and still maintain professional integrity. The number of such activities grows broader as professionalization increases. The personnel officer, the fiscal officer, and the economist, as well as the scientist, take pride in professional standards which they must maintain irrespective of the interests of immediate policy. Moreover, professional organizations have frequently proved themselves far more effective than the Civil Service Commission in defending employees who have met punishment for stubborn devotion to professional standards.

However, in a vast and crucial area of government, the problem of decision and control extends beyond the realm of professional integrity. The men at the State Department desks evaluating news from behind the Iron Curtain, economists working on tax policy, or hydro-electric engineers helping to determine public versus private power policy, are in realms profoundly and continuously dependent upon personal judgment and conscious or unconscious political preference. While this may be less frequently the case among government scientists, recent history has shown that their involvement in decisions affected by judgment and viewpoint is, at times, inescapable.

The dedicated public servant will attempt to exercise such judgment objectively and without partisanship, but this is not quite the same as the vaunted neutrality which public servants are alleged to have. The fact is that able men are rarely neutral in sentiment about important issues in which they share responsibility. Real neutrality would border on indifference and indifference soon becomes incompetence.

Moreover, professional integrity and standards bind together only particular groups within agencies, or groups which cut across many agencies, but they offer little amalgam to personnel structure as a whole or to the managerial problem within a department.

BUREAUCRATIC SELF-REGULATION

Beyond the standards of particular professions or skills, standards may develop for the public service as a whole, an *esprit de corps* which permeates the corporate body and provides a basic moral code of behavior for all who belong to the group. There is a considerable body of competent opinion which feels that formal legislative, executive, or judicial regulation or external accountability can never be sufficient alone to control such a large group as the federal service, with its otherwise inescapable centrifugal tendencies. There can be no substitute for its own self-conscious group pride, a group discipline, self-imposed because of the continuous need of approbation from one's colleagues. Such an ethic relates not only to issues of integrity but to an affirmative attitude of responsibility and initiative.

Like most characteristics of this kind there are potential liabilities along with the assets. Within the federal service there are special "corps" which have a sense of tradition and elite pride, such as the Foreign Service and parts of the armed services. There is basis for the view that such "self-conscious" groups have built up a sense of separateness which has reduced their political responsiveness and has had a stultifying effect upon quality and attitudes of personnel. It has developed unfortunate tendencies toward "in-growth."

Studies of some foreign bureaucracies which developed pride of internal cohesion, tradition, and strength have suggested that while such bureaucracies tend to be above reproach in matters of honesty they take on objectives of their own and can become formidable obstacles to conduct of the policies of elected political officials. This is claimed to have been one of the weightiest liabilities of the Weimar Republic, a burden of the Blum government in France, and to have altered the goals of the leaders of the Cooperative Commonwealth Federation when they took office in Saskatchewan.

The extent to which the potential advantages of such an *esprit* can be realized while its dangers are minimized would seem to depend, in large part, upon the effectiveness of the political authorities. The group ethic can be consumed in institutional self-centeredness or it may be oriented to a responsiveness to political change and political supremacy.

The existence of grievance committees, employee review boards, and other collective bargaining procedures in government may similarly have constructive or negative results, depending upon the fairness of the government's basic labor policies, the quality of leadership among the supervisors and their ability to imbue the employees with a sense of purpose regarding their work.

Where top leadership is strong and control and responsibility are clear, all these "informal" elements we have listed—professional ethics and bureaucratic self-regulation, collective bargaining, even pressure group activities—may be constructively utilized for morale, efficiency, and vitality. But when central leadership is weak or uncertain, these elements may exercise additional centrifugal pulls and compound administrative confusion.

Some Consequences of the Conflict and Diffusion

The constitutional and political environment establishes the conditions and limitations of public administration. What is casually referred to as poor administration may in fact be simply an adjustment to controlling circumstances. Basic difficulties for achieving meaningful personnel management flow from the political culture we have described. A few deserve mention.

FRAGMENTATION OF THE EXECUTIVE

To maximize their own powers, congressional committees frequently tend to split off from control of the executive branch the bureaus in which they have special interests. In a few cases independent agencies of various kinds may be established. More frequently, the devices are 1) to fix legally the internal structure of agencies which, among other things, will have a powerful influence upon the character of personnel which can be employed; 2) to give direct statutory authority to officials at the bureau chief level, bypassing both President and heads of departments; 3) to spell out detailed administrative and personnel procedures by law;* 4) to appropriate funds in minute detail so as virtually to remove executive discretion or flexibility; 5) to impose a formal or informal "legislative veto" by committees on administrative decisions; 6) to give direct administrative "instructions" to middle- as well as upper-echelon officials; 7) to plant "sympathetic" personnel in key positions.

Such procedures do violence to the spirit of the Constitution because they rupture the unity and responsibility of the executive and prevent its internal coordination. Responsibility becomes so diffused that in a sense it ceases to exist. As Chester Barnard, a foremost practitioner and student of executive management, has pointed out, the breakdown in responsibility stifles initiative and furnishes "incontrovertible alibis for not doing what the specific situation calls for."

Effective hiring, firing, and accountability for personnel is split off from control of the executive together with determination of administrative method and even program responsibility. Units and agencies are encouraged to ride off in their own separate directions.

Such processes encourage direct dealings between executive bureaus (rather than their politically responsible leaders) and congressional committees, as if the system of government required that bureaus report directly to committees of Congress rather than to their own chiefs and, through them, to Congress.

There is a normal propensity toward autonomy in all governmental units which such relations vastly accelerate. The United States Corps of Engineers, for example, which neither the Secretary of the Army nor the President of the United States has been able to control, likes to refer to itself as "the engineer consultants to, and contractors for, the Congress of the United States," almost an oblique way of saying they have gone into business for themselves. The Hoover Commission pointed out that this is encouraged by the statutory responsibility of the Corps for preparing river development plans. The Secretary of the Army is not responsible for its selection of projects. As early as Jefferson's administration, Fisher Ames was complaining that congressional committees had usurped the role of "ministers" of state.

As Don K. Price describes it,

---

* In recent years some 20 to 25 civil service laws have been enacted annually. There are now more than 1500 separate statutes affecting personnel, most of them enacted after 1930.

typically, the executive bureau and the congressional committee find themselves natural allies, with the purpose of guarding their common specialty
against coordination. . . . The real issue is then between the executive
bureau and the congressional committee, on the one hand, and on the other
hand, the Congress as a whole and the President.

These relationships cut off control of bureau chiefs from department
heads and in turn divide department heads from the President. There
have been numerous cases of permanent bureau chiefs whose influence
in Congress so far exceeded that of their more temporary department
heads that they were in a position to make the latter dependent upon
themselves. The case of J. Edgar Hoover would occur to even the casual
newspaper reader. In a different way, this would be true of that eminent
civil servant, the late William Jump of the Department of Agriculture.
This is not to imply that either of these men did in fact use his vast
informal authority to the disadvantage of his superiors, but it is a not
uncommon practice.

A former Undersecretary of Agriculture, Paul Appleby, has explained
why "department heads take positions hostile to Presidential needs and
policy":

> The President cannot fully control Cabinet Members because the Cabinet
> Members cannot fully control the Bureau Chiefs. When a Cabinet Member
> is not in command of his bureaus, he becomes their servant, their champion,
> simply adding the prestige of his position to the uncoordinated representations
> naturally developed out of preoccupation with governmental and popular
> segments.

This makes more intelligible a somewhat hyperbolic statement attributed to former Vice-President Dawes that "cabinet members are the
President's natural enemies." The forces of dispersion feed on one
another tending toward administrative anarchy.

ENCOURAGEMENT OF PRESSURE GROUPS: A TRIPLE ALLIANCE

The centralization of authority over particular areas of government
action within a bureau and "its" congressional committee encourages the
profitable enterprise of the special interest lobbyist. He need not contend with those concerned with the over-all general interest of the government, but only with those as specialized as himself. He soon becomes
a member of the alliance himself, rather than petitioner. This brings
about direct and indirect control over personnel selection and activity,

as already pointed out, by private groups whose right to be consulted in the development of policy is not challenged but whose right to manage a portion of the government raises fundamental issues.

THE DISCREDITING OF GOVERNMENT

Fragmentation results in a form of government ineffectuality which has been found advantageous to, and encouraged by, particular groups. Those who have lost out in the attempt to stop a legislative measure can prevent its administration; they need not reach the President himself to do so.

Those interested in negative government tend to band about the Congress or its committees; those interested in positive government gravitate to the President. The divisions and splits tend to give support to those who allege incompetence of the civil service and the ineffectuality of government generally. They give support to the extraordinary view that an efficient government may be dangerous. In 1928 a leading business journal could express the editorial judgment that only if the public service was ineffective could Americans protect their freedom from encroachment of government. While this is not a widespread attitude today, and the business community does generally recognize and espouse the essentiality of an effective public service, the voices of obscurantism are still heard in the land.

The results help to sustain the frequent vilification of public servants individually and collectively. They tend to discredit government and government workers and thus injure the quality, the self-esteem, the traditions, and the effectiveness of public service.

SPECIAL DIFFICULTIES FOR THE HIGHER CIVIL SERVICE

The lack of clear control creates special dilemmas and hazards for the higher civil service. First it jeopardizes the necessary role of non-partisanship and interferes with the loyalty to political leadership which is indispensable to an effective and democratic civil service. If the political authorities of the day are in apparent conflict and the federal employee is not clear to whom he reports, it is not always easy to avoid appearing in a partisan role.

One textbook on administration states:

Organization charts of the executive branch tend to display reassuring straight lines of command and responsibility. In certain ways, however, a more appropriate comparison might be with a feudal pattern of higher and lower fiefs in which the vassals are sometimes torn between conflicting loyalties, and where designation of rank is often a very misleading index of actual power and influence.

Since congressional committees habitually deal directly with bureau chiefs or even lower levels, who are frequently permanent civil servants, they throw these men into one of several awkward roles. The civil servant may appear as a political spokesman for a particular policy or defendant of a particular course of action. He is frequently obliged to testify before committees who insist, "Now tell us your personal views, whether or not they agree with the administration's recommendations." Honesty may then throw the civil servant into a position of testifying against his political superiors, thus driving a wedge between top civil servants and the political authorities.

The bureau chief sometimes appears before a committee in an apparently higher role than his department head because statutory responsibility has been directly vested in him. The proper procedure is for the political officials to take responsibility for congressional relationships. It would not be difficult to persuade the executive branch of the desirability of such procedure, but at present it is not likely to prove acceptable to Congress.

AGGRAVATION OF DIFFICULTIES DURING A CHANGE OF ADMINISTRATION

Such difficulties become painfully apparent at times when the national administration changes political hands. Instead of the new political officials taking for granted the permanent civil service as ready to serve them with loyalty and integrity, inexperienced officials are prompted to distrust and suspect the inherited bureaucracy. They have difficulty thinking of many in the higher level group as neutral, for they recall that they have appeared as spokesmen or advocates for the previous administration's policies.

The initial atmosphere of distrust makes a new administration particularly vulnerable to congressional pressure in selection of key personnel, civil service procedures notwithstanding. As we have seen, under present conditions, the congressmen in their committee roles have more than a conventional patronage interest in particular posts. The employee represents a means of policy control and administrative control for the congressman.

In some measure, such devices as senatorial courtesy in confirmation cases make the administration helpless. But new and inexperienced administrators are likely to make more concessions than necessary before they learn that it is not merely a matter of selecting one employee rather than another, but that they are building forces of resistance into their own organization. When the Eisenhower Administration took over in 1953, an attempt was made to strengthen the political position of the Department of State by installing emissaries from Congress in some key positions. Instead of improving department-congressional relations, it simply diluted the authority of the Secretary.

A newly elected administration is likely to arrive with a rightful desire and expectation to take full and energetic control of the executive branch. Frustration is bound to come early. The temptation, before the reasons for frustration are understood, is to find a scapegoat in the civil service "holdovers" and to feel the urge to permeate the agencies with one's "own" appointments, with people "we know."

ADVANTAGES OF DIFFUSION

It is not here assumed that rivalries and friction are devoid of virtue. A society which has found that the apparent wastefulness of competition and dispersal of authority in economic life is more than compensated by resulting inventiveness and innovation can reasonably assume some similar phenomenon in political life. The myriad forces and interests in a pluralistic society must find expression in the political market place. Undoubtedly the crossfire within government helps keep the public awake and informed; it results in closer scrutiny over all actions of government; it assures a better hearing for minority viewpoints. It may, if properly directed, increase the range of alternatives and visions presented to the executive and legislature. It may be a means of maintaining a broadly representative bureaucracy.

Multiform accountability also has its distinct virtues. The conduct of a democratic society is not an exercise in logic, and some deliberate friction and counterweight arrangements are necessary to maintain a shifting equilibrium even at the sacrifice of consistent majority rule. Our tradition is of the many and the various.

Diversity Without Anarchy

But there are limits. We must avoid the danger of making pluralism a cloak for anarchy. After democratic debate, pulling and hauling, evaluation and compromise, we must arrive at some form of resolution. Few would argue that the sources of bureaucratic control need be—if indeed they could be—unitary or monolithic, but this should not rule out establishment of means of coordination and identifiable accountability.

Clearly, the various sectors of the American bureaucracy are intensely policed, checked, and double checked, by many sources, official and unofficial, even if such sources were limited to those we have enumerated, which, of course, they are not. We have no problem of quantity. But is the fact that all units are continuously answerable to a variety of influences peering over their shoulders a substitute for general direction and supervision? The exercise of administrative power is pluralistic, but it should be an ordered pluralism.

Avoidance of the spoils system is not enough; honesty in personnel is not enough; *esprit de corps* is not enough; individual competence is not enough—important as all these are. What seems indispensable is the capacity for and the practice of central management throughout the government. This means making available the tools for responsible leadership and the capacity for direction and supervision by political authority of a democratically accountable government service. Happily the matter has been receiving increased public attention and progress is visible.

Progress Toward Central Administrative Management

Americans are pragmatic. The practical necessities of the twentieth century have caused some significant improvement in the machinery for management of the federal government. Virtually every American President of this century has publicly complained about lack of administrative tools to cope with expanding executive responsibilities. As it became increasingly apparent that federal administration could continue to be neglected only at great peril, there developed a gradual acceptance of the concept of central management in the Presidency and in the departments.

This development was less influenced by constitutional doctrine or political philosophy than by the inescapable fact that if tools of management were to be effectively placed anywhere, they had to be located at the points of executive operations. There were no practical alternatives. Valuable things have been done; much remains to be accomplished.

For most of our history the President had no staff services to assist him.

He was a man with one or two secretaries, presumably able to call upon the departments for additional aid when needed. Not until after World War I was it recognized that while executive accountability is ultimately centered in a solitary individual, the office is an institution whose tangible and intangible attributes provide the means through which the President may carry out his constitutional obligations. In addition to the symbols and traditions of office, the Presidency is for many purposes an organization, a group enterprise with strong elements of continuity and permanence despite the periodic change of Presidents who are in charge of the enterprise and determine its character. It furnishes the managerial assistance and the staff tools for executive coordination and control. To meet similar needs, organized central staff services have grown up in the offices of departmental Secretaries.

Central management staffs are not designed to take over or perform any of the functions of individual departments or other operating units; such facilities do not in any way reduce or modify the responsibility of the heads of individual departments or bureaus. In the case of the Presidency, they deal with problems which cut across the entire national government, or in the case of a department, the whole of that organization, and which are not the primary or peculiar responsibility of any particular unit. They handle such activities as budget and personnel management, organization and procedures, planning, program coordination, and related staff functions. They are, in short, the instruments through which a responsible administrator can coordinate and control a large number of separate enterprises without undertaking to operate them himself.

THE BUREAU OF THE BUDGET

The historic landmark at the presidential level was the Budget and Accounting Act of 1921. For the first time suitable means were provided by which the President could properly discharge the responsibilities of an executive with regard to the expenditures and fiscal affairs of the agencies.

The President was made responsible for transmitting to Congress a consolidated financial program in the form of a single executive budget (although the Congress did not commit itself to pass a consolidated appropriation bill) and provision was made for a central budgetary agency. The head of the Bureau of the Budget was made directly responsible to the President, although the agency was formally located in the Treasury.

The President's increased ability to organize and control the executive budget simultaneously increased the ability of Congress to come to grips with the complexities of its appropriation responsibilities.

THE EXECUTIVE OFFICE OF THE PRESIDENT

The next and decisive landmark was the establishment in 1939 of the Executive Office of the President. Although staff assistance had been growing up around the President, here at last was official recognition of the need for formal organization and institutionalization of the central management machinery of the government. Since then the Executive Office has grown in status and importance as one of our foremost assets for the management of constitutional government.

Many important changes have taken place in the organization of the Executive Office of the President during its 25 years of formal existence. It is now made up of approximately 1450 employees (exclusive of personnel of the Central Intelligence Agency, and those who care for the executive mansion and grounds). In addition to the White House Office, which includes the President's aides, administrative assistants, and secretaries, the main units are the Bureau of the Budget (which has always been the institutional core of the Executive Office, responsible not only for the executive budget but also for administrative organization and methods), the Council of Economic Advisers, the Office of Science and Technology, and the Office of Emergency Planning. The National Security Council is a Cabinet level inter-agency coordinating committee with formal status in the Executive Office.

There has never been included in the Executive Office a real central management arm for personnel, obviously one of the core elements of administrative management. Until 1953 there existed a Liaison Office for Personnel Management, a token of President Roosevelt's unsuccessful attempt to obtain a bona fide office of personnel management. It was a makeshift arrangement, providing that one of the President's administrative assistants should act as "contact" with the Civil Service Commission. For some time it was considered only a part-time job. In 1953, in accordance with a Hoover Commission recommendation, the Liaison Office was superseded by a Personnel Adviser to the President in the person of the Chairman of the Civil Service Commission. The Task Force on Personnel and Civil Service of the second Hoover Commission (1955), however, recommended abandonment of this arrangement, and in 1957 President

Eisenhower reverted to the designation of a special assistant for personnel management. In 1961, President Kennedy dropped the position and named the chairman of the Commission as Presidential adviser on personnel policies throughout the Government.

U. S. CIVIL SERVICE COMMISSION

The United States Civil Service Commission was established shortly after the assassination of President Garfield, primarily to help avoid the evils of the spoils system. The Pendleton Act provided that the members be appointed by the President and serve at his pleasure. Rule-making authority rested in the President alone. But the structure of the arrangement, the political realities surrounding it, and its historical purpose kept the Commission from operating as actual staff of the President. In time the necessity of developing close relations with congressional committees added to the difficulties.

The three members' appointments were subject to Senate confirmation; at least one of the members had to be a member of the opposition party; and its structurally separate position was tagged "independent" from the beginning. (It has been alleged that the Congress found in this action its precedent for a later wave of independent commissions, usually regulatory in character, by which executive responsibility has been curtailed.) Nonetheless, the Commission generally regarded itself rather loosely as an agency of the President.

For more than a half of a century there were no sharp issues in the dichotomy as the Commission's activities were limited to merit system protection of a relatively small portion of the government service. But as civil service coverage was widely extended and broader concepts of personnel management began to enlarge the Commission's arena, congressional committees increased pressure on the Commission to play a role independent of the President with a massive surge of restrictive legislation. In 1956 the House civil service committee exhorted the Commission not to accept presidential control and warned, "Congress expects to hold it entirely accountable." * Although the Senate committee, under the leadership of Joseph S. Clark, presented a quite different view, in that year Congress enacted legislation which provided fixed six-year overlap-

---

* This was not without precedent. In the latter part of the nineteenth century, congressional spokesmen were even arguing that "heads of Departments ought to be independent of the power of the President."

ping terms for the commissioners previously serving at the pleasure of the President. Theoretically it is now possible for a majority of the Commission to be from the opposition party during the first two years of a new President. In addition, authority to approve super-grade positions was transferred from the chairman, designated by the President, to the Commission as a whole. Such additional impediments are characteristic of the severe limitations on the Commission's efforts to operate as a presidential agency.

Until World War II, the Commission interpreted its task as performing personnel administration for the departments and agencies, rather than helping or guiding them in the task. In part, the theory was that the departments, being themselves under political appointees of the President, could not be trusted with the job of hiring and firing without jeopardy to the merit system.

Even after the departments began to establish personnel divisions of their own, as a result of an executive order in 1939, the Commission's resistance to decentralization was great and it continued to stress the negative protective and policing features of its responsibilities instead of undertaking to help the departments solve their personnel problems in order better to accomplish the programs for which they were responsible. Strict avoidance of patronage was sufficient to receive an "A" in personnel practice. Since the war, the trend has been toward more constructive goals. Greater general understanding of the importance of practicing broad personnel management has not escaped the Commission, but some of the underlying sources of difficulty remain.

CIVIL SERVICE AND FEDERAL PERSONNEL MANAGEMENT: A DILEMMA

Why has it never been possible to establish for personnel management the kind of direct, operationally-oriented, executive responsibility which has proved so successful in budgetary management? Surely it cannot be contended that the personnel function is not essential to adequate executive control and supervision of administration. There are, however, important complexities which plague the personnel problem and differentiate it from the other elements of the central machinery of government.

Part of the problem is simply a widespread misunderstanding of the scope and character of the task of personnel management in government. Even among those who have come to recognize the vital character of personnel work in modern industrial management, there is often a failure to make a transference to the problems of modern government. Many professional friends of civil service reform, perhaps still thinking of the old battles of the past or perhaps impressed by the continued prevalence of spoils at local levels of government, continue to see it primarily as a policing job. They are still mainly concerned with the establishment of iron-clad procedures to insure that "political favorites" and "ward heelers" are kept out and "honest choices" on the "basis of merit"—determined by a competitive examination—are admitted, and then protected from political dismissal. It is frequently assumed that providing "good" personnel in this fashion is adequate to get the program job done.

It took many years before it was generally realized that budget management was more than a set of accounting procedures to assure honesty, that it was basically a tool for program planning and administration expressed through indices of fiscal control. It is not yet as widely appreciated that personnel administration is something more than assuring honesty, fairness, and even technical competence, that control over the hiring, firing, location, and assignment of personnel is a basic managerial tool for program direction and coordination, an essential wherewithal to make possible the President's constitutional prescription to "take care that the laws be faithfully executed."

Another part of the problem is that many of the political "pros" and some of the interest groups have had a more sophisticated view of certain aspects of personnel policy and control than the reformers. As we have already indicated, patronage in the conventional sense is far from the only or even the primary cause of Congress' activities in the personnel field. The special interests and the particular power centers of individual congressmen, developed through the committee system, are not congenial to the principle of central personnel management. It might weaken their own "controls."

In addition, there is a body of opinion, both in and out of Congress, which holds that, as a matter of principle, personnel and personnel administration should be held accountable to the Congress directly rather than through the President. Unlike the executive budget, which the committees get an ample opportunity to go over, real executive management of personnel would not give congressmen the same opportunity for individual item approval, disapproval, or revision. Neither the nature of executive-legislative relations already discussed nor the traditional American distrust of "bureaucracy" encourages unified executive authority over personnel.

EXECUTIVE CONTROL VERSUS POLICING THE EXECUTIVE

Finally, there is a real and difficult substantive dilemma facing federal personnel management. On the one hand executive requirements demand that personnel administration be organized to meet the responsibilities of the Chief Executive and his department heads. If personnel control is not to be largely ritualistic, dedicated to techniques rather than to the program goals of government, it cannot be insulated from those who must use the personnel, who must make of their employees a working team to achieve desired ends, and who must be held responsible for their performance. This is the central argument for 1) maintaining central staff services for personnel policy in the Executive Office, and 2) decentralizing actual personnel selection and all other aspects of their management to the responsible operating officials, the department heads.

On the other hand, there are special factors which tend to exclude personnel administration in government from this type of executive control. Unless guarantees against spoils and the caprices of politics, in the form of tenure and related elements of reasonable security, can be offered, government will not be able to attract or retain the calibre of men it must have. The long history of political spoils in this country, still egregious at some state and local levels, and the original purpose of the federal civil service laws, combine to place very heavy emphasis upon these safeguards. This supports the negative functions of preventing malpractice rather than the positive goals of personnel management. Preponderant concern with this consideration tends sharply to reduce the degree of personnel control entrusted to the politically accountable officials.

Thus a conflict, at least in basic emphasis, is recognized. One viewpoint maintains that unless we can rigorously protect the merit system from the appalling inefficiencies and insecurities of the spoils system, and maintain its attractiveness to the kind of men and women we must have to staff our government, modern personnel management authority would do the Chief Executive and his department heads little good. Another point of view insists that the only purpose of having competent and honest personnel is so that they can collectively serve the positive objectives of the government under control of the executive. If we forget this, we create a situation wherein the instruments or the techniques become more important than the purposes and may even destroy the latter.

Those who emphasize the second point of view claim there is no incompatibility between good personnel management controlled by the program operating officials and a strong merit system. In any event, they feel that it is far better to take a few risks than to sacrifice management for policing. In the long run, they say, we are likely to get a better quality of person into the merit system through the leadership of operating officials accountable for program achievement than through a separate outside agency which becomes the symbol of "an old lady with a stick." They say that having personnel management outside the stream of program responsibility inevitably leads to red tape without any relation to the ultimate aims of government.

The other side, of course, denies these contentions. They believe that the tradition of the spoilsman in this country is still too strong to be overlooked and it continues to be nurtured by our state and local governments. If we relax the safeguards of the merit system, we are in danger of losing the important advances made since passage of the Pendleton Act. The federal service does not yet have enough public respect or status to produce much righteous wrath if a new administration were to undertake to violate the merit system. On the contrary, they point out, our political campaigns always ring with denunciations of the "dictatorial bureaucracy," its "demand for more power," its "incompetence" and its "corruption." It almost comes as a surprise to many people (and a disappointment to some) that most federal employees are not given the heave-ho immediately after a new administration's inauguration day.

Furthermore, the argument runs, the practical facts of American political life, such as the conflicts described earlier, make it impossible for the Chief Executive to take effective control over personnel, however we might give him the forms of such control. A weakening of the protective aspects of the merit system would probably open the door wide to depredations by individual congressmen, and the executive might end up in a poorer relative position than it is today.

We have put the opposing views in extreme terms for purposes of clarity. The extreme positions are not dominant. There should be general acknowledgement of the enormous achievements of the merit system and recognition that a zealous preoccupation with a policing system was originally essential if its firm establishment was to be attained. Furthermore, it was only about 30 years ago that we began to understand enough about administration to talk about "personnel management" in the sense it is now employed. Now there is a change in our circumstances and in our needs. Can we not move toward new goals without sacrificing the gains of the past?

THE NEED FOR RECONCILIATION

The great challenge is now one of reconciliation, how to achieve a positive managerial approach to personnel in the federal system without abandoning necessary safeguards against spoils. Or, as William Seal Carpenter said:

> What the modern reformers must undertake is nothing less than the reconciliation of the principle of merit and fitness for appointment and promotion in the civil service with the requirement that the chief executive shall at all times be able to control the amount and quality of the administration for which he is by law responsible. In other words, the chief executive . . . must be enabled to utilize the personnel under the merit system to the best advantage to accomplish the efficient purposes of government. . . . The authority of the President having been established to function through department heads, it becomes necessary that the line of command and supervision from the President down through his department heads to every employee, and the line of responsibility from each employee of the executive branch to the President, shall be clearly outlined.

Challenges to the Civil Service System

The federal civil service system, as Herbert Kaufman shows in Chapter 1, has been subjected to numerous waves of criticism from many sides. The contemporary issues have a more specialized focus.

HOW HIGH SHOULD THE CIVIL SERVICE GO?

In the original enthusiasm of the upward and onward movement of the merit system, students of administration generally assumed there could not be too much civil service. Now the view is more common that the concept of a neutral civil service may have lower limits than was once supposed. In line with strengthening the capacities of the President, within the context of our political system, it is increasingly asserted that not only top management but some of the middle management—the bureau chief level and equivalent—may have to be available to the President for appointment of non-permanent employees who are willing to accept posts in government for a limited period because of enthusiasm for a particular program or an administration.

A THIRD CATEGORY OF FEDERAL EMPLOYEES?

Dean Paul Appleby has pointed out that,

for a half-century or so while political science was developing as a distinct discipline, much of its literature tended to accept as substantially real a separation of powers which excluded from administration any—or at least any important—policy-making functions. Under such a theory of separation, a civil service system was justified, accepted, and probably to a small extent over-sold.

Sophistication in these matters came to the politicians long before it came to the academic observers. While the latter were still describing a completely polarized universe between "spoils" and "merit system," the political world was demonstrating that there was at least a third category. These were men to whom an administration owed no party rewards and who sought no patronage but who combined a special competence with an aggressive dedication to the program policy they were brought in to help administer.

The politicians had long noted the now generally accepted fact that policy formation goes on at almost all levels of administration. More important, in the American context, the form, content, and survival of programs are up for continuous battle. Unlike the British executive, the American President does not have any automatic control of program and policy during a term of office. In the absence of a responsible party system, an election simply establishes the stage of the continuous battle and indicates how some of the weapons will be distributed.

As the President is steadily embattled, directly or indirectly, over almost all parts of his program, including those regarding which he may assume he won a "mandate" with his election, he must depend upon a devoted and affirmative commitment to his program on the part of his administrators, certainly those who are "exposed" to Congress, and thus far it has been exceptionally difficult to prevent the bureau-chief level from being continuously so exposed. Thus the President often needs from these men more than a formally efficient neutrality, or even an honest willingness to do the job as well as possible because it falls in the line of duty.

Furthermore, as Herbert Emmerich has put it, "If the President is in a constant state of siege, the department heads may be said to be faced with a chronic state of mutiny in their bureaus." One explanation lies in the professional specialization of many of the bureaus which results in resistance to control by outsiders. This, plus the inherent desire for independence and freedom from executive management which characterizes most bureaus, and congressional and interest group encouragement of autonomy, sets up bulwarks against integration too difficult for the department head to cope with. This is especially true if the permanence of the bureau chief adds to his stake in such separateness. In the absence of a class of mobile top-level administrative "generalists," it has not been easy to remove or transfer a bureau chief even though he is uncongenial to his superiors.

Among those who take a general position that virtually no jobs below the Secretarial level ought to be exempt, one of the basic arguments is that the differences between our two major parties are never "fundamental" enough to inhibit the ability of civil servants to carry out the policies of either party with energy and integrity, that the policy leeway admissible to any new administration is usually not very broad. This is in general true, if by "fundamental" is meant the kind of deep ideological cleavages which divide some less stable nations. But that should not allow us to underrate the significance of our own differences. Differences on public power, land management, health insurance, public housing, and similar unresolved policy questions are real and great enough to appear quite fundamental and they can become impassioned issues on which may depend the success or failure of an administration.

The President's own beleaguered position in relation to Congress and the vulnerability of his control over the executive branch frequently make him greatly dependent upon administrative officials who are not only competent but ready to do battle and are therefore, perhaps, expendable. In the absence of "collective responsibility" and party control, the President must frequently protect himself by exposing lower officials to frontal attack and using them for negotiation and pursuit of political strength.

David Levitan was one of the earliest students to advocate official recognition of a third category of government employees to cope with the American situation. He said administrative officials should be (and, in fact, are) divided into three groups: 1) career employees, recruited under civil service regulations with permanent tenure who expect to spend all their normal working years in the federal service; 2) political appointees, appointed because of party identification into established political offices or as part of the President's immediate official family; 3) professional employees who combine the characteristics of the two other groups. They could meet the standards of civil service regulations without difficulty but "the distinguishing feature about these employees is that they do not expect, nor are they expected, to make the federal service their life's work; yet they are not appointed because of their party connections, but because of their professional qualifications and announced clear-cut identification with the policies of the Administration in power."

A British scholar, R. N. Spann, after studying the United States civil service, found demonstrated merit in this new element. He wrote:

> The experience of the 1930s has had some permanent effects on the American civil service. The New Deal raised the prestige of government employment. It, and the emergencies which followed, have also caused some reconsideration of the problems of recruitment . . . [and] emphasized the need for better management. . . .
>
> But the New Deal was also a triumph of the Patronage. It indicated, in spite of some lapses, that discretionary appointment could be used to good purpose. Recruitment by contact had produced men of talent. It also became fashionable to speak of the need for "loyalty" in the servants of the new State, a word which carried different implications in the America of the 1930s from those which it has today. More important, it became clearer that, in the social and political context of the United States, a considerable number of the higher offices of an active government were inevitably "political." Whoever occupied them would be held to account by Congress and others for what was done and could assume no protective garb of anonymity. Choosing acceptable occupants, or making them do some fighting to get themselves and their programmes accepted, discarding them if they failed, looked like the sort of adjustment to changing circumstances that a President must make to keep the ship afloat. Some regretted this and wished, for example, that Congress could be made to behave like the House of Commons. To others it seemed the form of government native to the American temperament. . . .

In addition to the apparent political necessity and policy advantages of this type of practice, which has in fact been going on in some degree for a long time in the American service without formal acknowledgement, it has been supported as a source of additional vitality and democracy for our public service. By keeping considerable portions of the bureaucracy fluid it avoids the dangers of the "closed group" and helps to keep the bureaucracy broadly representative of almost all social strata as well as to make more readily available the experience and talents of the outside business, scientific, and academic communities.

The frequent interchange between public and private life has contributed to democratization of the nation through wider citizen understanding of, and participation in, governmental activities. Especially in view of our apparent inability to develop in the career service an administrative class of "generalists," this type of reserve pool appears to offer an effective base for the support of the civil service. We are fortunate that no social, professional or traditional barriers yet divide the civil service from the private citizen, that so many of the latter have seen it from the inside. In a dynamic economy and in an open pluralistic society, there are other constructive choices besides a general "spoils system" or a permanent "closed group" of civil servants.

The problem of reconciling the value of a permanent civil service core at the top levels of public management—for its irreplaceable experience and governmental knowledge and the need for continuity—with the effective control required by the President and his department heads is enmeshed in the peculiarities of American political institutions and is not merely a management question. It is not unreasonable to assume that only if the President's controls and the authority of department heads over their bureaucracies are far stronger and more direct than they are today, can new administrations generally be expected to accept fully and readily a permanent civil service in the upper reaches of administration. So long as this control is lacking, it is probably inescapable that the President and Secretaries will seek to substitute for the machinery of effective control by enlarging the number of trusted and familiar associates and personal adherents in key posts. But in reality how much direct control can the executive obtain in the context of our executive-legislative relations and broadly diffused social power?

Under these circumstances, even an administration fully aware of the advantages of the experience and governmental know-how of civil servants may feel it must give up some of these advantages if they impede its need for control and for committed supporters. If, therefore, it were possible to obtain real personnel management control within the executive line, would this not ultimately contribute to strengthening the merit system and extending the career service?

Recent Explorations in Quest of Efficiency and Accountability

"It is a strenuous thing this living the life of a free people," said Woodrow Wilson. A democratic society derives its vitality in part from continuous self-examination and readjustment. The job of reorganization is by its nature never consummated.

In effective administration a good deal of reorganization is continuous, resulting from necessary day-to-day action and decision. But more basic structural reform is episodic, usually requiring special attention to accumulations of obsolete impediments and conscious re-examination of old assumptions.

The United States government has regularly subjected itself to such periodic re-evaluations, beginning with the establishment of a reorganization committee by the Continental Congress in 1780. The crucial significance of such reforms goes far beyond the dollar-and-cents value of increased efficiency into the vital relationship between structure and control.

Two historic reports of the past three decades resulted in some effective action and wide public discussion, and left a deep imprint upon our administrative doctrine and institutions. These famous reports were the products of the President's Committee on Administrative Management, sometimes referred to as the Brownlow Committee, which reported in 1937, and the Commission on Reorganization of the Executive Branch of the Government (the Hoover Commission), which reported in 1949. This was followed by a second Hoover Commission which reported six years later.

Significantly, despite the passage of a dozen years marked by the disruptive effects of a great world war and the different auspices of the studies, they were in full accord in their central thesis. This thesis reaffirmed the basic constitutional doctrine of the unity of the executive. Both stressed the theme that efficiency, as well as accountability, depends on the establishment of clear responsibility in an effective Chief Executive as the center of energy, direction, and administrative management. He must have a clear line of managerial control down through the operating departments, along with the assistance of adequate managerial and staff agencies.

The temper of both studies was indicated by Paul Appleby in an appraisal of the Hoover Commission reports:

> It is not widely enough recognized that the reality of responsible government is dependent upon the ability of the President to control the executive branch. It is not widely enough recognized that, in spite of all the popular talk about "presidential power," the Chief Executive is, of all chiefs of important modern States, weakest with respect to his executive government.

The recommendations of both study groups are numerous and detailed and, since almost all deal with problems of government organization, most of them impinge in greater or lesser degree upon personnel management. We confine ourselves here to those matters which relate most directly to the organization of responsibility for personnel administration. On these matters there was agreement on the important principles and some disagreement on methods of implementation.

THE BROWNLOW COMMITTEE RECOMMENDATIONS

The President's Committee formulated the principle that the administrative position of the Chief Executive required positive and continuous management, through the aid of staff services, rather than his sporadic indications of approval or disapproval as in the past. The President was recognized as perhaps the sole influential integrating core in the government as contrasted with the multiple centrifugal forces in Congress, the departments and agencies.

Personnel control is a primary element of continuous management and supervision but it cannot be effective unless accompanied by control over organization of work and the delegation of responsibility. The President's Committee advanced the proposition that the task of reorganization is inherently executive in character since the "division of work for its effective performance is a part of the task of doing that work." The Hoover Commission agreed. Compromise progress along this path was made by permitting the President to advance reorganization plans subject to veto by the Congress within a specified period.*

The Committee reproached Congress for its habit of vesting executive functions in bureau chiefs beyond control of the Chief Executive. The Hoover Commission likewise pointed an accusing finger at Congress for breaking the chain of command and, in effect, destroying effective responsibility. Limited progress has been made in this area. Both reports called attention to the excessive number of agencies which theoretically reported directly to the President and the impossibility of his maintaining direct supervision over so many separate units. They demanded amalgamation into a smaller number of agencies with direct lines of control.

Directly to the point, the Committee said that "federal personnel management . . . needs fundamental revision." It asked that the Civil

---

* The Reorganization Act of 1939, which first granted this method of reorganization to the President, specifically exempted the Civil Service Commission.

Service Commission be replaced by a single Civil Service Administrator to whom would be transferred all the Commission's duties, powers, and authority. In addition there would serve a part-time, non-salaried Civil Service Board consisting of seven members drawn from private life and appointed by the President, with advice and consent of the Senate, for overlapping terms of seven years. The Board would serve as adviser to the Administrator and "act as the watchdog of the merit system and to represent the public interest in improvement of personnel administration." It would also appoint the examiners to conduct a competitive examination to fill the vacancy of the Civil Service Administrator, when it should exist, and certify to the President the name of the three highest candidates from which he could make the selection subject to consent of the Senate.

In addition to the duties indicated, the Administrator would "act as the direct adviser to the President upon all personnel matters . . . and would assume initiative and leadership in personnel management." It would be his duty to stimulate and aid the departments and bureaus in establishment of able personnel staffs. "Personnel management at the departmental and bureau level is exceedingly important." It would further enhance the role of departments by having the Council of Personnel Administration—which included personnel officers in the departments—strengthened as an instrument for the formulation of constructive policies.

Other personnel recommendations included extension of the merit system "upward, outward, and downward to cover practically all non-policy-determining posts" and steps to strengthen the attractiveness of the government as a career service.

The principles underlying these recommendations seem reasonably simple. They attempt to advance the presidential role in personnel management. They recognize the well-known inefficiency of the commission form of organization for administrative purposes and particularly its unsuitability for a staff agency to the President. They recognize that a committee's real utility can be in an advisory capacity, as a channel to the public, and for watchdog purposes. The recommendation to strengthen the personnel work of the departments was in accordance with the principle of decentralization. These principles seem hardly challengeable from the viewpoint of administrative science. Far less acceptable is the unusual suggestion that the President be obliged to select one of his chief staff aides from a panel of three arrived at by competitive examination. The Committee's major vulnerability in this field was that it saw virtually no limits to the merit system principle.

ACTION DESPITE CONGRESSIONAL REJECTION OF RECOMMENDATIONS

President Roosevelt transmitted all the Committee's recommendations with his full endorsement. Those portions of the personnel recommendations which required congressional approval did not receive it. Fear of presidential authority and fear that a one-man administrator would not adequately protect the civil service undoubtedly contributed to the rejection.

The report was enormously influential, however, because many of the reforms could be effected by executive action alone once the climate of opinion was made ready by broad public discussion. Since 1938 important steps toward decentralization of personnel administration have been fairly continuous, and the principle has been given at least lip service everywhere.

An executive order in 1938 required each executive agency to set up its own personnel office headed by a director of personnel. Before that time departmental personnel activities had been confined to some necessary clerical operations.

Although in 1949, the Hoover Commission found that in many cases their activity was still limited to formal paper work, there has been considerable improvement. World War II, with its enormous expansion of the federal service, forced the Commission to delegate recruiting and classification to the agencies and to regional offices. As the departments came to be staffed with professional personnel officials whose knowledge and influence gave them a much greater voice in the councils of the Civil Service Commission, the Federal Personnel Council (formerly the Council of Personnel Administration) was invigorated. After the heat of the debate on the Committee recommendations had subsided, the merit system was extended to many additional positions both by executive orders and congressional action, notably the Ramspeck Act of 1940.

THE HOOVER COMMISSION REPORTS

The first Hoover Commission was quite different from the Brownlow Committee. It was created by a Republican Congress (the eightieth) rather than a Democratic President. Instead of three men, distinguished for their professional and scholarly expertness in public administration selected by the President, it was composed of 12 members—six Republicans and six Democrats, four chosen by the President, four by the Presiding Officer of the Senate and four by the Speaker of the House. The staff of the Brownlow Committee had been made up almost entirely of academicians, but most of the Hoover Commission task forces were recruited primarily from the business world. The Commission had the enormous prestige of being headed, actively and prominently, by an ex-President.

The basic tone and principles affecting all nineteen of the Commission reports is clearly stated in the first, *General Management of the Executive Branch*. Its fundamental position on the management of the President's Office is well on the way to becoming doctrine in the field of public administration.

The position is clear. "The President, and under him his chief lieutenants, the department heads, must be held responsible and accountable to the people and the Congress for the conduct of the executive branch." It noted that authority to meet these responsibilities was lacking and staff services to exercise the authority were inadequate. Its over-all recommendations therefore included:

> Establish a clear line of control from the President to these department and agency heads and from them to their subordinates with correlative responsibility from these officials to the President, cutting through the barriers which have in many cases made bureaus and agencies practically independent of the Chief Executive.
>
> Give the President and each department head strong staff services which should exist only to make executive work more effective, and which the President or department head should be free to organize at his discretion.

After finding that the government had not built "a corps of administrators of the highest level of ability with an interest in the program of the Government as a whole," the Commission recommended that steps be taken to develop mobile "generalist" administrators who could be moved about among the bureaus and departments.

The implementation of these generalizations as they relate to the organization of personnel responsibility was contained in several recommendations. The Commission softened the proposals of the Brownlow Committee, which had proved unacceptable to Congress. It proposed the creation of an Office of Personnel within the President's Office. The director should serve "in a coordinate capacity with such officials as the Director of the Office of the Budget" and would be the principal staff adviser to the President in connection with civil service problems. It proposed that this director should be the chairman of the Civil Service Commission. At the same time it was recommended that "the Civil Service Commission should be reorganized to vest in its chairman the responsibility for the administrative direction of its work." The two other commissioners would remain on a full-time basis and the three would continue to be responsible for recommendations to the President about civil service rules and for issuance of regulations and standards and to act as an appellate body.

The Hoover report also recommended that "the Civil Service Commission should place primary emphasis on staff functions, rather than upon processing a multitude of personnel transactions" and that "primary responsibility for recruiting and examining Federal employees should be placed on the departments and agencies" all of which "should be required to have on their top management staffs a director of personnel."

Even further decentralization was urged by having the President direct agency heads to "make sure their personnel offices place primary emphasis on advising operating officials, and that most personnel activities [be] carried on by operating officials." The Hoover Commission was quite clear that it intended a maximum merging of personnel activities with line operating responsibility, but it left much to be desired in clarity regarding the practical and desirable limits of such assimilation.

A variety of measures was urged to develop a better qualified upper level career service, particularly to encourage a group of broad-gauged and mobile administrators who could be transferred from one bureau to another and from one department to another.

THE VIEWS OF COMMISSIONER POLLOCK

One of the commissioners, James K. Pollock, undertook to sharpen the personnel report and wrote a vigorous addendum which proved so cogent that it has received almost as much attention as the report itself. He asserted that, while there was no disagreement over the idea of decentralization, the Hoover Commission had not gone far enough, for it had recommended that personnel administration be decentralized under "standards approved by the Civil Service Commission." He felt this was much too vague and might not permit thoroughgoing decentralization, that procedural standards in the hands of the Civil Service Commission were likely to prove inflexible, artificial, centralizing, and so produce "a dead hand in personnel administration." He felt that the responsible heads of the agencies should be free to develop personnel programs "suitable for their varying needs."

Dr. Pollock agreed with the Commission's unanimous rejection of "the Civil Service Commission form of organization because it has served only to perpetuate the evils of inaction, delay, and administrative meddling which have characterized its operations for so many years." But, he protested, the compromise recommended would prove unworkable and he endorsed the single personnel administrator proposed by the Brownlow Committee. He was convinced that protection of the merit system could be as effective under a single administrator as under the commission form of organization.

Pollock felt that the methods suggested to develop a high-level career system of general administrators were inadequate for the objective with which he fully agreed, and added:

> I believe with equal emphasis that the service must be opened to the steady and balanced infusion of new blood from the main streams of American business and professional communities. Such an exchange is necessary to prevent an isolated, inbred bureaucracy, unaware of, and therefore unresponsive to, the views and purposes of elected officials.

"SENIOR CIVIL SERVICE"

The second (1955) Hoover Commission's report on personnel and civil service elaborated upon the development of a stronger generalist higher career service, an expanded non-career political leadership, and the relationship of the two groups. It urged that the number of non-career executives be significantly increased because it was too small for the tasks to be performed and also as a means for protecting the integrity of the career service. Career administrators should "be relieved by non-career executives of responsibility for advocacy or defense of policies and programs." The political appointees should, however, be confined to the departmental, as distinguished from the bureau, level.

The most prominent and disputed recommendation was for the creation of a body of mobile career administrators to be known as the "senior civil service," who would be available at top posts across the government. Appointment to this group, from among exceptionally qualified career civil servants, would carry with it status, rank, and salary for the individual regardless of the particular position he might be assigned to fill:

> The primary objective is to have always at hand in the government a designated group of highly qualified administrators whose competence, integrity, and faithfulness have been amply demonstrated, who will make it easier for non-career executives to discharge their responsibilities. . . . A secondary but related objective is to make the civil service more attractive as a career to able men and women.

The "senior civil service" plan was not received enthusiastically in most quarters. Scholars and experts agreed with the objectives but generally thought the design too rigid and unattuned to political realities to fulfill its goals. For example, the Commission had stressed "political neutrality" and explained, "This means they must avoid such emotional attachment to the policies of any administration that they cannot accept change and work in harmony with new leaders." Critics demurred that political (party) neutrality was one thing, but lack of program commitment was quite another, and the latter was of dubious value or practicality in a top administrator. Many also felt it would curtail the healthy lateral entry of professional people from the outside world into the higher civil service and also fail to make the career service generally more attractive.

Congress had its own obvious reasons for opposing an "elite corps" of mobile civil servants. The assumption that it was primarily lack of time or knowledge of political officials which caused career administrators to represent their programs before congressional committees did not take into account that congressmen insist on carrying on continuing negotiations with the permanent officialdom.

President Eisenhower undertook general support of the plan. In 1958 he established by executive order a Career Executive Board, as an adjunct of the Civil Service Commission, to develop standards and procedures to introduce a Career Executive Service, a watered-down version of the "senior civil service." The action came under immediate attack from a House subcommittee which requested the President to suspend the program. When he failed to comply, Congress struck out the appropriation for the Career Executive Board and prohibited the Civil Service Commission from using any of its funds for this plan. The executive order was then rescinded.

PROGRESS AND MORE PROPOSALS

Nonetheless, the work of the Hoover Commissions, added to the Brownlow studies, did generate considerable progress and a healthier widespread concern with personnel issues. In 1949 the Chairman of the Civil Service Commission was made responsible for administration of the Commission. In 1953 he was appointed Personnel Advisor to the President, an arrangement which was reinstated in modified form in 1961 after a four-year lapse. There has been a salutary internal reorganization of the Commission. The Commission initially objected to the Hoover recommendation that "primary responsibility" for recruiting and examining be transferred to the agencies from the Commission, where it had been since 1883, for fear this delegation would not provide the necessary protection against "personal political favoritism and discrimination." Nevertheless, the movement toward decentralization continued. As far back as 1947, President Truman issued an executive order making Department heads responsible for personnel management although authority over standards and procedures remained under the Commission. There has been vast expansion of the authority of boards of examiners operating under the departments and delegation has increased.

Both before and after the Hoover Commissions, the Civil Service Commission attempted to advance the development of broadly-gauged mobile career administrators. A special recruitment program for promising young college graduates—the Junior Management Assistant Program—was aimed at this objective. Machinery was established to encourage transfer of career employees to higher vacancies in other agencies. A special examination for "Federal Administrators" limited to those already in federal employment who had reached the rank of GS-12 was set up. And it was the influence of the Commission which caused President Eisenhower to give his support to the senior civil service idea.

In 1952 the Commission announced the beginning of a "career development program," but it was not until 1958 that Congress, after much resistance, authorized expenditures for executive training by all agencies. Although such training and educational programs have been sharply criticized as spotty and inadequate, there is no doubt that more is being done than ever before.

The constructive interest stimulated by the several reports even reached into the halls of Congress. In 1958, Senator Clark of Pennsylvania introduced a bill substantially adopting the central thesis of the first Hoover and Brownlow reports. It would have created an Office of Personnel Management in the Executive Office of the President, to be headed by a single director, which would take over most of the functions of the Civil Service Commission. The Commission would remain as a separate agency mainly to protect employee rights. The principles underlying the bill were: 1) that personnel administration is an executive function for which the President is responsible under the Constitution; 2) that the President needs a staff agency similar to the Bureau of the Budget to assist him in his personnel responsibilities; 3) that wider responsibility for personnel administration could be delegated to the departments. The opposition expressed at the hearings centered on the familiar theme that an independent commission is needed to safeguard the merit system against political discrimination. The bill never reached the Senate floor but was favorably reported by a majority of the Senate Civil Service Committee.

Clearly, the central issues remain lively and myriad proposals are being submitted. In 1964, the influential Committee for Economic Development, composed of leading businessmen and educators, issued a thoughtful report on "Improving Executive Management in the Federal Government." It concentrated on the top-level career and political executives, some 8,600 positions (5,500 civilian), as defined by the Committee. In considerably modified and more practicable form, it borrowed some of the concepts underlying the Hoover Commission's recommendations. Its major recommendations were: 1) establishment of two new and higher career super grades (GS-19 and GS-20), with entry limited in numbers to those with superlative achievement records and highest potential, involving suitable salary recognition and distinctive "rank-in-person" status, and that "means be sought to increase the number of transfers at these levels between agencies"; 2) establishment in the Executive Office of the President of an Office of Executive Personnel, under a director serving at the pleasure of the President, to which would be transferred the functions of the Civil Service Commission involving classification, recruitment, training, development, and separation for all personnel above grade GS-15 (the super grades)—the Office would be the center for dealing with all upper echelon civilian career personnel including those not under the Classification Act, and "it would be the

main source of advice to the President on upper-level personnel policies"; 3) assignment in each agency of the upper-level personnel functions to a member of the agency's top management group in daily association with the agency head.

The case for extending upward the grades of the career service is
strong, to attract and retain the best quality, to allow more recognition
of superlative performance, to permit more flexibility in the use of such
men, and hopefully to improve chances for a proper working relationship with successive political officials. A strong staff agency for personnel does seem needed at the Presidential level. Questions do arise,
however, with respect to the operational functions which the CED would
assign to the Executive Office and in the proposed bifurcation of the
government's personnel management between the Civil Service Commission for the ordinary grades and the new agency for the top grades.

The CED asserts that the CSC is inherently handicapped in undertaking
positive dynamic measures to improve upper level personnel management. It is not clear, however, to what degree Congress would permit
the proposed Office of Executive Personnel more freedom for creative
measures. The CED correctly decries that "a Congressman or Senator may
exert more influence on appointments and key promotions in the agencies with which he deals, as a member of an appropriations sub-commit-
tee or of a substantive committee, than the President who is charged
with constitutional responsibility for the results." It has often been
Congress which has prevented strengthening the top-levels of the agencies
for personnel management by its restriction of what it calls "overhead,"
rather than agency reluctance.

These latest proposals, especially considering their auspicious origins,
deserve and will undoubtedly receive considerable discussion in the
future. In any case, it now seems clear that some degree of consensus
has been emerging among the experts and scholars. The President needs
regularized staff assistance in the Executive Office to carry out his personnel administration responsibilities. The career service needs to be
strengthened, augmented, and made more attractive at its higher levels.
Simultaneously, the non-career executive group needs considerable bol-
stering. But an intellectual consensus is not quite the same as action,
and the historic bases of resistance remain formidable. The basic issue
of reconciling a top-level career service with adequate political control
of the entire structure remains as troublesome as ever.

THE OMISSION IS THE CRUX

The basic issues of American politics were, of course, beyond the mandate of both the Brownlow and Hoover groups (as well as that of the CED in 1964). They confined themselves to reorganization of the executive branch, unfortunately not entirely a separable matter. This caused omission of some problems which lie at the heart of public administration and which severely delimit the efficacy of purely administrative reforms. Foremost among these is the central problem of American government which conditions all the rest—executive-legislative relations.

Directly and indirectly, the Brownlow-Hoover-CED groups pointed accusing fingers at Congress as the principal architect of disorder and irresponsibility in the executive branch. But their cautions to Congress regarding the perils of its failure to observe elemental canons of administrative efficiency and effective government runs counter to more powerful propulsions set in motion by constitutional tensions.

In England, the issue could not arise in this form because of a real separation of powers in regard to the conduct of the executive branch. In the United States the hortatory approach to Congress sometimes gives the impression that the problem is that congressmen are evil or stupid, which is largely untrue and extraneous. The problem lies deeply imbedded in the character of political institutions which conditions the behavior and the relationship of Congress and the executive. The conflict may be tempered through the strengthening of knowledge and understanding contributed by these important public studies. But it appears doubtful that they have, as Don K. Price asserts, "persuaded Congress that it can control policy more effectively if the Executive Branch is more effectively under the direction of the President," or that, even if persuaded, the results could be much different as long as committees remain autonomous.

Whatever gains are made in the efficient organization of our personnel management services will probably be insufficient to overcome the fracturing of executive control which stems from these profound sources. It is unlikely, in view of its own structural diffusion, that Congress can long desist from the sort of actions which caused the first Hoover report to say:

> Authority is diffused, lines of authority are confused, . . . [and] . . . the line of responsibility from each employee of the executive branch up to the

President, has been weakened, or actually broken, in many places and in many ways.

The basic causes of such actions were not, and could not be, touched by either the Brownlow or Hoover recommendations. They are as alive today as ever. It may be worth considering whether the next large-scale official study of the organization of the executive branch should not include, and perhaps start with, a study of the organization of Congress.

However, that is all the more reason for developing the very best possible organizational tools of administrative management within the executive branch. The maximum degree of executive unity which could possibly be achieved by such formal measures would still leave a great deal of diffusion of authority. Even full approval of the kind of recommendations we have discussed would not result in the President being made administratively too strong. They will deserve the approbation of history if they prevent the authority of our Chief Executive from becoming perilously weak.

Harvey C. Mansfield

3

Political Parties, Patronage, and the Federal Government Service

The Dilemma of Party Patronage and the Public Service

When the presidential election results signal a turnover in party control the voters sanction a change, and to party men a change means, most immediately, patronage won or lost. The new President may wonder what to do with the movement he has successfully headed. Congressmen and lobbyists may ponder their new bargaining positions and their clients' expectations. Civil servants await the outcome with apprehension, hope, or resignation. Party men think of the offices to be filled.

Accommodatingly, the Democratic Eighty-seventh Congress in 1961, the Republican Eighty-third Congress in 1953, the Democratic Seventy-third Congress in 1933, all following in turn the precedent of Republican action when Harding was elected in 1921, asked the Civil Service Commission for an up-to-date list of appointive federal positions exempt from merit system coverage. The number of these in the 1960s was of the order of 225,000 in the continental United States, plus some 150,000 overseas. Yet in 1954 and in 1962—in each case, a year after the new

HARVEY C. MANSFIELD is Professor of Political Science at Ohio State University, and is frequently a consultant to various government commissions and committees. In 1953 he was a member of the faculty of the National War College. Since 1956 he has been Managing Editor of The American Political Science Review. Professor Mansfield is the author of numerous books and professional articles, including two others in American Assembly publications.

administration was installed—it appeared that the number of patronage appointments the national party headquarters could count as having been made to positions of any consequence was in the range between two and three thousand—scarcely one-tenth of one per cent of the total federal civilian employment. Patronage is on the decline, if not on the way out. By all accounts the good old days of wholesale replacements, still at least partially preserved in states like Indiana, Kentucky, and Oklahoma, and in many local jurisdictions, are gone. What has come over the system?

The Constitution divides and separates the legal powers of government; the party system is the informal instrument we chiefly rely upon to hold the bits and pieces together and make the formal institutions work. Parties furnish a mechanism—no doubt clumsy, but we have evolved nothing on a national scale more apt for the purpose—of popular participation through elections. They make the voters' choices usually manageable if not always significant. They provide a modicum of common interest among the top officials of government, and a vehicle for the cooperation and compromise necessary to carry any legislative program through to the statute books. Well or ill done, these are indispensable functions if popular government is to be orderly and responsive.

Next to the influence of the separation of powers, therefore, the relations of the majority party to the administrative establishment are fundamental in shaping the future development of the federal government service. We do not know how to do without parties, even if we would. Yet, whatever may have been true in Andrew Jackson's time, today too much depends on the calibre of governmental performance for us to be complacent with anything short of the best obtainable. Notoriously, partisan appointments afford no guarantee of fitness for public service.

How can a major political party of the sort we have known—Republican or Democratic—live without patronage? How can the sort of federal establishment we want to see live with it?

Early in this century, it was the machine politicians, on the defensive, who saw the dilemma in these questions. A genially plainspoken Tammany philosopher discoursing on "the curse of civil reform" (*Plunkitt of Tammany Hall*, p. 18) put the spoilsmen's argument in classic form:

> First, this great and glorious country was built up by political parties;
> second, parties can't hold together if their workers don't get the offices when

they win; third, if the parties go to pieces, the government they built up must go to pieces, too; fourth, then there'll be h - - l to pay.

He went on to predict flatly that Anarchism would be the outcome. Party workers without the prospect of jobs would lose their patriotic interest in serving their country and become disaffected citizens. Despite this Cassandran prophecy, the civil service laws made headway.

Today, when national party institutions appear to be in no immediate jeopardy, but when the bloom is off the civil service rose, it is those most concerned for effective and responsible government who are having second thoughts about the role of the party and the goal of complete impartiality in government service. Though we dislike bosses, we need more party cohesiveness and discipline than has lately been in evidence in national politics, to bridge the separation of powers, to surmount deadlocks, to contain group demands, and assert a national interest. Though we have rebelled against the spoils system, when we elect a new administration we expect it to make a difference—which can only be brought about through an administrative establishment willing to give full support to the new policies. Are we losing a necessary means to these ends with the decline of federal patronage in a political climate increasingly uncongenial to it?

It is not necessary to overstate the dilemma to make the point. Patronage is evidently on the wane, but it has by no means disappeared. And the federal service, if not all we could wish it to be, has come a long way in the past thirty years. But the accommodation of the two is still unresolved in practice and in principle. The dilemma is inherent in two contradictory notions, both widely accepted, both embraced in public policy. Moreover, since World War II it has had to be confronted not only in the stress of a change in party control but also in circumstances of nearly full employment for skilled workers, when competent people do not have to work either for a party or for the government just in order to have a job.

A solution in principle for the role of the party in the federal service is not so simple as it once seemed, either. It is not enough to make a moral issue of the matter and demand that the rascals be turned out and honest people be put in office; honest people may honestly differ on any issue of policy or on the qualifications of an honest man. It is not enough to urge, as "good government" advocates have been wont to do, that "politics" and "administration" are two different realms of activity and only need to be cleanly and clearly separated. On the controversial frontiers of governmental functions, at times of widespread policy shifts, and even in the day-to-day conduct of old-line operations, policy questions for administrators emerge. We cannot take the politics out of policy. We look increasingly to the administrator for the formulation of new policy. He is generally an indifferent administrator who is indifferent to the policy he carries out. The criterion of "policy-making" posts, as a formula for defining the area of "legitimate" patronage, admits of no ready application in practice, and invites argument in principle, too.

It is not enough, again, to lump together all politically inspired appointments as "patronage." Before passing judgment on any individual case it is relevant to inquire into the sponsorship and the ultimate purposes to be served by an appointment, whether it is of high or low degree.

Finally, it is not enough to look at the effects of federal appointments on the federal service alone. The parties have their roots in the states and localities, and their branches ramify through the organized pressure groups. The importunities of local politics and of economic interests for federal appointments are as likely to disrupt as to strengthen the national party unity and discipline that patronage is supposed to promote. Historically, federal patronage policies and practice have been largely concerned with the nourishment of state and local party organizations.

PATRONAGE

Patronage was not invented or discovered in America; nor is it peculiar to government. In the general sense of appointments to office made for reasons of party or factional affiliation or personal gain, rather than because of personal qualifications for the posts, it has been practiced from time immemorial in diverse civilizations and in a variety of forms. Tradition credits the Chinese with inventing the sale of public offices as a device for raising funds for relief in a national disaster. Its advantages were so apparent as to recommend it to rulers long after the particular justification disappeared. In Europe and England the feudal system's mingling of economic and political power and perquisites not only made for an easy rationalization of the disposal of governmental and ecclesiastical offices for gain or for whim but also led to the legal recognition of life tenures and personal property in office.

In a more extended sense patronage merges into the broader pattern of the spoils system, that is, the manipulation of public authority for the special benefit of officeholders, their sponsors, business associates and friends. Of this system the distribution of public offices for partisan advantage is the most publicized feature, but in large cities the utility corporations, public works contractors and suppliers dependent on the favor of city authorities, have often been called upon to augment the supply of jobs. A large proportion of these may be short-term affairs, handed out shortly before election times. The spoils system encompasses a host of other forms: unduly restrictive specifications for contract bidding, favoritism in contract awards, and preference or discrimination in the inspection of contract performance; special treatment for inmates of institutions; discriminatory enforcement of the criminal law and of building, health, zoning, and other codes; differential tax assessments; tariff, franchise, and license privileges; "honest graft" in the acquisition of real estate; and the like. People will pay the powers that be to secure favors or to work off grudges, and party organizations within living memory have derived revenue by all of these methods.

Limiting ourselves here to appointments, some characteristic variations on the general form of patronage are worth noting for the light they shed on party needs and motivations.

What a full-time professional party worker wants, if he can get it, is a sinecure, a salary with such nominal official duties as not to distract him from his real work. Every American government accordingly has some paired positions drawn on the model that in England (for somewhat different reasons) separates the titular or ceremonial from the working head of the state. The front man takes the honor and the top salary, while the deputy does the work of the office. Cabinet posts—the Postmaster Generalship comes readily to mind—and assistant secretaryships, ambassadorships, department heads in state governments, and city commissionerships, have often been used in this way. But such conspicuous places are frequently unavailable or unsatisfactory for the purpose because public controversy over some aspect of the department's work will focus too much public attention on the office for the incumbent (or his political superior) to treat it any longer as a sinecure.

A less visible position with functions that have atrophied with time and technological change is safer in this respect. A county government in a metropolitan area where the tax base is high but the city does most of the work of government is a likely place to look for such positions.

In the national government the offices of Register of the Treasury, Treasurer of the United States, and Director of the Mint typify the category. But sinecure posts are sitting ducks for professional reorganizers; the office of Register was abolished after 150 years by one of President Roosevelt's reorganization plans. Besides, the prevailing moral climate is unfavorable to sinecures if their existence is publicized. Since in any event there are not enough such places to go around, the professional party worker, if he gets a public office, must usually reckon on dividing his time between official and party duties.

At the lower echelons particularly, the number of workers on whom the party needs to call, and for whom consequently it would like to make provision, is greatly in excess of the supply of full-time jobs that can be so used. Experience indicates, however, that a large proportion of these workers are needed only for short periods around the dates of primary and general elections, and that fringe benefits in the form of correspondingly brief interludes of a few days' public employment, on the highway department rolls, say, or as election inspectors, or (until 1950) as census takers, will suffice as incentives or rewards.

Along with providing a living, or part of it, for some of the faithful, which can most conveniently be done in relative obscurity, the party needs some other suitably prominent positions to bestow on citizens selected as representative of groups to which the party wishes to make an appeal. It is not necessary (and it may or may not be helpful) that the individuals so chosen be themselves party workers. A record of voting regularity is enough. For the purpose of this use of patronage is to symbolize in the minds of other members of the target groups the depth and genuineness of the party's interest in them.

A third need of the party for patronage, beyond building and sustaining an organization of professional workers and attracting blocs of voters, is to minimize the divisive influences of faction and personal ambition within its ranks. It cannot stifle ambition without jeopardy to its own future, from internal decay or external invasion. In a pluralistic society it must expect to reckon with factional rivalry among competing clusters of power. Ambition and rivalry are closely linked, wholesome within limits, and destructive unless harnessed to the larger welfare of the party. Patronage is sometimes a harness.

The counterpart of this particular need is when patronage is used to disrupt the unity and balance of interests of the opposing party. President Roosevelt doubtless had larger ends than this in view when he named Stimson and Knox to head the defense departments in 1940. But when Governor Chester Bowles in 1950 appointed the incumbent Republican senator from Connecticut, ex-Governor Raymond Baldwin, the party's best vote-getter in the state for two decades, to a place on the state's highest court, and so not only eliminated a proven campaigner for the opposition but also made room for another Democrat in the Senate, professionals on both sides recognized a spoiling raid successfully executed.

Patronage used to pacify rival power within the party, in the interests of a united front, does not necessarily require appointing the rival himself to anything; and it may prove self-defeating. If the rival has a secure and independent base of his own, say in the Senate, or as an undisputed state party leader, he may prefer to keep it and distribute to trusted supporters the patronage that is his due. In this way the appointing power not only risks surrendering control over the policy areas he gives up with the patronage, but may encompass his own later undoing as well. So President Kennedy may have reflected in 1963, after appointing Senator Eastland's candidate in 1961 to the newly created federal district judgeship for Mississippi.

The reason for this apparent paradox lies in the possibilities of conflict among the objectives to be served by patronage. The party, to accomplish its collective purposes, needs organization; and this implies a system of direction and control, an allocation of responsibilities and prerogatives, and some recognition of rank and status among the membership, in order to secure concerted action. The distribution of patronage is a means to this end, tending to reinforce the *status quo*. But the party also needs leadership, and this is commonly provided by some form of limited competition in which those at intermediate levels may legitimately aspire to higher places. Still others may be content with secure, if secondary, positions. All these are competitors for political power, whether they are ambitious to rise or only aim to be secure where they are. They have their own private and individual ends to serve. The award of patronage to them, while it may temporarily keep them harnessed to the organization's goals, also enables them to bide their time, to build their separate power bases or islands of safety, and so later to defy or overthrow the central authority of the party. For the loyalties of patronage appointees go only secondarily to the formal appointing authority; primarily they stay with the immediate sponsors who procure the jobs. This is the lesson in the rueful remark of a disillusioned President, that for every office he filled, he made nine enemies and one ingrate.

The same conflict in objectives may be observed in the use of patronage to cement the ties between the party and various economic interests and pressure groups. Many real estate people, for example, want an indulgent administration of FHA loans; many livestock people want to control the grazing rights on public lands, and so on. The party wants the voting and financial support of realtors and ranchers, among others. An obvious basis of mutual accommodation is the appointment, to key administrative posts in these governmental service areas, of dependable party members who will be sympathetic to the clientele viewpoints. But what are ends to the party are only means to the pressure group. The alliance being one of convenience rather than of principle, the party may find itself abandoned if a decline in its fortunes otherwise produces (or forecasts) a victory for the opposite party next time. The pressure group may prove unable—as John L. Lewis learned about his mine workers in the 1940 campaign—to control the votes of its members; the party may be saddled with responsibility for scandals in administration which it had no real means of preventing once the patronage appointments pleasing to the pressure groups were made.

The analysis so far suggests some fairly obvious generalizations. Party patronage, like money and love in other human relations, is an object of desire, a prize of power, and therefore a potential means of getting people to work together. Considering the needs of the party and the private interests of the participants, it would be utopian to expect a party to relinquish patronage except as it is excluded by stronger forces or as it finds superior substitutes. But as with other mundane incentives where motives are mixed, the use of patronage involves risks, not precisely calculable, of accomplishing the opposite of the unifying effects claimed for it.

NEUTRALITY, EXPERTISE AND EFFICIENCY

The rationale of a merit system is commonly rested on the priority of the needs for neutrality, expertise and efficiency in government service, above all other considerations. Here is where the professional administrator takes over. He needs protection, sympathy and support from the people and the politicians because he is what they cannot be and does what they cannot do. He cannot be recruited or kept in the service unless he is treated with respect. As they supply consent, so he supplies rationality to government action; and in varying proportions according to circumstances, both elements are indispensable to the wholesome survival and progress of the nation.

More specifically, it is said that the public servant should be neutral in party affiliation and inactive in politics because he must be impartial in judgment. Government is the servant of all, and once its policies are decided, social justice requires that they should be carried out without personal or partisan discrimination or preference; indeed without even the suspicion that might attach to the actions of an official with known partisan views. Again, the public servant should be expert, because the tasks committed to him are technical and complicated, and only a personnel system based on merit will provide the needed training and competence. Finally, considerations alike of financial costs to the taxpayers, social justice to the people and good faith fulfillment of promises to the electorate, combine to require efficiency in governmental performance. Efficiency has no partisan label, serves no ulterior purposes. The economical application of available means to avowed and approved ends is the province of scientific management.

Taken literally this would be a government of Little Lord Fauntleroys. Without going into all the modifications and reservations that a worldlier realism would attach to the doctrine of neutrality, several features of it may be noted.

In every field it occupies, the administrative establishment is vested with some discretion—more in the case of temporary wartime agencies, in the case of the independent regulatory commissions, in the case of foreign and military policy, atomic energy, and secret intelligence; and less in the case of tax and postage rates, customs classifications, military pay, and veterans' benefits. Where there is discretion vested there is choice and the power of choice. Any question of choice, not settled by precedent or previous instruction, is a policy question, and may emerge at any level of the administrative hierarchy; though what is a policy question to the man below may appear an administrative detail to the man above. Administrators have power; and so long as that is so, party leaders and pressure groups, whether operating directly or through bases in the White House or in the Congress, will contend for the control of its exercise. Patronage may be a means as well as a prize of control.

Second, because administrators have power, the nature of their loyalties cannot be a matter of complete indifference to those who would control their actions. The importance of their loyalties varies a great deal with circumstances. The time is past when religious tests imposed absolute bars to public employment. But under revolutionary conditions unswerving attachment to the regime may outweigh all considerations of technical competence. This was obvious in Hitler's Germany and Stalin's Russia; it has been true at times in our own history, too. George Washington is commonly credited with making fitness for office the test of his appointments, but he applied that test only among those already favorably known for their attachment to the principles of the Constitution; by a prior test he excluded all Tories. Similarly, the Congress after the Civil War imposed a test oath designed to bar from public office and the practice of law all who had participated in "the late wicked Rebellion." At the other end of the scale, and in peacetime, we need care very little about the political views of the impersonal Post Office truck driver who gathers the mail from the boxes of deposit, or the linotype operator in the Government Printing Office who commits a congressman's speeches to imperishable type. In between are many degrees of balance among conflicting considerations. Must a brilliant scientist, as a condition of employment, be enthusiastic about the project on which he works? Must the director of the Bureau of Standards believe in the right of a battery additive manufacturer to sell a worthless product if customers will buy it? Must a theatre commander believe in the policy of limited war he is told to wage?

Careful distinctions are needed here among types and objects of loyalty—to the Constitution, to a superior officer (military or civilian), to a sponsor, to a party, to a clientele, to a policy or program, to a professional code or standard, to a conscientious ideal. To the extent that control and direction are in issue and uncertain, we may generalize that the question of loyalty is apt to be paramount and other qualifications secondary. So a new administration not yet secure will be more sensitive to party and personal and program loyalties, while a long established one will be more tolerant of free-thinkers and nonconformists. So also the outward emblems and symbols of loyalty will be worn and observed in the early stages, and be cynically manipulated or discarded as hypocritical later on. Similarly, a new agency with a new job to do —the sec in 1934, the nlrb in 1935, the Lend-Lease Administration in 1940, the opa in 1941, the eca in 1948, the Peace Corps in 1961—is usually staffed with people who believe the job can be done and is worth doing, precisely because they will put their hearts into it. A change in policy or control later, as in the nlrb after the Taft-Hartley Act, or in public power development under the Eisenhower administration, is heralded by the appointment of people who do *not* believe in the previous policy.

Third, the argument for expertise and neutrality is in fact more than a utilitarian plea for better technical performance of government services. At bottom it is also an argument that administrators are better qualified than others to rule. They know better than politicians or the lay public, it is said, what can and cannot be done, and how, and at what cost, and when and were. Their loyalties are not attached to parties or private groups and therefore their motives are purer; they can be trusted to serve the "public interest." They can see better than others what needs to be done, and hence, it is implied, are better fitted to decide what should and shall be done, which is the essence of ruling, of governing. This is the classic argument on behalf of a bureaucracy. It is not an anti-democratic political theory if entrance to government service is open and ultimate checks are kept in the hands of the constitutional authorities, so that political responsibility to the voters is maintained. It *is* an argument for more power and autonomy for civil servants, however, as a group and in their individual official capacities. Since a political party is also a group contending for power through patronage in the government service, the argument for neutrality is not fully understood unless it is seen as a rival bid for power by the bureaucracy itself against "outside political interference," such as patronage introduces.

SUMMARY

To sum up the problem here: the separation of powers and the nature of our party system make the federal administrative establishment an inevitable object of rivalry for control. The power of appointment—the substance of it, regardless of the form—is a hallmark of control. That control used to be exercised chiefly through the political parties, in the name of rewards or discipline. In this century it has increasingly been absorbed by the appointive officials themselves, in the name of expert and impartial service. We look to them for initiative and guidance in the creation of policy and program as well as for the conduct of day-to-day affairs. We need their service, we need the parties, and the parties need support and discipline. Pressure groups operate through the parties as well as directly on and through the government. They press for the satisfaction of particular desires, and are held in check chiefly by internecine competition or by the overriding strength of a more broadly based organization such as a party. In a society characterized by the interaction of countless groups, we need order as well as responsiveness. And we must also have the capacity to mobilize the full strength of the nation in behalf of commonly felt objectives, at home and abroad. What then, under our special circumstances, is the continuing role of party and patronage in the federal service?

Characteristics of the Party System

Whatever may be true of them elsewhere, political parties in this country are organizations to conduct election campaigns and, if possible, to win them. This is their central characteristic, and from it, taking into account our constitutional system, the influences of history and custom, the demographic contours of our people, and the economic and social dynamics of our times, most of their other known characteristics can be derived. I say "known characteristics," because so much is unknown in any precise sense. We have the gross statistics of voting behavior, broken down geographically, and the tabulations of the pollsters. We have detailed accounts of particular campaigns, and of particular areas over longer periods. We have the documentary records of conventions and speeches, and the fragmentary returns in response to financial reporting requirements. And we have the journalistic and biographical impressions of supposedly knowledgeable observers and participants. On these inadequate foundations we have also a great deal of speculation and generalization, some insight and more dogmatism—for everyman here can be his own curbstone expert—but very much less than a detailed scientific description, let alone a satisfactory synthesis. There are probably exceptions to most of the statements that can be made.

PARTY ORGANIZATION

Elective offices are filled from defined geographical districts, states and their subdivisions, ordinarily by majority vote of all those registered voters who present themselves timely at the polls. It follows that the prime basis of party organization must be geographical, that the party needs an organization to match every district from which an elective office is to be filled, and, because of the multiplicity of local elective offices, that the center of gravity in the party is nearer the bottom than the top. In addition, primary elections are often used to fill the lowest level of party offices as well, and this may mean further geographic subdivision of the organization. Within any defined district, the typical form of party organization is a committee, with a chairman.

Building from the bottom then, the party aims to have a committee for each of the 3,000-odd counties in the United States, each member representing a township or other district within the county. The test of a local committeeman is his ability to carry his district for his party, or if that is not possible, at least to beat off any challenger for his place in the party election in which he is chosen. This puts a premium on his capacity to produce at will the decisive margin—usually not over ten per cent of the voters in his district is enough—to ensure victory in a test. Personal acquaintances may suffice for this, particularly in stable rural areas, but the more dependable reliance for a city machine has historically been upon strategically distributed petty jobholders and their families, and upon the controllable employees and dependents of enterprises, not all of them legitimate, which in one way or another were in turn dependent on the favor of the city administration.

The state central committee ordinarily is comprised of a member from each county chosen by the county committee; the county chairman is an obvious choice. Alternates or women co-members are sometimes added, and special arrangements are sometimes needed to reflect more adequately the heavy battalions of voters in metropolitan counties. Because the local units are numerous and committee memberships are prized, both state and local committees are apt to be unwieldy, and smaller executive committees are the rule. Because county lines were fixed long ago and urban-rural jealousy permeates the parties, state committees like state legislatures are commonly stacked against the cities.

Between the local and the state organizations there must be some machinery to handle the nominations and campaigns of Congressmen and state senators whose districts usually embrace several counties but are not statewide. A conference of the county leaders concerned may suffice, especially for the latter. For congressional districts, however, a special convention may be held, including the county leaders and others; the state chairman may or may not have a significant voice; and in any event the congressional candidate or his backers must expect to supplement if not supplant the county organizations with a personal machine committed to his interests. Federal patronage is one way of supporting this effort.

Up through the state level, party organization follows geographical lines and, with the reservations noted, forms a hierarchy in the familiar shape of a pyramid. Above that level, however, the pyramid is truncated and bifurcated, and the organization is confederate. What holds the party together nationally is chiefly the prospect of winning or keeping the Presidency, and secondarily, of organizing the House and the Senate. To that end majorities must be mustered across state lines, and across constituencies quite differently arranged in the three cases.

The national organization to produce a majority was historically the Congressional Campaign Committee of each party, but its functions are now confined to furnishing assistance—speakers for rallies, data on issues and voting records, and small grants of funds—to those party candidates for the House (a considerable proportion) who think their campaigns will be helped by activities from that source. After the election House members who served on this committee have an important voice in the distribution of House patronage.

The eclipse of the Congressional Campaign Committee is due in part to the fact that after senators came to be elected directly—instead of being chosen by state legislatures—a corresponding Senatorial Campaign Committee was established in each party, to perform similar functions for candidates for that chamber. But earlier and more importantly the eclipse was the result of the loss of control by the House, through the congressional caucus, over the nomination for the Presidency. The rise of the national convention and the mid-nineteenth-century party realignments led, after the Civil War, to the establishment of the National Committee of each party, with its focus on the White House.

The national committee is composed of two members (one a woman) from each state, chosen by the state's delegation to the national convention. Unlike the state committee its principal officers, chairman and treasurer, are only formally elected by the members, and not from among their own number. The designation of these officers is the prerogative of the presidential nominee, and he owes his nomination, in turn, to the convention and not to the committee. Before he is nominated (unless he is an incumbent President seeking re-election) the committee must be neutral as between potential candidates; after the convention it is his servant, as his campaign manager is its chairman. Collectively it settles the time and place for the next convention. But unlike the state committee, which often decides on the party's slate for statewide offices, the national committee has little to do with the choice of the presidential nominee. Individually its members advise the President on federal appointments in their states where no senator or congressman has a vested interest, and otherwise promote the party's fortunes as they see them, with more or less attention to the chairman's guidance. The convention, meeting once in four years and preoccupied with the nomination, is rarely in a position to instruct or discipline the committee. The committee head-quarters, moreover, under the chairman's control is the great collector and dispenser of campaign funds and organizational center for national party activity. Its relations with the congressional campaign committees may be close or distant, but it outshines them though its light is only the reflection of the presidential sun.

This account is enough to show that though the roots of party strength lie in the states and localities, the route to national party power is not from the state to the national committee, as in the states it runs from the county to the state committee. The party strength of the President, and of the losing party's Presidential nominee, rests partly on shifting com-binations of state organizations, often cemented by the award or promise of patronage, but also on two other resources that the state organizations cannot deliver: the financial and other support of wealthy individuals and natural pressure groups, and the hold on the popular imagination of the voters that the mass media enable them to seek, outside party channels. For an Eisenhower, as for a Roosevelt, this hold gives a popular President an additional constituency of several million voters whom the parties cannot otherwise reach, and whom the party leaders—as both Tafts, father and son, learned painfully—dare not ignore.

PARTY COMPOSITION

Who makes up the "party"? There is no precise answer to such an apparently simple question. Not all those who voted for, say, Johnson in 1964 make up a party. Many Democrats who doubtless would have voted for him if they had gotten to the polls did not get there, for the total vote, though large, was still not much over three-fifths of the potential elec-torate. Many who did vote for him are doubtless not Democrats. Not just those, either, who register as Republicans or as Democrats in states where a party affiliation must be declared as a condition of voting in the pri-maries. Outside the South, many more regular Democrats and Republi-cans turn out in November, when no party affiliation need be declared, than in the primaries. And, finally, not just the active party workers, part-time and full-time, who go beyond the call of civic duty to vote, and in one way or another put their shoulders to the wheel. The most satisfactory definition in principle is the hardest to apply in practice, for the test is partly subjective and partly depends on evidence that is locked in the anonymous secrecy of the ballot box: those who think of themselves as party adherents and pretty regularly vote the straight ticket. But even this does not tell how many lapses are too many.

This analysis indicates clearly that, however defined, the two parties do not, between them, comprise anything like the whole adult population, even excluding—as the election laws in substance commonly do—idiots, paupers, soldiers, and students. Beyond this it is difficult to speak with confidence. But common observation and a few statistics suggest the existence of four broad categories with characteristic attitudes toward parties and patronage: 1) a small number, and much the largest part of them at relatively humble levels, who seek to make their careers in the party; this is the hard core of professionals to whom patronage will seem like bread and butter, or like shelter and a car—a place to stay and a means of getting somewhere; 2) a much larger number, perhaps 80 per cent or more of all those who vote at general elections, whose party allegiance is well settled; to many of these it will seem natural that the winning party should take care of its workers, though they want no patronage for themselves, may speak cynically of politicians, and be unwilling to tolerate dishonesty or incompetence in public office; 3) a considerably smaller number, perhaps 10 to 20 per cent of those who have voted in recent presidential elections, who are "independents" of one sort or another: some stay at home more often than they vote, but may be brought out by a sufficiently attractive personality, while others have no settled party attachment and think that the difference between party and candidate alternatives is often not worth the bother of voting, but may be brought out by a clear issue or an appealing candidate; these have no use for parties or patronage, but, being movable, may have a decisive influence on the outcome of an election; 4) a much larger number, some two-fifths of the adult population, who from apathy, inability, ignorance, too frequent moving to establish a residence, or other cause, do not vote at all and are disregarded in most calculations of practical politicians.

There is some movement among these categories; the trend line of the third has been gradually but persistently upward for years, while the percentage in the fourth took sharp drops in 1920, 1936, 1952, and 1960. Patronage would seem to be of importance only to the first category.

PARTY SUSTENANCE

The most thorough and comprehensive study so far made of campaign finances (Alexander Heard, *The Costs of Democracy*, 1960, p. 7) estimates the money outlays in 1952 at about $140 million; of this nearly $20 million was spent by national organizations, over $67 million by statewide organizations, and over $53 million through district and local activities. It is not possible to allocate these amounts even approximately among national, state, and local candidates, since so many of the organizations overlap in their objectives. No correspondingly careful or statistically comparable estimates exist for later years. There is no comprehensive central collection point for statistics. Legal reporting requirements, where they exist, are very loosely drawn. The actual amounts therefore are unknown and unavailable. They probably increased for 1956, 1960, and 1964, as television came into wider use. They are several times as large as the crude estimates offered in pre-war years. But Heard concludes that "the long-run dollar increase appears no greater than rises in the price level and the national income." Partly because of the unrealistic limits of the Hatch Act—a maximum of $3 million a year for any single committee—the gathering and spending of campaign funds is diffused among a multitude of committees.

The party needs funds locally to sustain the army of poll watchers, canvassers, and runners who must be mustered at election times; other local expenditures are for communications and office space and help— temporarily swelled at the same time—and for the cost of holding meetings and advertising. Expenses for these purposes apparently vary widely from county to county and state to state. Very modest sums, often taxed to the candidates themselves, suffice in stable rural areas. But in doubtful and "pivotal" states, to which the national headquarters attaches especial importance, they may run up to figures much beyond local resources. The national committee operates a grant-in-aid system to help out in these states.

The party needs funds nationally to support the national headquarters offices—usually both in New York and Washington—including substantial publicity, research and communications staffs, and for travel, printing, entertainment, and meetings. But the largest categories of national party expense are for TV and radio network time and newspaper advertising space, and for grants to state organizations that are the objects of special anxiety. The national treasurers raise funds from

Jefferson, Jackson, and Lincoln Day dinners, from individual and organizational contributions, and a variety of other sources. The Republican finance committees in Connecticut, Pennsylvania and Ohio can be counted on to make upstream grants-in-aid. Would-be ambassadors give evidence of their ability to meet the entertainment costs of diplomats at European capitals by donating to the party. Unions, banks and corporations are forbidden by law from giving to party campaign funds, but unions can campaign through affiliated organizations and corporation officers can donate personally. A corporation attorney, making a gift, may later get reimbursement through a bill for "legal services." Business men, from sentiment as well as from financial motives, are the principal givers. Many contributions and expenditures never get onto the party treasurer's books at all because some well-disposed citizen picks up the check, say for a hotel luncheon rally, or a printing bill, and pays it directly. So a large proportion of the gifts from business sources end up in one form or another as deductible business expenses on tax returns; it may well be that the largest campaign contributor is ultimately the U. S. Treasury.

It is probably significant that the scale of campaign expenditures has gone up at the same time that federal patronage has declined, but it is doubtful that this has meant any net gain for the Treasury. It does, though, point up the increasing dependence of the party on business contributors for its sustenance, in comparison with patronage that it can control directly.

THE MACHINE AND ITS ALLIES

The interdependence of local party machines and their business allies was noted long ago. Lincoln Steffens, the muckraking journalist contemporary of Theodore Roosevelt, probing the "shame of the cities," raised the question why influential business men in a corruptly governed city were generally faint-hearted about municipal reform and supported instead a municipal boss they could deal with. Steffens found his answer in a recurring pattern of economic and political relationships. The party machine, the underworld syndicates, and the local utilities and contractors were semi-sovereign principalities within the city, each with some outside connections, and linked by the common motive of gain. The machine exploited the spoils opportunities and had rewards and punishments at its disposal through control of the city administration; to keep that, it needed jobs, money, and voters—more or less interchangeable forms of currency. The underworld needed toleration from the police, the prosecutor, and the courts, and could pay in money and votes. The utilities and contractors needed franchises and business the city could give, and could pay in money, jobs, and votes. By marking out spheres of influence and supporting a concert of power each element in the combination could obtain what it wanted. Besides, a number of other business and professional interests, some respectable, some shady, banks and bondsmen, lawyers and newspapers, found profitable customers in the combination and saw only prospects of mayhem or economic ruin in bucking it. "The major interests," says Peter Odegard, "are content to leave minor spoils, such as jobs in the public service, to the party agents as long as these agents direct the affairs of state in a manner to promote the interests of the powerful oligarchies which control the economic and social destinies of the community." It was only when all the franchises had been awarded, so V. O. Key concludes, and the major privileges sought had been legally granted, that the important business interests associated with the party machine were apt to become converts to the doctrine of economy and efficiency in government; and then a sharp decline in the scope of the spoils system occurred.

On the national scene, the historic allies of the party machine have been the banks, the railroads, the tariff beneficiaries, the post office and rivers and harbors contractors, and the targets of the tax and antitrust laws. Except during the prohibition era, the underworld appears to have figured only in a minor way. Time and circumstance have diminished the relevance of some of these. The introduction of the secret ballot made obsolete the system by which a railroad could send its foremen to the polling places with payroll lists to check off as the men voted; and Congress has not undertaken a tariff revision since 1930. But the expansion of public regulation and spending and the rise in the corporation income tax rate have made the federal government an effective partner in nearly every large business enterprise today. The old principle still operates, the concert of power is extended, the mutuality of interest between the party machine and business remains. A call of the roll might start with the airline and aircraft industries, the shipping and shipbuilding firms, the broadcasting networks, the electrical and electronics industries, the oils and chemicals, metals and motors. They are Defense Department suppliers, subsidy and certificate holders, and taxpayers all. In the modern-dress form of the alliance the party still aims to look after its friends who make themselves useful. The campaign contributions from business sources run to much higher figures, and the votes produced by those sources are mobilized not by the intimidation of employees, but through volunteer clubs and associations.

The relative need of the national party machine for federal patronage has correspondingly declined, just as it is has in reformed municipalities, and for the same basic reason.

THE MACHINE AS AN INTEREST GROUP

The party as a whole is an amorphous group, with diverse interests. It has often been remarked that on most issues in Congress, the voting division does not correspond at all closely to party lines. On most issues, that is to say, the legislators, who by definition belong to the inner core of party professionals, are reflecting views and interests that permeate and divide the lay adherents of the party as well. These group interests are more apt to cut across party lines than to follow them. When a vote is taken, each member finds his own salvation, in his conscience, in his constituency, in the urgings of party leaders, administration spokesmen and lobbyists, or elsewhere.

The main jurisdiction over party institutions and activities lies, in our constitutional system, with the states. State laws, if any (in some states they are silent, in others prolix), determine the forms of party organization, the times, places and manner of making nominations, the design of the ballot, the system of registration, the administration of elections, the count of the results, and a host of other details. Party regulars in control of state legislatures act as a special interest group in determining all these matters in which they are so vitally concerned; and, conversely, what they determine has an important bearing on the habits and standards and character of those of their number who make the plunge into national party politics. An Ohio congressman, for instance, was convicted in the late 1940s for violating the federal act prohibiting his taking "kickbacks" from an employee in his office. At the time of his indictment he professed astonishment that he was violating any law, and much of his defense consisted in urging, in effect, that "we do this all the time at home."

The line that separates the machine from its followers is in one respect much less sharp now than in the early years of this century. This is a symptom of the general relaxation of party discipline that has been associated with the spread since then of the direct primary, itself as much a result as a cause of the change. The change is in the degree of freedom of entry by amateurs, upstart newcomers, and other outsiders into what was once a much more tightly closed system.

In practice, organization leaders in the northern, border, and midwestern states (and frequently in the mountain and far western states, too) ordinarily put up a slate which is approved by the voters in the primary, especially for the obscure offices. But upsets sometimes occur in the case of prominent offices; party leaders viewing the necessity of running the gauntlet of popular approval for their choices in the primary no doubt temper their wishes and modify their choices accordingly; factional disputes among county leaders may result in no unanimous endorsement of a slate for state offices; the fact of organization endorsement may itself be a handicap in some western states and not be published even if it is privately made and circulated; and in one-party states where the dominant party's primary is tantamount to election (unless that party is controlled by one man or a small oligarchy), the "organization" must stay neutral among contesting candidates, and indeed may scarcely exist. On the whole it is still true that an organized minority of professionals within the party usually controls the nominating process. The controls are more difficult to apply to the more conspicuous offices, however, and must be exercised with more solicitude for rank-and-file sentiment. Whether what is left of them warrants calling the professionals a "machine" any more is even debatable in some states. In any event, there is more doubt than formerly about who is to be counted among them, and more room for newcomers to elbow their way in.

The weight of the influence of the state and local party machines as interest groups has naturally been on the side of maintaining federal patronage as part of a larger system. The vertical linkage among the party professionals from the local to the state and national levels, in fact, causes this to be taken for granted. If the county organization has helped carry the national ticket, it expects to be consulted by the national committeeman, the senator, and the congressman on federal appointments that can be used to strengthen its hold. If the county organization has lost, but the national party has won, the county leader leans more heavily on federal appointments to help him survive. If neither has won, the prospect of jobs at a later and more fortunate date will still sustain hope, and therefore some party work.

CONTINUING PARTY ORGANIZATION PRESSURES FOR PATRONAGE

This account of the party system has stressed the main characteristics of its organization and methods of operation—its geographical bases and local autonomy; the ties of structure and interest that link together its local, state, and national units into loose and sometimes uncongenial confederacies with ambiguous common labels; its persistent and contrary internal compulsions toward unity and faction; its sources of financial support and relations with business allies; and the vested interests of its inner circles of professional leaders, managers, and workers. The system serves these vested interests at public expense but it also serves two major public purposes, in administering the complicated democratic function of popular elections and in helping elected officials to control the bureaucracy. Patronage has historically been a prominent part of the price of these services, a currency medium with a twofold use: an end in itself to the recipient, and a means of control to the dispenser.

There is little reason to suppose that so long as parties exist their workers will cease to demand payment for their services or to seek to aggrandize their positions. The parties still need support for their battalions in the field and career incentives for their executives. Elected officials still need the leverage of parties to govern. Like any other public utility charges, however, the party's price and manner of payment depend less on the quality and cost of service than upon its bargaining power. In this respect, and without much change in formal structure, subtle and profound changes have occurred in the workings of the party system during the past half-century, and in its place in American society. The parties have been tamed. They no longer exercise their former degree of irresponsible power. They are astute to attend to rank-and-file sentiment. They no longer furnish many large-scale opportunities for personal enrichment. They must elbow their way among the other great twentieth-century national organizations, the trade and professional associations, the labor unions, the farm bureaus, as effective outlets for the satisfaction of social wants. They have been supplanted as charitable welfare agencies. They have other rivals than the newspapers in the field of political education. They must constantly conduct their affairs before TV cameras and in the presence of reporters, under public scrutiny and regulation. The governments they would control are vast organizations performing technical tasks of great range and complexity.

A symptom of these changes is the sharp shrinkage in patronage.

Patronage in Adversity

EVIDENCE OF DECLINE

Comprehensive or satisfactory statistical measures of the decline in patronage are not available. It is greater in percentage than in absolute numbers because of the growth of the federal establishment, and it is probably greater in the field than in Washington, if temporary appointments are excluded. But the central fact is attested by all competent observers, professional, journalistic and academic; and not only the fact but also the trend, which has proceeded with only minor and temporary interruptions and reversals since the beginning of the century at least, and at all governmental levels, national, state, and local. The nineteenth-century practice of a wholesale turnover in federal jobs with a change in national party control passed as the civil service act gradually took hold. The Eisenhower administration, in cutting the federal payroll by nearly ten per cent, wiped out nearly as many positions within and outside the classified service as the total of theoretically exempt appointments.

The legislative symptoms of this trend, from the Pendleton Act in 1883 to the Hatch Act in 1938, are reviewed elsewhere in this volume. The extensions of civil service and other merit system coverage, by legislation and by executive order, through most of the departmental services in Washington, from there to the field services, and also, by virtue of strings on federal grants-in-aid, to state services supported by federal funds, are impressive and largely irreversible. Especially significant recent additions are the field services of the postal, internal revenue, and customs services. The most conspicuously laggard area, as might be expected, is in the administration of justice.

THE MORAL ATTACKS

The attacks against patronage began on the theme of moral protest, and by present day standards understandably so. Traffic in offices was part of the spoils system and outright dishonesty, now a criminal offense. The importunities of office seekers led to Garfield's assassination and Cleveland's complaint that they left him no time for proper public business. Even today, the moral aspect is the easiest to exploit. Partisan claims to office as rewards are readily pictured as special privilege, alike by the opposition which has an axe to grind, and by reform groups with an axe to swing. Partisan appointments are news items that may put an administration on the defensive. Party activity is not, like military service, a source of prestige and a claim on public gratitude. This moral attitude tends to make open solutions to the patronage problem impractical and to put a premium on subterfuge, cynicism, and circumspection among party professionals.

THE UTILITARIAN CHALLENGE

Following and reinforcing the argument from morality came the utilitarian protest: patronage makes for inefficiency in government service. This charge might come from an articulate section of the public, aware that it is not well served. So the veterans of World War I forced a reorganization of the old patronage-staffed Bureau of Pensions into a Veterans Administration under the classified service—and then proceeded to impose a veterans' preference on that service. Veterans of World War II were saved the same experience, therefore, only by a drastic anticipatory housecleaning in 1945-6.

The utilitarian theme came also from the scientific management movement in business and government. There was no room for patronage in the calculations of the experts who made surveys, proposed procedural renovations and structural reorganizations, and claimed potential savings. The taxpayers' associations and business lobbies talk along these lines, too, though in a showdown, if a choice must be made, they will generally be found to think first of control and to prefer a friendly administration to an efficient one.

These are the external spearheads of the attack, and historically they provided the main impetus. Latterly, as the government has expanded and increasing numbers of appointments have been delegated to executive agency heads and their subordinates, the traditional distrust of executive power in Congress has operated as another influence in the same direction. It is not entirely a dog-in-the-manger attitude that leads congressmen sometimes to prefer a civil service system to uncontrolled executive appointments. The WPA from its beginning was exempt from civil service, and no small part of the eagerness on the Hill after the 1938 elections to see it abolished may be laid to the apprehensions of a growing number of members that it might be used to build up organizations unfriendly to them in their home districts.

PROFESSIONALIZATION A FORCE

The strongest force working against patronage recently, however, is probably the internal one, the presence in government service of so many people who were not patronage appointees themselves, who suppose they got their own jobs by some test of fitness and want to see similar tests applied to others. The instinct of craftsmanship, the impulse to self-improvement, is very strong among such people. They do not like "politicians" or understand them; they are uncomfortable working near them. Many government workers are in skilled trades and belong to unions. They apply union tests of fairness to employment procedures. Others, such as scientists, accountants, and economists, belong to professional associations and respect professional standards. Still others, like the G-Men, foresters, public health and social welfare workers, are in self-contained agencies which develop strong corporate traditions and career loyalties of their own. To all of these, patronage appointees are alien and unwelcome intruders. Winning the consent of the electorate through maintenance of the party in power is a goal remote from their interests and unsuited to their talents.

Party politicians are out of their depth in these waters. Professionalization and unionization create formidable barriers to their entrance and promote conditions unfavorable to their survival. Professional employees already in the service are likely to be the first to learn of prospective vacancies in their agencies, and, through professional and personal contacts outside, to know where recruits like themselves may be found. The net effect of these internal pressures is accordingly toward autonomy for the bureaucracy, toward the exclusion of partisan considerations, toward the application of rational and professional standards of appointment and work. The internal pressures in fact fuse with the external pressures, for people in the service with a professional outlook subscribe readily to the moral and utilitarian arguments as well. Under this combination of influences, patronage merely for the support of the parties has yielded ground.

EFFECTS UPON THE PARTIES

The decline of patronage has affected the parties, broadly speaking, in two ways: first, in their capacity as organizations to nominate candidates and run election campaigns, and second, after the elections, in their capacity as organizations to run the government. In the first respect they have accommodated to the changes piecemeal and gradually, with less evident damage than their anguished protests forecast. Death and retirement have done away with a generation of bosses who would be as unfitted for the current environment in most places as the captains of industry in their time. New and more respectable types of party leaders have replaced them, and the organizations remain, though with altered methods and means of support. No longer able to place large numbers of workers on public payrolls, unless very temporarily, they depend much more on direct monetary contributions from business sources. This transition has been helped by the nearly full employment of post-war years, which has simultaneously reduced the number of the needy clamoring for jobs and vastly increased business wealth. And no longer able (or perhaps finding it unprofitable) to maintain the year-round social and welfare activities once elaborately organized on a neighborhood basis, they have turned to the mass media and to ubiquitous campaigning by the leading candidates—both means of exploiting attractive personalities—to make contact with the voters, save for the brief periods of canvassing for registrations and on election days. As with other technological changes, the old methods took more unskilled labor, the newer ones take more money. They take more out of the candidates, too, as planes and helicopters make possible more gruelling speaking schedules over wider areas. Not since 1920 has a major party won a presidential campaign by relying chiefly on its regular organization to deliver the vote. Dewey's defeat in 1948 was widely attributed to his mistaken calculation that such a strategy would be enough to win the election.

The parties have found another partial solution for the transition in large scale *ad hoc* volunteer groups which raise funds and campaign for the heads of the tickets, more or less independently of the regular party organizations. At least since 1928, when the Hoover-Curtis Volunteers effectively supplemented the established—and lukewarm—machines, such crusades have been a prominent feature; in 1952 they were spectacular. They enlist enthusiasms, tap resources of money and people, and exploit other systems of group and social relations, largely in existence already, that are not available to the regular parties as such. Dependence on business contributors and volunteer organizations is another sign of the crumbling of the monopoly that machine leaders once had over nominations and elections; but these supporters, so far as they are moved by mundane incentives, do not expect to be paid off in patronage. Their rewards, if they are successful, are in closer access to centers of official influence and other intangible satisfactions. With these aids, in sum, the parties, considered as campaigning organizations, have been able to take the changes in stride, to take credit (after the event) for the extensions of the civil service, and to persuade themselves that honesty and competence are frequently the best politics.

In their second capacity, as organizations to run the government, the parties have been affected by the decline of patronage in ways more difficult to delineate confidently. These have to do with the relative bargaining positions of the President and his official family on the one hand, and the members of Congress on the other, vis-à-vis the bureaucracy and the pressure groups. Each aspect is involved.

The President's Stake in Patronage

As the power of appointment is one of the main constitutional powers of the Chief Executive, his practical capacity to exercise it and the considerations he finds it prudent to bear in mind in doing so, are crucial tests of the power of his office and of his personal political stature. On these depend his ability to influence the course of events and, ultimately, his place in history.

Much depends in the first place, therefore, on the President's own concept of his role. In the Whig tradition of the Presidency, he was more a presiding officer than a protagonist of policies, keeping as far as possible above partisan controversy while disputed issues were fought out and compromised by the interests directly concerned, generally in Congress. This was the Coolidge concept, and it was what Admiral Dewey had in mind when he acknowledged his qualifications for the nomination in 1900, because "all you have to do is sign the bills Congress passes." In this concept, the President has little actual stake in the appointing power beyond his choices for the cabinet and the Supreme Court, and his ability to gratify some personal friends and followers in small ways. For the rest, if most of his authority is exercised by others anyway, they might as well (and no doubt will) determine what appointments shall be made, too.

An opposite concept was asserted by Jackson, Lincoln, Wilson, and the two Roosevelts. In their concept of the office the President clearly has a stake in as broad a reach for the appointing power as he can actually control, since it is a means for getting his way. But by the same token, he should be glad to save the time consumed in routine appointments (as in the military establishment, short of the top posts) that do not affect his control. And he should be more than glad to be spared the responsibility for appointments he cannot really control, transactions in which he and his office are being used by others for their purposes rather than by him for his own.

Much of the President's practical capacity to use the appointing power to his advantage depends, in the second place, on the kind of staff help he has in considering personnel questions. His personal acquaintance will not go very far. If he has few resources and little imagination in his own office for the task of finding suitable appointees to propose, he must perforce fall back on the role of choosing among suggestions from outside sources, if indeed they leave him any choice. In such a decision the weight of the sponsor must often be as influential a factor as the intrinsic merits of the candidate. The consequences of disappointing several sponsors may nullify the advantage of gratifying one. The strategic importance of the initiative is considerable, therefore, and good staff work is indispensable in keeping it. The great growth of the federal establishment has magnified the dimensions of the difficulty. Congress has been cool to proposals for enlarging the Executive Office staff along this line. The President's advice comes from a personnel assistant with a few helpers in the Executive Office, from the heads of departments, from his party's national committee, and from members of Congress.

Much of a new President's ultimate reputation for the calibre of his appointments—especially of a President who enters after a turnover in party control—depends, in the third place, on the commitments he gives and obtains during the "transition" period. The weeks immediately following election day, and on into the early spring of his first year in office, are crucial, for by and large he will be stuck—or blessed—during the rest of his first term, at least, with the results of his early choices for most of the key places in his administration. The choices must be made under great pressure of time, for programs will not move until the selections are made and confirmed. Commitments must be given to many people whom the President does not yet know well, if at all. Later necessary replacements will be harder or easier to obtain, depending on the tone set initially.

To cope with this responsibility, Eisenhower in 1952-53 organized the "Commodore Operation," relying on two of his most trusted campaign associates, Herbert Brownell and General Lucius Clay, who in turn drew on other resources, including the management consulting firm of McKinsey and Company, for suggestions and appraisals of names. Eisenhower on the whole was content to select his cabinet officers and agency heads, and to leave to them the choice of their subordinates—a method that brought an unusually large proportion of successful business men into office, and a round of complaints from the national committee head-quarters and congressional sources that their claims had been bypassed or ignored. (See the Brookings Institution study by Laurin Henry, *Presidential Transitions,* 1960.) Kennedy in 1960-61 commissioned the so-called "talent hunt," in charge of his brother Robert and his brother-in-law Sargent Shriver, to recruit the political executives for his administration; he kept to himself the choices for posts considerably further down the line than Eisenhower had tried to. (See Dean E. Mann, "The Selection of Federal Political Executives," *American Political Science Review,* March 1964.) Both these efforts, far more systematic and ambitious than those of any previous President, were financed from personal and party funds. In recognition of the financial burdens of this sort, imposed on an incoming President before he takes office, the Congress in 1963 authorized federal appropriations for future Presidents-elect for these and related costs of transitional preparations.

These intrinsic limitations go far toward explaining the personnel policies of twentieth-century Presidents. Over the long pull they have found it more important to extend the classified service and recognize agency career systems than to provide bread-and-butter patronage support for the party's rank and file. This has favored departmental profession-alization. They have moved earlier and further in this direction in the scientific and technical services than in the Post Office, Treasury, and Justice Departments. They have also moved sooner in the Washington establishments, where individual congressmen and committeemen could only claim quotas, than in the field offices, where state lines mark vested interests in specific jobs. On the other hand, they have seldom been enthusiastically out in front of these trends. They have fought out patron-age quarrels with individual antagonists on occasion, but have avoided general engagements on patronage policy. They have acquiesced to tradi-tion and the counsels of prudence in recognizing party and congressional patronage claims to existing exempt positions. In this connection they have felt the necessity, in the interests of fairness and peace, of establish-ing and generally observing some settled routines and designated channels for political job clearances. They have found some freedom of action by creating new exempt jobs at the beginning of their terms, and some virtue by covering the positions under civil service near the end of their terms. And without exception, each of them has made political appointments freely when opportunity offered to advance his policy or control by doing so. It is quite possible, consequently, for a President at one and the same time to have a general interest in removing a class of positions from the patronage category and a particular interest in using some jobs in the class for patronage purposes.

Against this general background, the President's continuing stakes in the use of patronage can be traced somewhat more sharply. They involve chiefly 1) his control over administration policy and the furtherance of his legislative proposals, 2) his influence on the standards of quality in governmental services, 3) his control over his own party, and 4) the reverse aspect of these, the consequences for him of a system that puts the disposal of much patronage in other hands.

On the first point, two classic cases can be cited. In 1913, President Wilson, and in 1933, President Roosevelt, delayed action on the recommendations of Democratic members of Congress for all but the most urgent appointments until the end of the first extraordinary congressional session. Each pleaded that he had no time to consider appointments until his legislative program was out of the way, and each saw his program for the session substantially enacted. Observers in each case saw a cause-and-effect relationship between the patronage whip and the policy control. This wholesale technique of leverage is only applicable when a new President comes prepared with a program, and it can be used only once. It did not work for Kennedy, though a judiciary act gave him more new judgeships to fill than had ever before been authorized at one time, and the Peace Corps opened up additional jobs. But in a specific instance press reports noted a federal judgeship in Kentucky as the price of a vote in the House Ways and Means Committee in 1963 that helped move his major tax cut proposal to favorable floor action.

The President needs freedom in making appointments to executive posts to advance his policy goals, even if no immediate question of congressional support is involved. Roosevelt's appointments of Marriner Eccles to the Federal Reserve Board, of Henry Wallace as Secretary of Agriculture, and of Harry Hopkins to the WPA and (later, during the war) to the Munitions Assignment Board—like Kennedy's naming of General Maxwell Taylor as Chairman of the Joint Chiefs of Staff—were at once major indicators of lines he wanted to follow and instruments for marking out those lines more concretely than he could have done himself. The last example, and Truman's dismissal of General MacArthur, show that the importance of sympathetic administration, for purposes of policy control, is not always confined to civilian posts.

The more common form of the problem involves congressional relations as well as departmental administration; and it emerges when the President's party has organized the Congress as well as when he faces opposition control there. Either way, he must muster bipartisan support for controversial measures in order to overcome recalcitrants on his own side of the aisle in both chambers.

In foreign policy, for example, Eisenhower's general tone and direction were presumably indicated in his selection of John Foster Dulles as Secretary of State. The appointment itself—like cabinet choices generally—was not seriously contested; but neither did it assure that policies agreeable to the President and the Secretary would prevail. Secretary Dulles, to be sure, had wide discretion to bring new people into ranking subordinate posts, to employ temporary special assistants, and to reassign career officers. The main domestic obstacles to his policies came not from departmental sabotage but from the Hill. Dulles's principal opponents were in the President's party in Congress: Senator Knowland, the majority floor leader, on Far Eastern policy; Speaker Martin, ranking Ways and Means Committee members, and southwestern and mountain state senators like Goldwater, Malone, and Dworshak on tariffs and trade; the Appropriations Committee chairman and a midwestern group on foreign aid; and so on. These opponents presumably spoke their personal convictions as much as their constitutional views. They had secure home bases and were not to be dislodged by promises of patronage or threats of reprisal. If the President's policy was to win out, then, the votes of Democrats and uncommitted Republicans were needed. Patronage was not the only means to this end, and the State Department was not the only place to look for it. But if patronage appointments would produce the decisive margin of votes on crucial bills, only purists could conscientiously condemn the President for making them, or wanting to keep them available in case of need.

Similar examples and lessons could be drawn from the experience of Eisenhower's Secretary of Agriculture, Ezra Benson—or from the prolonged drives, in which Kennedy and Johnson were engaged, to secure passage of the civil rights and tax reduction bills in 1963-4. They can be drawn, too, from secondary issues as well as from great causes: from the ultimate success, for instance, of Interior Secretary Udall in getting the wilderness sanctuary bill through in 1964, over the opposition of the Democratic chairman of the House Interior Committee.

Within the administration, appointments of political executives to subcabinet posts, places in the Executive Office, and the like, are a further means of policy control for the President, as well as of balancing party interests. They are also relatively congenial vehicles for usually short-term tours of service in the executive branch by members of the "Establishment"—leading figures in business, finance, and the professions —despite the complications of senatorial confirmation, conflict-of-interest troubles, salary sacrifices, personal incompatibilities, and so on, that may be encountered. Kennedy compounded these difficulties when he named three men to ranking positions in the State Department before selecting Secretary Rusk to head the Department, and again when he appointed two Republicans, McNamara and Dillon, as Secretaries of Defense and Treasury. In the latter cases an additional layer of screening and nego-tiation for the second-line appointments was introduced; some Repub-licans were brought in, some Kennedy preferences were vetoed, and vice versa, some compromise choices were made. But with few exceptions the results strengthened the President's holdover policy.

Because the transactions involved in political appointments, whether for policy or partisan ends, have ramifications, it is pertinent to ask whether the total price of patronage is not still too high. This leads to the second point.

The President has much at stake in his administration's reputation for probity and competence in public office. The Truman Administration, for recent instance, had an uneven record in this respect, which the Republicans, with the slogan of "the mess in Washington," effectively exploited in the 1952 campaign. From motives of prudence and public spirit alike, the President must be a guardian of quality standards for the public service. If positions are filled according to merit system procedures, he is largely absolved of personal responsibility. If he makes a patronage appointment, on the other hand, the public responsibility is his, whoever the actual sponsor may be; and the danger is particularly great if the appointment is non-competitive—that is, if the sponsor supposes he has an exclusive right to name the appointee.

Theodore Roosevelt gave the classic formulation to a policy designed to defeat such assertions of monopoly and achieve the best of both possible worlds. He would set the standards for offices not under civil service, he said, and accept political endorsements if the candidates met his standards, and not otherwise. It was TR's special combination of talents, perhaps, to dramatize a popular policy in a moral imperative, to believe whole-heartedly in the morality he preached, and yet to be able to find an alternative principle to justify an apparently inconsistent course when his first morality operated inconveniently. So he was able to pick and choose among the patronage recommendations of senators who needed his support; to find no candidates meeting his standards among the en-dorsements of senators he was bent on undermining; and to accept at face value the say-so of senators whose support he was courting. On the positive side of recruiting he was also unusually energetic in seeking out nominees who in addition to recognized competence would make a defi-nite appeal to some definite group with movable votes. Approaching Jacob H. Schiff, then a patriarch among Wall Street bankers, he asked, so the story goes, "Who is the best Jew I could appoint to be Secretary of Commerce and Labor?" And thereafter, turning his criteria around, he lauded his choice, Oscar Straus, as the ablest man for the post in the country. His successors may envy his professional touch, and find his formula no certain guide in settling particular cases.

Appointments to the independent regulatory commissions, because of their bipartisan make-up and statutory independence, afford a special test of the President's concern for personnel standards, and so do his judicial appointments. In both cases the record is very spotty. The prominence of the position and the amount of publicity attending the appointment appear to have a positive correlation with the calibre of the appointee. In the case of federal district judges, the senators and the state party organizations always take an active interest.

Regulatory commission appointments are monitored, if not sponsored, by the trade organizations in the industries under each commission's juris-diction. The Federal Trade Commission, the Maritime Commission, and especially the Tariff Commission, have furnished unhappy examples of the effect on personnel standards of putting first emphasis on a dependable industry orientation in their membership. That way lies not only the abdication of policy control but also usually mediocrity and, occasionally, scandal.

On the third point, the utility of patronage in enabling the President to be master in his party household is on the wane, as has already been seen. J. M. Blum, in a brilliant analysis of *The Republican Roosevelt* has shown how TR, soon after ascending from the Vice-Presidency, set about destroying Mark Hanna's power over the Republican party and ensuring his own nomination in 1904. The crucial step in the process consisted in selecting three of Hanna's staunchest midwest supporters— the state leaders firmly entrenched in Colorado, Kansas, and Missouri— cutting off their federal patronage, awarding it to a selected successor in each state, and then systematically building up the successor's influence. Before Hanna died, early in 1904, he had been driven to a public endorsement of TR's nomination. Nowadays it would be hard to find a comparable example. The clearest remaining evidences of the old system are the behavior of southern delegations at Republican conventions and the anxiety of state organizations over the appointments of federal district judges and district attorneys. Yet Eisenhower won his nomination in spite, not because, of southern patronage, and the patronage appointments of his first year appeared to be rather tokens of the power of others than assertions of his own control. Kennedy found no solution in patronage for the factional struggles that beset his party in New York, Massachusetts, Ohio, and California. But the old system dies hard. Recent Democratic administrations have depended heavily on alliances with big city machines, cemented with patronage. And Senator Taft certainly did not think the system defunct when he made it a major stipulation, in his famous Morningside Heights breakfast agreement with candidate Eisenhower in the summer of 1952, that there should be no discrimination against his supporters in the appointments of the new administration. This leads to the fourth point.

The major reason today for restricting the scope of patronage ostensibly available to the President for purposes of maintaining control of his party is probably the fact that except in limited circumstances patronage no longer ensures control. It works in the case of those who have little power of their own, and is not needed there if other incentives are present. It does not work in the case of those who have other sources of power. The clearest example of this is Senator McCarthy. When he broke with the administration in the summer of 1953, there were press editorials urging the President to cut off his patronage and bring him into line. This advice ignored the fact, as the event showed, that Senator McCarthy had already learned how to live without the President's blessing.

The argument, moreover, does not rest there. The very existence of patronage, nominally in the President's hands, is, as a long history shows, a standing invitation to other powerful figures to convert it to their own uses and ends. It will take a very strong President to retain more than a small fraction of patronage, especially below the top appointive positions, to serve his purposes. And the consequences of conversion by others are the diffusion and disintegration of administrative loyalties that in theory belong to the President. At lower levels it often leads to alliances between bureau chiefs and their congressional committee opposite numbers, such as have given the Corps of Engineers its long immunity from presidential control in river and harbor functions.

By a parity of reasoning the President may himself choose to neutralize what is ordinarily a patronage post in order to preclude others from controlling it, or to forestall partisan criticism of the appointee's performance. Better the loss of the patronage than the blame for the way it is used. This appears to be one explanation of some appointments of military men to civilian or diplomatic posts—of Roosevelt's naming an Army Engineer to be WPA Administrator in New York City, for instance; of Truman's bringing the internal revenue collectors into the civil service; and of Kennedy's appointment of a Republican, Henry Cabot Lodge, as ambassador to Vietnam.

Congressional Stakes in Patronage

Congressional influence over federal appointments has its constitutional sanction in the power of the Senate to advise and consent to all the President's nominations, unless by law another mode of appointment is fixed. In practice, informal understandings about prospective appointments are also frequently the essential, if unwritten, stipulations on the part of individual members in entering the general agreement that secures the passage of appropriations or legislative bills desired by the administration, whether or not the subject matter of the legislation appears related to the offices in question.

The Senate very early learned how to exert a collective bargaining power in behalf of its individual members in their negotiations with the executive in these matters. By the unwritten rule of "senatorial courtesy," still strong but now not quite so frequently observed as formerly, all senators will do each other the courtesy of uniting to reject, regardless of other considerations or circumstances, any presidential nominee to a federal position in a senator's state, if the senator terms the nomination "personally obnoxious" to him, and providing the senator is of the President's party, and that party has a majority in the Senate. Presidential nominations sent to the Senate are parcelled out to the Senate committees according to their subject matter jurisdiction—postmasters (until they were put under civil service) to the Post Office and Civil Service Committee, judges and district attorneys to the Judiciary Committee, and so on—for reports, and hearings if necessary. This and the near-monopoly control they have over the fate of legislative bills referred to them give the committees also, and especially their chairmen, a bargaining position far broader and stronger than the rule of senatorial courtesy affords, standing alone. It helps to explain, too, the superior prestige of the committees which get the bulk of the prized nominations.

Historic patronage procedures have emphasized the offices that are crucial to the maintenance of power at home. These are the offices that provide a livelihood for party workers and that go far toward ensuring local federal officials who will be as friendly as circumstances permit in administering the law as it impinges on constituents who are the objects of special concern to the party. It is important to the members of Congress that the local offices be in sympathetic hands; it is imperative that they not be in hostile hands. Now that most of them are under civil service and no longer available for party support, each member is on his own to find the means of survival elsewhere—in labor unions, in the American Legion, in a television audience, in a state machine, or in such an arrangement with local businessmen as Vice-President Nixon was called upon to defend so dramatically during his campaign in 1952. The shift is more in the channels than in the ultimate bases of support.

In varying proportions these same interests and some others as well are forwarded by appointments that members are able to secure for their protégés in agencies located in Washington. No rules of equitable apportionment prevail here, however, beyond the inescapable ones that committee chairmen fare better than others and (which is much the same thing) that old inhabitants rate more than newcomers. Since seniority in the Senate is more apt to be found in the South and in sparsely settled states that are politically stable in allegiance, this tends to offset the advantage of senators from more populous states with more local federal offices. So during the decade of the 1920s, Senator Reed Smoot of Utah, from the vantage point of his chairmanship of the Finance Committee, was able to swell the ranks of the Utah State Society in Washington to abnormal size. He developed a private network of federal officials loyal to him, infiltrating and cutting across the hierarchy of Washington agencies.

The hazards of life in Congress give all members a common concern for a shelter in case of accident. So it is that any member or ex-member of either house whom the President nominates to any position requiring Senate confirmation is automatically deemed fit for it, and, unless in the case of a Supreme Court appointment, he is ordinarily spared even the formality of a hearing. This rule stands on the same footing as the rule of senatorial courtesy. Not all lame ducks, by any means, are taken care of in this manner, but the practice is common. Not all the advantage of it lies on one side, either; sometimes the office seeks the man. Recent legislation makes members eligible to participate in the federal employees' retirement system on favorable terms, and this was justified at the time as a more rational and equitable form of social security that would reduce the pressures from prospectively retiring members.

The importunities of politics must frequently tempt members into abuses of official influence in connection with appointments. The traditions of both houses not only tolerate but in many ways encourage a wide latitude of individual interpretation of the nature and limits of duty and responsibility in the pursuit of their careers as representatives. The heterogeneity of their backgrounds hinders the growth of conventions of behavior sufficiently broad and compelling to be adequate by themselves to protect their collective reputation. One such that is generally observed is the canon of caution against intervening in the official processes of justice, when a constituent is caught in the toils of the criminal code; but this covers only a little of the ground. The framers of the Constitution also foresaw the likelihood of conflicts of official and personal interests, and wrote prohibitions against two forms of them into the fundamental law. One prevents a member from holding simultaneously "any office under the United States," and the other forbids a member, during the time for which he was elected, to take any civil office "which shall have been created, or the emoluments whereof shall have been increased, during such time." But the collective stake of the members in keeping the prestige of Congress acceptably high in public esteem is not satisfied by these. The color of virtue has therefore been further safeguarded by a series of self-restraining statutes. The earliest is one that forbids a member to have a financial interest in a contract or contractor with the United States. The Civil Service Act (1883) and the Corrupt Practices Act (1925) forbid members to pay money, or promise or use official influence in obtaining a federal job in return for votes or electioneering support. The former act also forbids the solicitation of classified employees for political contributions, while the latter purports to limit expenditures by candidates, and, in addition, requires periodic reports of campaign expenditures. The Hatch Acts (1939 and 1940) reinforce these restraints by putting a reciprocal prohibition on "pernicious political activities," *i.e.*, electioneering, by federal employees and state employees paid from federal funds, except those in policy-forming positions. So jobholders in the executive branch are forbidden directly to do what congressmen are forbidden to ask them to do, while the latter remain otherwise largely the judges of their own conduct in patronage matters.

Pressure Groups' Stakes in Patronage

In contrast with parties, pressure group organizations are concerned first and last with government policy. Their interests in offices and appointments are strictly instrumental. It is in fact precisely because the party's order of priority as between policy and offices is exactly the reverse that there is so much room for pressure group activity in our politics. For interests with a specific and settled policy orientation find no dependable vehicle in the shifting and compromising combinations that a party must often form in its search for a popular majority. Policies and appointments are closely linked, nevertheless, and so the two types of political organization are in constant contact, usually in cooperative, but sometimes antagonistic, relations.

In spite of their antithetical principles of organization, one striking parallel between the two can be drawn: in both types of organization the smaller units show the greater homogeneity of interests, while as the units grow progressively larger the quest for consensus requires compromise or silence on divisive issues; in the very largest the common denominator of agreement may be almost emptied of policy content. It is not uncommon, for instance, to find congressional districts so predominantly marked with one or two major interests that their congressmen are stereotyped, whoever they may be: congressmen from well-to-do suburban districts on the fringes of large cities, from coal-mining districts, from industrial districts, from farming districts, and so on fall into this category. It is still possible, though not so common as formerly, to find whole states similarly marked; their imprint lies on their senators. Increasingly, however, industrialization and other forces have diversified these larger communities. Tourist inroads have marred the once simple politics of Florida and Arizona; oil discoveries are doing the same to

North Dakota. A senatorial candidate stumping a state must be sensitive to more cross-currents of interest than most of the congressional candidates on his ticket. And the presidential candidate can hardly open his mouth in safety on any topic without hedging his words.

So, characteristically, in each of the three great segments of our economic life—agriculture, labor and business—we find one or two huge nationwide associations (built on competing principles of organization if there is more than one) that attempt to be all-embracing in membership: the American Farm Bureau Federation, the AFL-CIO, the U. S. Chamber of Commerce, and so on. They speak with a mighty voice on topics on which their members are united; that is their reason for being. All farmers want cheap credit and high prices for what they sell; all unions want high wages, freedom to strike, and government support for collective bargaining; all businessmen want lower taxes. But on specific issues in their general fields these inclusive associations are often tongue-tied and paralyzed by internal disagreements. Some farmers are dairy-men or raise cattle or poultry, and want cheap feed; other farmers grow hay or corn. Dairymen want a tax on oleomargarine, while soybean and cottonseed interests oppose it. Some skilled workers make watches and want the tariff on Swiss watches raised, while others work for the assemblers of imported watch movements and want the tariff lowered. The petroleum industry is divided between the domestic independent crude producers and the integrated companies with foreign holdings. The National Association of Manufacturers wants a sales tax which the National Retail Merchants Association fights. The AFL-CIO seldom endorses a presidential candidate, and proclaims a "non-partisan" policy, because some of its international vice-presidents are ardent Republicans while others are the best of Democrats. Accordingly, in each of the three fields a multitude of smaller but more homogeneous associations has arisen, each of them organized around a commodity, a product, a craft skill, an industrial employer, a limited geographical area, a method of doing business, or other specifically identifiable interest.

The major economic lobbies focus most of their energies on votes in Congress, on decisions and programs of administrative agencies, and on appointments to key positions in the federal establishment. In these matters, party leaders play the role of brokers among the spokesmen of competing interests. And in connection with appointments it would be logical to expect that the most inclusive pressure groups will be most concerned with the cabinet and subcabinet posts—the NAM and the

Chamber of Commerce with the Treasury and Commerce Secretary-ships, the Farm Bureau with the Agriculture Department, the AFL-CIO with the Labor Department and NLRB appointments—while the more specialized associations pay attention to appointments in the subordinate divisions and specialized agencies. So the mine workers concentrate on the chief of the Bureau of Mines, the real estate people on the FHA, the commercial banks on the Comptroller of the Currency and the Federal Reserve Board, the savings and loan league on the Home Loan Bank Board, the airlines on the Civil Aeronautics Board, and so on.

The consistent theme in the interplay of pressure groups on government, both when they operate directly and when they work through party intermediaries, is the effort to create autonomous and controllable fragments of government, each with a jurisdiction corresponding to the area and scope of the pressure group's interest—autonomous, that is to say, in the sense of independence from the rest of the government, and controllable from the point of view of the pressure group. Viewing government as an instrument, the aim of a pressure group is to have a "little government" beholden to it for its existence and powers, responsive to its policy dictates, endowed with sufficient legal authority and funds to carry through its programs, and able politically to ward off or disregard the impulses and restraints that come from the coordinating centers and mechanisms of the larger government as a whole. Ideally, such an island of power consists of the pressure group membership which forms the clientele and supports its private government, a separate public agency dedicated to the service of that specific clientele, and a ring of outposts, agents, allies and dependents, reaching into the other centers of power—the White House, the relevant legislative committees and appropriations subcommittees of Congress, the cognate divisions of major executive departments, and the headquarters of the more inclusive pressure groups—that may impinge on its interests. In practice, the realization of this structural model is always in some degree frustrated, both by the competition of rival interest groups seeking similar arrangements for themselves and by the overriding necessities of national policies that obtain wider bases of support and obtrude across the private preserves of the pressure groups. Nevertheless, the number of cases that approximate the ideal for long stretches of time is sufficient to warrant the characterization.

The utility of such a structure for the ultimate policy goals of the pressure group obviously depends on the appointment of persons sympathetically disposed toward those goals to the executive positions, at least, in the public agency involved. This is the primary stake of pressure groups in federal appointments. It will be a great practical convenience to them if they can infiltrate the operating levels of the agency as well.

The pressure group stake in the federal service can hardly help being a challenge to the interest of the bureaucracy in regulating what it regards as its own internal affairs. Bureaucratic standards of laudable conduct are linked to the performance of agency objectives and the development of professional skills; they put a premium on loyalty to the agency and its avowed public purposes. Veterans' preference clashes with these standards by inviting its holder to "soldier on the job," to treat his place as a reward already earned rather than a trust to be discharged. Other types of pressure group apointments clash with these standards by lodging in the public service people whose first loyalties are to private careers and organizations outside. As trustees of the public interest, professional bureaucrats inevitably look upon these as they do upon party patronage appointees—alike intruders endangering the standards they live by. From motives of self-defense, if no more, this drives the professional bureaucrats to reassert their autonomy where and when they can.

Alternatives to Patronage

The abuses of patronage and other types of party spoils are now generally regarded as evil, like other forms of prostitution. They are among the manifestations of human frailty that are deplored but still tolerated in the degree that they do not too seriously interfere with social goals and cannot readily be stamped out altogether. But no one (unless an immediate beneficiary) seriously advocates a return to nineteenth-century spoils practice. When first introduced here, that was a democratic reform to break up the power of a ruling aristocracy, as Carl Fish pointed out many years ago, but it has long since lost its respectability. For the present generation its decline is a moral achievement not to be surrendered.

The relaxation of party discipline that has accompanied the decline is perhaps a more arguable blessing, for discipline seems to promise responsibility, and superficial observers of party activity, at least, see little enough of that. But the form of discipline most familiar to American parties was long ago labeled "bossism." With us, the strictest party discipline, in the states and in the Congress, has historically been associated with the utmost irresponsibility toward the public welfare. It is debatable whether this tends to prove that political power should never be concentrated in one man's hands, or only that the men in our party history who have been able to concentrate it have been the wrong men, or in the wrong places—party bosses working in secret rather than elected Chief Executives whom the voters could turn out. The exceptional cases, like Huey Long on the one hand or the elder LaFollette on the other, where the elected executive was also the actual boss, are not decisive either way. On balance, the freedom of political choice and alignment that has flowed from the competition of many groups has seemed a net gain. With party bosses apparently on the way out, people today would have to be shown that the enforcer of discipline can himself be made popularly responsible before they would think it safe, let alone worth paying a price, to reconstitute their power.

The growth of businessmen's contributions to party funds, which have taken the place of patronage as the financial mainstay of party activity, has been received with more ambivalence. The practice is regularly decried, but it flourishes. Laws are passed to restrict it, but major loopholes are deliberately left. Vast sums are required and can legitimately be spent for propaganda and education through the modern techniques of publicity, and the citizens are still attracted by pageantry. But financial contributors may prove to be Indian givers, and when the method of repayment is the distortion of public policy to private advantage, it is understandable that onlookers should be uneasy. If the power of money is a root of evil, is there another way to support the public functions that parties perform without endangering democratic control of government policy on the one hand or the integrity of the federal service on the other? Alternatives are worth looking at even if they raise as many problems as they solve.

One school of thought proceeds on socialist premises: since the function is public, and liable to abuse under private control, let the government do it. We have, of course, come some distance in this direction already. All states now furnish the ballots that candidates or parties once had to supply on their own; the states and localities furnish the polling places, the equipment, the administrative officials. Outside the South, at least, they conduct the party primaries as well as the general elections. A few western states publish and distribute to voters informational pamphlets of biographical materials about candidates and arguments pro and con about referendum issues. Conceivably the federal government might take over the conduct of congressional elections and primaries, provide for the election of delegates to national party conventions held at government expense, put radio stations at the candidates' disposal, and so on. Or it might give each recognized party a subsidy allowance for these and related campaign purposes. Emancipated by these means from their dependence on private benefactors, it is argued, parties and candidates might then be able to dispense with patronage too, and devote themselves disinterestedly to the public weal. Despite an endorsement of elements of this approach, from a commission of eminent citizens appointed by President Kennedy to look into the financing of campaign costs, it has not so far caught on in this country. And unless it were coupled with some effectual means of preventing private campaign expenditures over and above the government's provision, it would hardly fulfill its own premises.

Along another line it is urged that if parties were effectively committed to definite program responsibilities, they would have to find the means of enforcing a discipline adequate to meet those responsibilities. This indicates movement toward a parliamentary government system. In England, the necessary discipline is obtained by a central party headquarters control over nominations to seats in the House of Commons. Assuming that our traditions of local control over nominations are unshakable, this would require at the minimum that the President be given power to dissolve the House of Representatives when it refused to enact measures he advocated. This threat supposedly would provide the disciplinary weapon. The same general end would be served if in addition to, or in lieu of a part of, its present membership, it had a substantial number of seats filled by election at large over the whole country, on the same ballot with the President. He might then have a controlling influence over the nominations to these and so have a bloc of supporters in the House tied to his political fortunes. Any such program as this would, of course, require constitutional amendments, the ultimate consequences of which would be difficult to predict with certainty. It also assumes that we could have, simultaneously, a two-party system and those two parties programmatic in character. We have already seen how the electoral system works against this as a permanent condition.

More modest innovators point to the fact that we have had a number of cases of popular state governers who have been elected and re-elected without the assistance of—often in the teeth of—the regular party machines, and they have supported and extended civil service systems and lived with little or no patronage. Grover Cleveland, Robert M. LaFollette, Hiram Johnson, and Judson Harmon were classic instances. Senator Norris of Nebraska belonged to a later school. Earl Warren and Frank J. Lausche, more recently and less controversially, won successive terms in the governor's office, by drawing votes from both parties and capitalizing on their independence of machine support.

Can this formula of success be generalized? On the record, the answer appears to be no. The phenomenon of a man with a personality sufficiently magnetic by itself to draw a majority of the voters, and to attract enough of them to sustained and concerted voluntary activity in his behalf to substitute for a political party machine, occurs seldom. It is fostered, though by no means guaranteed, by the prominence of his office. Presumably, it would be favored further by a drastic extension of the short ballot principle to eliminate all elective executive offices except the Governor's, leaving him to appoint other officials, as in the federal government. It is fostered, also, by the availability of radio and television to convey the candidate's personality directly to more voters more quickly. But it does not tell us how, except by accident and luck, a man gets started on a career in public life, before he reaches a spotlight position; the parties provide some sort of ladder for advancement. It does not solve, either, the case of legislators, who are too numerous and anonymous to find a group salvation in this way. The logical end of this approach is a nation without parties—a situation the framers of our constitution apparently hoped for, but thought would be manageable only through a scheme of indirect election, like the Electoral College, to exercise by delegation the final stages of choice.

The only nation without parties is Utopia, and if we consider utopias there are other forms of election that suggest themselves. The school teacher may think of competitive examinations open to all, to fill public offices now elective. The psychologist may dream of aptitude tests suitable for the purpose. The man with sporting tastes will conceive a gigantic lottery for the business, as the Athenians once chose their Council and other officials. These methods might not work out so differently in practice. They have, at all events, one feature in common with the monarchical principle of hereditary succession to office, and in contrast with the system of party nominations familiar to us. They leave no room for the influence of popular preference on the choice. The consent of the governed might be given to such a system, but not to the particular individuals who for a time were to be the rulers.

If these quasi-automatic and impersonal schemes are rejected, the remaining realistic alternatives to party nominations and patronage, historically speaking, are based explicitly or implicitly on some aristocratic principle—the recognition of some determinate class as better fitted than others to rule. A governing priesthood is out of the question. A ruling military class has wrecked too many regimes in recent memory to be heard as a claimant; even in Soviet Russia the Red Army leaders were relegated to obscurity after World War II. The landed gentry lost their primacy in England with the rise of commerce and industry, and in this country with the westward migration and expansion. An intellectual aristocracy waits on a day of deference toward learning as an end in itself that has never arrived in this land of practical people. The prestige of science is higher, but a government of scientists has not gotten beyond the stage of talk about "technocracy" and the literature of science fiction. If we have had a persistently influential class, periodically but by no means always and everywhere conceded to be entitled (as a matter of right and not just as a matter of fact) to govern the course of affairs, it has not even been those whom Alexander Hamilton described as the natural rulers, "the rich and well born" but rather the business leadership of the country. Yet considering the relative ease and mobility of movement into and out of this group, it is dogmatic to use the term "class" to describe it. And it is a curious ruling class whose leaders often have to be drafted to take responsible governmental positions even temporarily. Successful businessmen do not look on government service as a preferred career; they want to influence government policy more often than they are willing to take government office. Moreover, recurrent depressions, agrarian protest movements, and the rise of organized labor have combined to impair the prestige of business leaders in government from time to time and prevent the crystallization of that automatic deference toward them as members of a ruling class that is the mark of an acknowledged aristocracy. Because their incumbency or interest in public office, as distinct from public policy, is usually so fleeting, they can hardly take the place of the parties as a direct and regular source of recruits for a permanent government service.

As a practical matter this review seems to confine the major alternatives to two, which are indeed alternatives of emphasis and direction rather than irreconcilable opposites. One is a bureaucracy substantially uncontrolled save as congressional mandates, court decisions, presidential directives and the orders of department heads give authorization, and set limits. Within these, professionally trained civil servants would be free to work out their individual and collective destinies, shaping administrative policies, programs and procedures by precedent and rule in the light of their conceptions of the public interest. This involves broad delegations of authority and trust in the experts to know best what should be done and avoided. It points toward a self-contained, self-governing and self-perpetuating officialdom such as the FBI has typified. The other is a bureaucracy continuously permeated, like the Department of Agriculture, say, by the varied and shifting influences that parties tend to channel into the administrative structure of government. The fact that both models can be found simultaneously in the same government, even in the same department, suggests that there is something to be said for each.

Elements of a Public Policy

An effort to reconcile the competing claims and clashing values of the various interests served in appointments to the federal service begins with recognizing two irreversible facts: 1) the vast bulk of the civilian positions in the federal government are in the classified service and 2) they will be filled by the several departments and agencies, working through the procedures permissible under civil service statutes and regulations. A small proportion in addition are covered under certain agency career systems, like the foreign service, public health, immigration border patrol, and coast guard services. A considerably larger but for present purposes less significant number are industrial workers or temporaries in this country and overseas, many of the latter being alien "indigenous personnel." Together these categories probably account for over 95 per cent of the total. As to nearly all of them (disregarding vestigial partisan traces in the Post Office and elsewhere) the parties have little or no contact or even concern. Pressure group influences affect a good many of them informally. Because of the number of positions and the regulations surrounding them, recruitment is effectively decentralized. The President and members of Congress, even with the staff help they have, cannot affect the disposal of individual cases in significant quantity. Their influence must in the main be exerted indirectly, through agency heads and principal subordinates, and the Civil Service Commission, by means of appointments to these posts and by policy changes in law, appropriations, and executive orders. The decisive criteria for individual appointments are inevitably those felt at the points of personal contact with employing officials down the line in all ranks of the hierarchy and across all agencies.

This means that insofar as the President and the Congress and outside observers feel a concern for the direction of broad tendencies in personnel management in the bulk of the civilian establishment, they need to make their concern manifest in considering such policy matters as expansion and retrenchment, pay and promotion and fringe benefits, loyalty and security clearance systems, Whitten riders, major appointments, concessions to pressure group interests, and the like. Ambivalence about the actual goals of the personnel system was once shown dramatically in two orders from the White House: one, revealed in the press on October 27, 1954, directed all federal agencies to advise the Republican National Committee of all vacancies as they occurred, whether in the classified service or exempt, and provided for notification forms and clearance and reporting procedures; the other, announced on November 22, 1954, opened the way for permanent status for thousands of "indefinites" currently on the rolls, and reaffirmed the traditional prohibitions against partisan influences on appointments in the classified service. The intervening years since then have not altogether resolved this ambivalence.

It means also that the range of appointments in which policy preferences can be expressed directly in the choice of appointees is very small. In any large organization governed by routines the maneuverable margin of the business that is subject to deliberate manipulation and control is small, and has a disproportionate symbolic significance for that very reason. In surveying from this angle the types of federal appointments that can be directly controlled, some broad distinctions are useful.

The most legitimate and least harmful positions to which strictly partisan appointments can be made are those which for reasons of ceremony and dignity must exist, and for technological reasons are sinecures or can safely be made so. The ambassadorships to major capitals are the most conspicuous places of this sort. Modern communications enable the State Department to dictate every move of the incumbents, and men and women of ordinary means cannot afford to take them so that they are closed to career foreign service officers anyway; these are ideal rewards for party contributors who are willing to live abroad. Lesser diplomatic posts make harmless outlets for appointments appealing to special voting groups. Memberships on international claims tribunals, which have a minimum of policy content in their work, carry salaries adequate to take care of lame ducks and faithful party workers. Comparably necessary and harmless positions in domestic agencies are much harder to find. A George Washington Bicentennial Commission, for example, doesn't come along very often. The historic practice of appointing federal district attorneys and marshals on party recommendations has been to the disadvantage of litigants and the reputation of federal justice, and puts too severe a strain on the parties' capacity for self-restraint.

The most difficult appointments, from the point of view of balancing party and congressional claims, public policy, and the special interests of practicing lawyers, are probably the judgeships, and especially the district judgeships. The President's choice of an Attorney General is crucial here, for on his judgment and tact largely depends the maintenance of quality standards.

Almost equally difficult are the appointments to the independent regulatory commissions, for these have nationwide jurisdictions and compact, highly organized clienteles endeavoring to capture them; and they are subject to party and congressional pressures as well. A President with a program has a genuine policy stake in their operations, and because of their statutory independence he has not many other means of influencing them.

The most important appointments for the President, from the standpoint of his control over the course of federal policy, are, naturally, his cabinet members, and after these the subcabinet and upper administrative places that they or he may fill in the departments, and the staff he assembles in the White House executive office. The dominant considerations for the first group are mostly impersonal, and better so. Sectional representation, factional and functional recognition, strength for negotiations with congressional leaders, public prestige, and identification with major policy issues, are all factors in this reckoning. For the second group the same sort of considerations apply, but as the number of places is considerably greater the subdivisions of talent and function must be worked out in greater detail, and balance in the total is correspondingly harder to obtain. For the third group adaptability to the President's personal viewpoints and working habits are the decisive criteria.

Of these three groups, the second is most significant in shaping the role of parties and patronage in the federal government service. It embraces the posts of central departmental management that lie between the cabinet heads and their bureau chiefs—the under and assistant secretaries and their deputies, the chief budget and personnel officers, the legal and policy advisers, the general managers and field operations supervisors. At these levels civil service standards and protections lose cogency, clashing with the outside pressures of party and special interest reaching inward and downward. For old-line operations the claims of civil service extend higher into this zone. For new functions and controversial operations the range for political appointments dips further down. In all this zone, when appointments are given to others to use, they are patronage; when the President and his department heads are able to keep them for their own purposes, they are policy-making positions. If they require Senate confirmation, the President's interest will dictate that they be abolished or made sinecures. If they have been in the classified service he will want them in Schedule C.

In the end, good government depends on a mixture of rationality and consent. It is not enough for a government to know what is best for the people. It is also fatal for it to take them on the road to disaster even if in emotion or error they have voted to go there. The special claim of the civil service is to supply rationality in government action, as that of the parties is to engineer consent. The delicate task of the President, insofar as he can, is to determine the mixture in particular situations and make his decisions accordingly. For purposes of policy control, and at policy levels—though no longer for the simple sustenance of party organizations—a place for federal patronage remains.

Frederick C. Mosher

4

Features and Problems of
the Federal Civil Service

Introductory

The "bureaucrat" is one of America's most cherished stereotypes. But viewed from the perspective of other societies, a most striking feature of our government is the very absence of a distinct governmental class—of a "bureaucracy" in the sense in which that term has long been used in Europe. In many important respects, government employment and public employees in the United States are surprisingly like their non-public counterparts. Here, the employees of the government and of all but the smaller private concerns work within frameworks of organization, systems of loyalty, duties, and discipline, and processes of human relationships that are fundamentally parallel.

The work of Americans is highly specialized in a tremendous range and variety of categories, and public and private employment are alike in their diversity. The federal service does include some activities which involve a monopoly of specialization, such as the military services, the Foreign Service, and the Post Office. For most of the remainder the occu-

FREDERICK C. MOSHER *is Professor of Political Science at the University of California (Berkeley) as well as a staff consultant of the University's Institute of Governmental Studies. He has had extensive experience in government, including service with* UNRRA, *the Departments of State, Army, and Air Force,* TVA, *and state and local governments. In 1962 he was staff director of the Committee on Foreign Affairs Personnel (the Herter Committee), which produced the report,* Personnel for the New Diplomacy.

pations are similar or identical among public and non-public agencies. Transfers from one to the other are frequent; the requirements of training and experience are similar. In fact, many employees feel a closer identification with their profession or trade than with their employer, whether public or private. The steamfitter may care little whether he is working for the U. S. Navy or for U. S. Steel; the forester may not be much concerned whether his employer is the U. S. Forest Service or the University of Michigan. Many of those now in private employment have at some time had government experience; and many of those in the public service have had private training and experience.

Similarities also lie deeper than these. For the most part, we live close together, whether publicly or privately employed. We dress alike, read the same papers, go to the same shows. Our children go to the same schools and colleges—as we did before them. We have similar values, similar prejudices, similar aspirations.

The views of the federal "bureaucracy" as a vast monolith of faceless clerks, or as a distinct social class, or as a political bloc are not just oversimplifications. They are mirages. There are within the federal service a number of subservices, each with its own distinctive membership and character, some of which undoubtedly resemble in more or less degree a "bureaucracy," defined either in the popular, pejorative sense or in the objective perspective of the social scientist. But there is hardly a federal bureaucracy as such; indeed the very title of this volume is somewhat misleading in its implication that there is a *single* federal service. There are many federal services, loosely linked but widely different one from the other. Many of these services bear more resemblance to like organizations outside the government than to other services within it in respect to the attributes of their employees, the kinds of work they do, the methods of employment, and the personnel problems they face.

How Is the Federal Service Different? ### Some Underlying Considerations

Why then does the federal service, the many different services of which it is composed, present special problems?* Why are not the practices developed in private employment practice simply transferred into

---

* Many of the special problems herein outlined apply also to other governments in the United States—the states and a great variety of local units. Our attention will, however, focus simply on the civil service of the nation.

the government? That there are differences is implicit in the publication of this volume; indeed, all of the accompanying essays treat in part relatively unique aspects of public, as distinguished from private, employment. The discussion that follows treats some of the differences that seem to have particular operational significance today. A few of these are differences in kind; others are differences in degree and, as will be noted later, for many of them the distance between public and private practices appears to be narrowing.

SOVEREIGNTY

Sovereignty may be an appropriate point of departure; it is the concept from which political theorists begin. Its definition, its ramifications, even its existence in democratic states, are the subjects of much debate. But the central sense of the word continues, for better or worse, to have much significance for the law, the practice, and the image of public employment. It connotes supremacy, the highest power in a given jurisdiction. The state, whether viewed as sovereign itself or as the expression of the will of a sovereign people, yields to no other power and demands the final allegiance of its members (citizens). Employees of the state stand in a special relation to it; they are presumed to be servants of a sovereign authority.

We need not here indulge in argument about the theoretic validity of sovereignty in a democratic state. The idea behind it, however valid, has shaped, in a number of ways, the nature of public employment. First, it is presumed to demand, on the part of public employees as individuals, a special kind of loyalty—a loyalty running beyond the immediate job and organization and to the government as a whole. This loyalty brooks no rival if another allegiance undertakes or threatens to compete with it. The problems involved in the enforcement of such a single-minded loyalty have long been a source of difficulties in our national government. They are illustrated in the variety of efforts to eliminate *conflicts of interest* between the government and private organizations. They are further illustrated in the *loyalty and security* programs which have been designed to prevent the employment of persons suspected of being loyal to other governments or associations, or having beliefs considered to be antagonistic to the interests of the United States.

Secondly, the sovereignty concept has contributed special problems to the negotiation and bargaining between governmental employees, joined in associations or labor unions, and their governmental employer. Many of the normal, socially-approved activities and weapons of unions in the private economy—the strike, the closed shop, the boycott—have been suspect in governmental jurisdictions, if not forbidden outright. Governor Thomas E. Dewey of New York in 1947 stated in simple terms his view of the sovereignty doctrine in this field: "A public employee has as his employer all the people. The people cannot tolerate an attack upon themselves." In spite of significant changes in labor relations in the federal government in recent years, the setting and the constraints upon the bargaining process in the public sphere remain distinct and unique.

POLITICAL NEUTRALITY

A third facet of the sovereignty concept has been its contributions to efforts to insure political neutrality and to inhibit political activity by public employees. This doctrine says, in effect: If the people are sovereign in a democracy and the public employee is but a servant of the people, he should be deprived of any special ability, deriving from his position, to influence the political judgment of the people. This argument is particularly potent in a country historically fearful of the powers of the government and its bureaucrats. Further, the civil service reform groups which have long urged the insulation of the public service from political influences and activity, have advocated laws and regulations designed to protect civil servants from influences and coercions of the parties. Since the late 1930s, the Hatch Acts have restrained civil servants from engaging in most political activities, other than the exercise of a silent franchise.

POLITICAL RESPONSIVENESS

Related to political neutrality is another concept guiding the conduct of the public service: that it should honestly and to the best of its ability interpret and carry out the will of the public as expressed through the appropriate political mechanisms. It should respond promptly and wholeheartedly to changes in that will. As long as one's view of the function of the appointive public service is that of execution of policies and programs elsewhere established, the concept of political neutrality is an appropriate corollary to that of political responsiveness.

It is now widely recognized that an important function of the public service is the development of policy, the making of policy recommendations, and, in many cases, the final policy determinations. How can such activities be reconciled with a system of political neutrality? This problem has contributed to the efforts to distinguish between the functions of policy development and policy execution, and the efforts to split policy jobs from administrative jobs. Among the holders of "policy" jobs, the idea of political responsiveness becomes dominant. They are separated from the regular civil service as to manner of appointment, tenure, and in other respects. They are presumed to come and go as sails shift in changing winds. "Administrative" personnel, on the other hand, are permanent civil servants, politically responsive in the sense that they respond to directives from above and also politically neutral in the sense that they have only the slightest voice, on the job or off, in determining the course of public policy.

The line between policy and administrative jobs is a hazy one, if it exists at all. Some offices, even departments, are almost exclusively in the business of making policy, yet employ many career personnel. And what may properly be termed "policy" is constantly changing as public issues and interest rise and fall. The problem of defining the Schedule C group, the political appointees in the administration, is the most immediate illustration of the general difficulty in applying these concepts. It is also illustrated almost continuously by such questions as whether it is appropriate to hire and give civil service status to a local political leader, or whether a departmental staff officer should be permitted to deliver speeches before local political clubs. It may be noted also that the distinction between public and private employment in this regard is probably one of degree rather than kind. But the size of the public establishment, the complexity of its problems, the difficulties of the political mechanisms, and the dimensions and variety of the public to be served make a vital difference.

REPRESENTATIVENESS

Another respect in which the federal service is distinctive in degree if not in kind arises from the idea that the service should be representative of the total population. Public jobs are distributed among sections, among classes, among functional groups of the population. The concept of representativeness has two connotations. The first is that public jobs should be distributed *equitably* among the total population. The second and more important connotation is that different groups should be "represented" in the policy-forming and policy-executing phases of administration through appointees who will effectively express their points of view. The idea of a politically representative bureaucracy, as a complement to the representative legislature, as a basic facet of democratic structure, is not yet widely accepted in formal terms, but as a consideration in public employment it has long been recognized. From the beginning it has been practiced in the selection of cabinet members and other presidential appointees. The system of senatorial confirmation and "courtesy" reflect it in part, as did the patronage system. The civil service system continues one aspect of it in its apportionment of Washington jobs. But more important than these, perhaps, is the continuing pressure for representation in the government by representatives of special groups and interests —persons who bring with them "built-in" understandings and attitudes and who may in some cases be answerable to the groups they are presumed to represent. The demands for agriculturists in the Department of Agriculture, for labor people in the Department of Labor, for businessmen in the Department of Commerce are examples. The special voice of the organized legal profession in the employment of lawyers, and of the organized doctors in the management of the various medical units, are others. To a considerable extent, the shape and nature of the public service is determined by the demands of various groups for adequate representation.

EQUAL TREATMENT

These demands are to some extent balanced by still another influence in the management of the government service, the doctrine of equal treatment. It has long been a basic tenet of our system of government and of British jurisprudence that people be treated equally under the laws. As applied to the initial appointments to the public service, the doctrine has come to mean equal opportunity to compete for jobs among the entire adult citizenry. It has lent support also to a variety of devices and protections to assure undiscriminating, equal treatment to those on the job.

The principle of equal treatment, coupled with that of the merit system, has had a great impact upon virtually all aspects of public employment practice. On the technical side, the two principles have necessitated a tremendous emphasis upon devices for evaluating work qualifications and work accomplishment and upon standardization of policies for dealing with both candidates and employees. Thus they have contributed greatly to the depersonalization of personnel administration.

It is of course true that these same forces and developments are present in many sectors of private employment. The principle of equal treatment is not monopolized by the government, nor is that of the merit system. But they have been engineered into general governmental employment practices as a response to public policy and legislative fiat. In private employment, their application has been less consistent and has emerged from the ebb and flow of management negotiations with organized labor.

SOCIAL PURPOSES

Against the ideas implicit in equal treatment and the merit principle, nonetheless, it has long been recognized that public employment might be used for social purposes other than, or in addition to, getting the job done in the most efficient manner. The word "social" is here used in the sense of "socially-approved" or at least "socially-permitted." Patronage, viewed as a device for maintaining political organizations by "rewarding the faithful," is a well-known example. The employment of persons on work relief projects in periods of depression is another, though quite different, instance in which merit and efficiency are subordinated to, or importantly conditioned by, other social objectives. Likewise, programs for the hiring, rehabilitating, and training of handicapped or disabled persons illustrate the application of objectives to public employment in addition to that of efficient performance. A long-standing example in our American experience has been the provision of preference in public employment for veterans.

MODEL EMPLOYER

A related observation about the public service is that the federal government, by virtue of its size but more importantly because of its position in American society, has the role or the potential role of leader or model employer. Not only is it an employer competing among all the other employers in our economy. To some extent—perhaps today too small an extent—the policies of the federal government have an influence on those of other jurisdictions of government and of private employers as well. Government employment standards and practices have long been considered not alone from the standpoint of their immediate application in the government but also of their possible impact upon the entire employment market. For the government to fall far "behind" or far "below" the standards of other employers is a source of shame. The more usual appeal of reformers in the public personnel field is that the government should stay in the vanguard and be an unquestioned leader in employment. This has meant that, among other things, the social objectives and standards of the government must be embodied in its employment practices before the government can expect them to become widely respected in the non-public field.

In a number of the areas of personnel administration, the federal government has in fact been in the lead or near it at one time or another. The civil service idea itself, the development of entrance examinations, and later the use of position classification were examples of this. The ideal of the "model employer" is, however, better illustrated in a variety of the social conditions of employment and labor: child labor; minimum wages; retirement; shortened hours of work (and their lengthening during the war emergency); leave policy; and salaries and wages among the middle and lower grades. Organized labor has lent vigorous support to liberalized government employment conditions, partly on the grounds that government's practice would constitute a "yardstick" for private industry.

Through its own personnel practices, the federal government may, by the force of example, give persuasive force toward social reforms it seeks in the non-public sectors of society. Conversely, by failing to practice what it preaches it may embarrass its leadership and severely weaken its case.

Perhaps the most vigorous current examples of federal efforts to be a "model employer" are provided by the drives in behalf of better opportunities for Negroes, for handicapped persons, and for women. The first two have in fact been going for a long time, and the third is more recent. All three were reinvigorated soon after the inauguration of President Kennedy and all have now become focal elements in the federal personnel picture. Since 1947 the President has sponsored a Committee on the Employment of the Handicapped. President Kennedy continued support of this Committee and added in 1961 a Commission on the Status of Women and a Committee on Equal Employment Opportunity. The Commission on the Status of Women, most narrowly governmental in scope, was supplemented in 1963 by a Citizens Advisory Council and an Interdepartmental Commission on the Status of Women. All of these organizations have published vigorous reports advocating the extension of opportunities to these groups. The Civil Service Commission has provided leadership in the implementation of many of their recommendations.

Significant gains have been reported in the hiring of the physically handicapped. In 1963, 19 of every 1,000 persons hired by the federal government had some physical disability, an increase from six per 1,000 in 1957. It has been achieved in part through the work of local coordinators of employment for the physically handicapped, appointed by the Civil Service Commission.

Negroes and other minority groups have increased their representation in the federal service, although there is still a long way to go. Between 1961 and 1962, Negroes accounted for 17 per cent of the net hiring in the federal service. Over half of these were placed in positions having salary ranges of $4,565 and over. Kennedy and Johnson appointment policies have been of great benefit to these groups.

Commission (and Committee) efforts have been far more successful in improving the employment outlook for the handicapped and the Negro and other minority groups than in the employment of women. The proportion of women in the federal service has remained nearly constant (24 per cent) over the last decade. Women are underrepresented at nearly every level of government employment; in total work force (less than one-quarter as opposed to one-third in private industry); in professional occupations (76.8 per cent of all women in the federal service are in the lowest five grades, all subprofessional, of the General Schedule); and at top levels (in 1962 only 24 of 2,000 positions at GS-16, 17, and 18 were held by women). Although Commission efforts have been successful in drastically reducing the number of agency requests for men only, and although appointments by Presidents Kennedy and Johnson have contributed greatly to efforts to bring women into high-level positions, the federal service is still far short of the goal President Kennedy envisioned in 1961: a "showcase of the feasibility and value of combining genuine equality of opportunity on the basis of merit with efficient service to the public."

PUBLIC SCRUTINY

It is of great significance that government activities are carried on under some degree of, or with some possibility of, public scrutiny. The degree varies widely among different types of programs and among the different personnel processes. But there cannot be much question that it is a significant environmental influence in the government, certainly more so than in most private enterprise. Government is not exactly a goldfish bowl, as it has been dubbed by some. But there is usually a good possibility that decisions in the field of personnel, as well as in other areas, will be revealed outside the office. The careful administrator will consider not alone how a decision may look on a memorandum and how it may look to his fellow employees, but also how it may look to his successor, to a congressional committee, and in a newspaper. Few other organizations, if any, must operate on the general premise of "open covenants" under the potential scrutiny of a hostile political party, an alert legislature, a galaxy of pressure groups, and a profession of newspaper, TV, and radio publicists who thrive on the discovery of injustice, malfeasance, and error.

The Management of Merit

Civil service employment involves many of the same activities and problems that face any large employer. But no other institution, private or public, approaches the federal service in terms of size (more than 2½ million civilian employees), geographic spread (50 states and about 125 foreign countries, colonies, and dependencies) and occupational diversity (an estimated 80,000 different occupations—representing just about every significant profession and calling known to man—are employed somewhere by the federal government). The government is in fact a loose aggregation of many different employers. But for some purposes and in some ways it operates as a single employer. The balance between agency operation and discretion on the one hand and central standardization, operation, and control on the other has long been the object of debate in the government. As will be shown below, the balance has swung dramatically in the last quarter-century away from the central office.

There are, nonetheless, strong centripetal and standardizing forces. The "board of directors" of the U. S. government in Congress, and some committees and some members of that body have long taken a rather unusual interest in the administration of federal personnel—unusual, that is, for a board of directors. Their inquiries sometimes lead to the passage of laws. Some of these laws apply only to specific categories of personnel—the Postal employees, the Foreign Service, manual workers, and so on—but the laws applicable to the general competitive civil service are usually sweeping and apply to hundreds of thousands of individuals in all sorts of occupations and programs. Some of them are fairly general in nature; many are specific and detailed; and some, though general in purport, are so phrased as to require highly specific procedures to make them effective. Most of the important phases of personnel administration are based upon laws of wide application—examinations, classification, pay efficiency ratings, veterans' preference, retirement, layoffs, and so on. Within or pursuant to the laws, the President has issued a variety of executive orders and the Civil Service Commission a large volume of more detailed instructions, all usually having application to a great proportion of employees in whatever agency they may work.

There are other more or less continuing forces in the direction of centralization and standardization of practice. One of these is the budget and appropriations process, which, among other things, forces each agency every year to bring together comprehensive information and plans about its operations and to defend them before their headquarters officials, the Bureau of the Budget, and the committees of Congress. Another is the President and the government-wide objectives and programs he supports. In recent years presidential impetus has been the dominant factor behind the drive for fair employment practices, greater employment of women, increased productivity of governmental manpower, and collective bargaining in the federal service. Personnel procedures are to some extent standardized by fiat from some of the central staff and service agencies (the Bureau of the Budget, the General Services Administration) as well as by rulings and judgments of the Comptroller General and the courts. Finally, non-governmental organizations having interest in various aspects of public employment tend to exert a standardizing influence on employment policies—at least to the point of criticizing wide and unequal disparities in practice. Among those with great influence in this direction are the veterans' organizations, many labor unions, and professional associations.

Thus, the government continues to operate, in many ways, as *one* employer—one having enormous size, scope, and variety, but still only one. The ground rules are very nearly universal in application and in some fields, such as reductions-in-force, they are very specific (some would say distressingly so).

For the first half-century of its existence, the Civil Service Commission constituted the bedrock of centralized operations in the federal merit system. Viewed by itself and by many others as the mainstay and watchdog against partisan political practices in public employment, it both carried out many personnel operations itself and reviewed those operations which were performed in the executive agencies. In many respects, the most significant development in federal personnel administration since 1933 has been the decentralization of personnel powers from the Commission and the accompanying revolution in that agency's role and operations. Much of this development was the product of necessities of speed and scale rather than of design. Most of President Roosevelt's New Deal emergency agencies were set up outside the civil service, at least partly because of the alleged cumbersomeness of civil service recruitment. In the late 1930s, the majority of these appointees were blanketed into the civil service system. In 1938, following the recommendations of the Brownlow Committee of 1937, the President directed all departments and agencies to set up personnel offices and thus equip themselves professionally to handle their own personnel work. Then, with the vast personnel requirements of World War II, personnel authority was delegated to the war agencies; the central system simply could not keep up with demands. After the war, efforts to re-centralize personnel matters resulted in widespread criticism, culminating in the report on personnel of the first Hoover Commission in 1949. Its central theme was decentralization of personnel administration. The great bulk of operating activities has moved from the Commission to the operating departments and agencies and from Washington to the field. Perhaps the most significant single event in this recent history was the passage of the Classification Act of 1949 which vested in the departments and agencies full authority and responsibility for evaluating and classifying jobs, according to standards promulgated by the Commission and subject to its periodic post-audit. In terms of work volume, the most striking decentralization has been in the fields of recruiting and examining, the traditional citadels of Commission activity. Of the 300,000 appointments to the competitive service in 1962, more than 85 per cent were recruited and examined by boards of examiners within the departments and agencies themselves.

Today the bulk of federal personnel work is performed by the operating agencies of the government, and a large proportion of it is done in their field establishments away from Washington. Personnel "programs" are, by and large, agency programs, not Civil Service Commission programs. And they comprehend, in addition to classification, recruitment, and examining, which have already been mentioned, the lion's share of training, placement, promotion, evaluation, labor relations, and other common personnel activities. Some of the principal debates on decentralization today relate not to the relative prerogatives of the Civil Service Commission and the rest of the executive branch, but, within individual departments and agencies, between their headquarters and regional offices and between the regional offices and the local installations.

In consequence of this transformation, the role and the complexion of the Civil Service Commission itself has been drastically revised. It is still in operation, but its largest operating activity—the conduct of security investigations for most of the government—did not exist thirty years ago. Today the security program accounts for almost half of the Commission's budget. Its other operating activities include some examining and the administration of the federal retirement system and of some other employee benefit programs, such as life insurance and health. It also continues to carry on some of its traditional functions—enforcing the basic laws of the civil service, the Hatch Acts, the Veterans' Preference Act, and others; hearing and deciding on employee appeals against agency decisions; issuing civil service regulations; and inspecting agency personnel management performance. But more than ever before, the Commission today is serving in a staff capacity as adviser, consultant, and planner at the levels of the President, of the departments in Washington, and of their installations in the field. It has been given, or has assumed, leadership in stimulating improvements in personnel programs in general, in eliminating discriminatory practices, in promoting efficiency, and in projecting a favorable "image" of the public employee and of public employment in the nation. And in recent years, these roles of leadership and of staff consultant have had growing importance.

Yet the Civil Service Commission* has many faces: its roles are confusing and in many senses contradictory. It is at once policeman, prosecutor, defender, and judge. It is an advocate before the Congress and an agent of the Congress; a security sleuth of, and a "union" for, employees; a rule-maker, an inspector, a disciplinarian, and a management consultant to other agencies; an adviser to and instrument of the President; an insurance agency; and a public relations office for the government in general. As indicated above, the Commission has considerably shifted its emphases in recent years. But many of the older functions, the older roles, remain. That it has been able to make this shift and still carry on its traditional responsibilities with as much grace and aplomb as it has is a considerable achievement of its leadership and its staff.

The Quest for Quality—Problems of Entrance

From their beginning, civil service systems have directed primary attention to recruitment and selection. At first, in fact, these were the only major functions of the Civil Service Commission. The extension of its activities into other areas of activity did not really begin until the time of World War I. It is thus no accident that when Americans think of civil service they think first of entrance examinations. This is the principal activity which provides the civil service system with direct contact with the general public. Examining and recruiting for the federal civil service

---

* The term is used here generically to include the members of the Commission and its entire staff, headquarters, and field.

has become an enormous, continuous business. In recent years, the government has announced an average of more than 20,000 examinations per year—about eighty every working day. It processes nearly two million applications and hires between two and three hundred thousand new employees annually.

OPEN COMPETITION

The basic procedure of civil service selection is about as old as the merit system itself. Its major steps are:

on the basis of requests for eligibles from agencies, examinations are planned and scheduled;

examinations are publicly announced;

candidates submit applications;

applications are reviewed and candidates are notified as to their eligibility;

examinations are given;

examinations are graded and eligible registers are set up for those that pass in rank order of grade;

in response to an agency request, the top three names on the register are certified;

the agency selects and appoints one of the three.

Although there have been a number of variations in this procedure—including additional steps and shifting of sequence, particularly in recent years—the fundamental elements remain about as stated. The most important addition has been the requirement, for those who have passed the examination, of an investigation of security and suitability—by all odds the most laborious, time-consuming, and expensive step of all.

The crux of the process is the examination(s), and it is here that personnel administration in the public sphere has concentrated a large proportion of its energies and resources from the very beginning. The competitive procedure rests on the premise that the future performance of individuals in different kinds of work can be comparatively predicted with reasonable accuracy by tests of their qualifications and attributes given in advance. Starting from the simplest beginnings 80 years ago, testing has developed into an imposing applied science, comprehending measurements of: intelligence; different kinds of aptitudes, knowledge, and memory; performance of different kinds of tasks; attitudes; physical and athletic ability; character; and personality. The typical civil service examination comprises a battery of different kinds of tests, most of which are graded in quantitative terms; the various grades are then combined according to some formula of weighting to provide a composite examination score. It is of course presumed that all of the attributes measured, and the weights assigned to each, bear a valid relationship to the qualifications required for specific jobs.*

The procedure claims a number of advantages. First, it is *open*. Everyone can have a "crack" at a job, providing only that he meets the minimum qualifications which are themselves intended to be based upon what the job requires. Second, it is *competitive* in terms of the criteria of ability to perform the work of the job as such criteria are reflected in the examination itself. Third, it is *objective*. It systematically excludes political, personal, and other considerations. It separates the appointing agency as well as the examiners themselves from the individuals examined, making collusion or discrimination on the basis of factors other than merit difficult if not impossible. Fourth, it still permits the appointing agency a degree of *discretion* in its selection (one out of three), but only among candidates of proven qualifications. Finally, it is *efficient;* it takes advantage of the best available examining techniques, makes possible mechanized, mass examining, and avoids duplicating efforts among different appointing agencies.

Against these alleged advantages, critics of the civil service system make many counter-charges. One has been that the process is laborious, lumbering, and expensive, especially for a government of such vast size in an era of rapid change. Its slowness is such as to discourage the best qualified applicants and to detract from its effectiveness in meeting the changing needs of the using agencies. The very objectivity and impersonality claimed for it do not permit sufficient attention to human factors in employment such as personality, compatibility, dedication, and initiative. The employing agencies, not infrequently dissatisfied with the caliber of candidates from whom they may choose, complain that they are deprived of an essential ingredient to their responsibility for their programs—the determination of whom they may hire.

A related series of criticisms has gone to the heart of competitive examinations themselves. In a system of such vast size, there must be a great *distance* between the examiner and the hiring officer and consequently a tremendous difficulty in adapting the examination to the requirements

---

* The subject of job testing and the problems associated therewith would warrant a volume—or a five-foot shelf. Let it suffice here to emphasize that civil service testing has advanced far beyond the paper and pencil examinations with which Americans commonly associate the civil service, and that in the development of testing technique, the federal government has been in the forefront.

of individual jobs. And persuading the hiring officer that the examination is so adapted is equally difficult. This is particularly true in those occupational fields of highly specialized skills and knowledges for which a central examining agency could hardly be equipped with qualified staff. Further, testing technicians recognize that even the best examinations are fallible—subject to a margin of error. There is doubt in some fields whether tests are reliable at all, and some have alleged that tests are negative indicators; that they measure the wrong kinds of things. Yet, the traditional competitive procedure requires that every passing candidate be ranked in accordance with his exact grade and that he be certified for possible appointment in accordance with his proper rank order. An 85 is superior to an 84.7 and below an 85.2.

The Civil Service Commission has, in recent years, shown flexibility in bypassing or overcoming many of these difficulties without doing too much violence to its underlying legal and idealistic principles of open competition, equal opportunity and objectivity. Foremost has been the decentralization already mentioned. Long ago, the Commission set up regional offices in major cities across the country, and a large part of this examining work has long been conducted at the regional level. The regional offices now account for about twice as many of new civil service appointments as the Washington headquarters. Second has been the delegation to boards of examiners, operating within the agencies and their field installations, of the bulk of day-to-day recruitment and selection. These steps have made possible quickening the response to personnel needs, bringing the selection process closer to where the work will be done and also closer to the labor market upon which it must depend. The examining operations of the Civil Service Commission headquarters have been reduced mainly to professional and administrative fields, for which it is desired to tap a nation-wide employment market to produce eligibles in demand by a number of different federal agencies (such as the Federal Service Entrance Examinations, described below, and the management series).

The procedural restrictions involved in civil service examining have been relaxed for different categories of jobs. One device is the offering of continuously open examinations, particularly for semi-skilled and clerical jobs, such as typing and stenography. Under this system, it is possible for a candidate to apply, be examined, and appointed all on the same day. Another is the so-called *unassembled examination,* in which applicants are rated on the basis of their credentials in education, prior experience, evidences of achievement, and letters of recommendation. Such examinations are widely used for professional and specialized positions. The technique known as *selective certification* is frequently used to permit agencies to ask for candidates from general civil service registers who have particular specialties of education or experience to fit particular job needs.

THE SHIFTING SIGNIFICANCE OF COMPETITION

Despite these many steps to simplify and expedite entrance to the federal services on the basis of merit, the U. S. government is still hard pressed to recruit enough highly qualified personnel for many of its professional, scientific, and administrative posts. The civil service system has historically given great attention to the improvement of its techniques for selecting the best qualified among those who apply. But open competition among candidates can be futile if there are not any qualified applicants to begin with or if the best qualified potential candidates do not apply. There is evidence that in some fields this has been the case. In a few specialties, this is a reflection of a basic shortage in the society as a whole, a deficiency in the educational system. In others, it appears that the government has not been getting its share of the best available—they are drawn into other fields of employment. In these crucial areas, the competition among applying candidates is less significant than that between the government and other potential employers for the cream of the crop who are available.

Increasingly in recent years, the focus of federal efforts in recruitment has been to strengthen its competitive position in the labor market. This new approach to federal recruitment entails a near-reversal of two implicit and basic assumptions of the civil service which were grounded in the nineteenth century. The first of these was that the government was operating in an employers' labor market and that, in such a market, its position was a favorable one. Its fundamental procedures assumed that there were, and would continue to be, an ample number of qualified persons seeking federal employment—that is, unemployed or underemployed, or filling jobs considered less desirable than those in the government. A companion assumption, probably inherited from Andrew Jackson, was that government jobs (with certain exceptions) were basically simple, requiring no special knowledges and skills.* Armed with these two assumptions, the Civil Service Commission recruited passively by announcing

---

* There was apparently once much truth in this belief. It has been estimated that, at the close of the nineteenth century, only two per cent of the federal civil service were professionals. Most of these were probably lawyers and engineers.

examinations in small print in newspapers and on Post Office bulletin boards and by awaiting applications. Except in wartime, there appears to have been little positive effort to advertise opportunities and to seek qualified applicants before the Great Depression of the 1930s.

For the upper level jobs today, no assumptions could be more deceiving or more damaging. In many fields, these jobs are the most demanding, the most difficult, and the most important in their impact upon the society. Yet the assumptions have lingered long in civil service procedures, in the views of the Congress about the civil service, and, most important of all, in the minds of many influential individuals outside the government, including a significant share of scholars.

In recent years, a major focus of Civil Service Commission effort has been to combat these old assumptions. It has fostered continuing federal-university relations, "Career Days" on campuses, federal-industrial conferences, active public relations campaigns, articles and speeches on the excitement and the attractions of federal service.

RECRUITMENT FOR JOB OR CAREER?

The open competitive system of selection provided by the Pendleton Act of 1883 has been referred to as "Americanizing a Foreign Invention" * (primarily a British one). The emphasis in this expression should be upon "Americanizing" because in some ways the American variations on the model were more important than the model itself. The British system contemplated the recruitment of its civil servants immediately upon the completion of their education and their retention in the service throughout their working lives. None were to come in except at the bottom; and the examinations were attuned to the educational system, not to the first job assignment. The Congress which passed the Pendleton Act rejected the concept of a closed career service with explicit intention. It removed from the bill a provision that would have permitted entrance only "at the lowest grade" and amended it to add an injunction that tests given for entrance be "practical in nature" and related to the duties to be performed.†
These changes undoubtedly reflected a fear of a closed bureaucracy and a desire to maintain the democratic tradition in the public service. They have colored the nature and the administration of the civil service ever since. For while it is true that many thousands of civil servants have

---

* Paul P. Van Riper, *History of the United States Civil Service* (Evanston, Illinois: Row, Peterson and Company, 1958), p. 96.

† *Ibid.*, p. 100.

entered and stayed in the service for their entire careers, it is also true that the civil service does recruit new people at all levels, and always has.*

It is also true that the historic practice of the American system has been to frame examinations according to the requirements of the duties of specific jobs and not to measure the qualifications for progressive advancement in a life-long career. Critics and reformers—even including some of the Commissions themselves—have for a very long time urged the development of a career-oriented personnel system, including entrance examinations tailored for the purpose.† Examinations were administered for what amounted to career experience for some technical and professional specialists such as agriculturists, geologists, engineers, and foresters. Nonetheless, for the first half century of its existence, the Civil Service Commission did virtually nothing in the direction of attracting and examining college graduates for careers in the public service.

In the light of this background, the movement which began with the New Deal toward a career system for college educated people constitutes in some ways the most substantial achievement—and reversal of tradition —in recent personnel history. This development was, in part, a response to the growths in size of the federal government during the New Deal period, World War II, and the Korean War. It was more importantly a product of the obvious growth in importance and difficulty of federal undertakings. And in part, it has been a response to the intellectualization of the society and the governments which guide and service it. The push for a positive program of career recruitment, long advocated by civil service reformers, was strengthened during these years by the persistent and repeated urging of a series of study groups, starting in 1935 with the Commission of Inquiry on Public Service Personnel. Its basic recommendations for a true career program were endorsed by and elaborated on by a variety of successors, notably the President's Committee on Administrative Management in 1937, and the First and Second Hoover Commissions in 1949 and 1955. All urged strengthening of recruitment

---

* In spite of this, some of the more professionalized bureaus of the government, such as the Forest Service, have developed closed career services in which lateral entry (i.e., direct appointment from outside above the bottom level) is virtually unknown. Paradoxically, in the U. S. Foreign Service, which was established in 1924 as a direct imitation of the closed British system, the majority of the top positions today are filled by persons who in fact entered laterally rather than in the orthodox manner.

† As long ago as 1905, the Commission in its *Twenty-Second Report* stated that "the great defect in the Federal Service today is the lack of opportunity for ambitious, well-educated young men" (p. 23).

and subsequent career opportunities for qualified, well-educated persons. The response of the Civil Service Commission to these emerging needs and recommendations was sporadic, sometimes hesitant, but, over-all, remarkable. Behind the leadership of Commissioner Leonard D. White, an early appointee of President Franklin D. Roosevelt, the Commission offered its first examination designed for unspecialized college graduates in 1934—the Junior Civil Service Examiner examination. This test, which was offered again in 1936, provided a vehicle for the entry of a substantial number of able and well educated individuals into the federal service. In 1939, the effort was resumed with the offering of the first Junior Professional Assistant (JPA) examination, which aimed more specifically to draw college graduates who had majored in particular fields. Altogether, the first JPA included some 22 types of specialized options, including one for Junior Administrative Technicians, designed especially for persons who had specialized in administration or political science. The JPA was continued, though with changes in emphasis and options, through the war and until 1947. It was then succeeded by the Junior Management Assistant (JMA) program, which was the principal vehicle for general college recruitment from 1948 to 1954. The JMA was different from its predecessors in a number of ways. It drew the hiring agencies into the examining process to a much greater extent than before; it involved a much more extensive and presumably more thorough examining process; it was integrated with a systematic training and career development program to a much greater extent than its predecessors.

The JMA was probably a more effective device than any of the programs which preceded it for attracting and selecting young career professionals and potential career executives for the federal service. But it fell into hard times, for reasons not attributable to itself, during the late Truman Administration and the first years under President Eisenhower. The principal reason was the rapid decline in prestige and attractiveness of the federal service in general during the early 1950s, a decline resulting from security investigations, the hysteria attending Senator McCarthy's charges, the effects of veterans' preference (particularly its impact upon staff reductions), scandals in the public service, and "politics." Between 1951 and 1953, the number of applicants for the JMA dropped from 19,000 to about 8,000.

In 1954 the Civil Service Commission staff conducted a thorough investigation into its whole college recruiting program, and the following year launched upon a new one which was different from those that had gone before—the Federal Service Entrance Examination (FSEE). This examination was designed as a vehicle for the recruitment and selection of college graduates and graduate students from a wide variety of fields of specialization—most of the major fields offered in colleges.* The FSEE test measured general intelligence and ability plus general information. It was supplemented by a test and program for Management Interns—a "blue ribbon" extension of the FSEE for the best qualified of applicants, leading to supervised intern programs in particular agencies. Applicants for Management Intern must pass the FSEE and then take more rigorous written and oral examinations. The select few who make the grade are appointed at higher levels and can anticipate rapid advancement to positions of high administrative responsibility.

After more than a decade of continuous experience, the FSEE and the Management Intern programs remain the basic general recruiting and selecting devices for federal college-level entrance. It may therefore be useful to discuss in somewhat greater depth their nature and content. The two tests represent the principal governmental response to the challenge of competition by other employers for young, educated persons aspiring to high-level professional and administrative positions. Although not restricted to upper division college students and graduates, the FSEE is clearly directed to them and they have constituted the bulk of those successful in the test. The test itself, a fairly brief short-answer exam of intelligence and general information, is sufficiently broad that college students and graduates can compete successfully regardless of their major field of study, and for most students it is now the principal means of entrance into the Federal service.† Through the device of selective certification, described above, a wide range of junior professional positions are filled from FSEE registers—park rangers, budget officers, tax accountants, geologists, mathematicians, air traffic control officers, to mention only a few.

The FSEE, which is one of the relatively few examinations which the Civil Service Commission itself still conducts, in many ways illustrates the degree to which civil service procedures and traditions can be adapted to the needs of the times. It is widely advertised on college campuses, and

---

* A number of other specialized examinations are still offered for majors in some fields, including the physical sciences, engineering, accounting, forestry and others.

† The FSEE replaced more than one hundred more specialized examinations.

active recruiting is stimulated by visits of agency personnel representatives to the colleges and through faculty members. The examination itself is offered a number of different times each year, scheduled in relation to the rhythm of the academic year. Entrance grades and salaries are high enough to match the offerings of other employers in most (not quite all) fields. The results of these efforts have been impressive. In 1963, nearly 230,000 individuals applied for the FSEE; 140,000 took the examination; 58,000 passed; and over 8,000 were appointed to federal jobs.

The Management Intern examination is a much more rigorous and "exclusive" process. Those who pass it are assigned to tailored intern programs of training and practice in agencies and can expect rapid advancement, if they are successful, to positions of considerable managerial responsibility. The examination is offered less frequently than the FSEE but is given on the same days. Applicants must pass the FSEE and, in addition, more difficult tests of general abilities, knowledge of public affairs, and administrative problems. Those who pass the written tests later take an oral examination. The majority of those successful are graduate students. In contrast to the broad sweep of the FSEE, only 23,000 applied for the Management Intern part of the examination in 1963. Of these, about 2,500 passed the written examination, 700 reached the eligible register, and 300 were appointed to positions.

Together the FSEE and the Management Intern examinations approach the career idea at the entrance level and are far removed from the traditional philosophy of the civil service. But they are not yet a complete answer to the problem of professional and administrative personnel for the government. In spite of the impressive numbers of applicants, there is evidence that large numbers of the best potential applicants do not apply. It is increasingly clear that the top students normally proceed to at least one year of graduate training and that the "cream" of these are not attracted by the federal service. The majority of those appointed from FSEE registers have little background in social, political, and administrative fields, and one may question whether high academic ability in languages, music, or English literature is sufficient assurance in itself of adequacy in dealing with the governmental problems of today and tomorrow. Finally, it must be noted that most governmental agencies have not yet established systematic provision for the development and advancement to higher positions of their best qualified people. The planned career system ends soon after its beginning, and most of those in government, soon after their entrance, must fend for themselves.

The Civil Service at Work—Its Utilization and Development

Among the personnel systems of nations of the world and also of most large private employers, the American style is *sui generis*.* Here one finds no administrative or managerial "class," clearly and legally distinct from other classes in the service, no career guarantees for budding administrators, no manifest distinction between management and labor. Instead, there is heavy emphasis upon professionalization and full expectancy that the bulk of top civil service posts† will be filled by specialists who have worked their way up in the specialized fields of their agencies. But perhaps the most important underlying feature in practice and psychology of the federal system is the stress laid upon positions and their work content as distinguished from—and to a considerable degree as governing—the people who "fill" them.

"THE JOB'S THE THING"

The rock to which federal personnel administration is moored is the classification of positions. The classification system, founded in 1923, has since grown to encompass the bulk of white-collar employees. The present framework for about one million workers, about 40 per cent of the total, is the Classification Act of 1949. This law does not apply to the half-million postal employees, to the blue-collar workers, most of whom are in the Defense establishment, and to the legally excepted groups such as TVA, the Foreign Service, and others. Most of these others are governed, however, by their own classification systems which are not fundamentally different in ideology and method from that of the general civil service.

Some form of job evaluation and classification is an inevitable requirement for efficiency in a large organization. Without it, planning, organizing, budgeting, recruiting, and many other management activities would be disorderly, perhaps next to impossible. The passage of the first Classification Act in 1923 has appropriately been called "one of the great

---

* The American national system is, however, generally comparable to those of American states and cities which have civil service legislation.

† In most agencies, these comprehend positions up to and including bureau chiefs. A 1958 study showed that, of 63 bureau chiefs, 26 had been trained as engineers, scientists, or technicians, nine were economists, eight were lawyers, and the remaining 20 came from administrative or business careers—M. Smith, "Bureau Chiefs in the Federal Government," in *Public Policy, the Yearbook of the Graduate School of Public Administration* (Boston: Harvard University Press, 1960).

landmarks in public personnel legislation," * and the improvement of classification methods over the succeeding years has been one of the major achievements of American public management.

Virtually all large bureaucracies, almost by definition, must employ some system for the classification of positions. The distinctive feature of American public practice is the degree to which it has become the primary and dominating element in personnel management with regard to such matters as initial appointment, assignment, transfer, promotion, and pay. Positions of comparable content, scope, and responsibility are grouped in common classes, and each class is presumed to require definable qualifications in terms of education and prior experience. An employee's current position determines his class, and his class determines his pay and, to some extent, his opportunities for advancement. An employee in a given class can gain a promotion only if he is moved to another position in a higher class or if his own position changes to such an extent as to warrant a "reclassification" to a higher class. The "class" is determining; competence governs only to the extent that the employee is able to change his class. The incumbent is not supposed to perform duties below or above the level of his class for any length of time without being either demoted or promoted, as the case may be. The emphasis is thus always upon the job, the work currently done.

Over the years, the classification system has been the butt of a good deal of criticism, particularly by line administrators who must work with it. These complaints have been directed toward its alleged inflexibility, the difficulty and slowness of keeping personnel assignments and promotions in tune with operating needs, and, particularly, staff interference with what are claimed to be properly the authority and responsibility of management. Some have charged, too, that the system is too impersonal, too objective to take into account the human element, the contributions that the individual, qua individual, brings to his work. In fact, there has been a running debate in federal circles as to the respective merits of the civil service "rank in the job" approach against the "rank in the man" concept which is considered to govern the military officer services, the Foreign Service, and the civil services of most European countries.

The direction of civil service developments since World War II has unquestionably been toward relaxing the severity of the position emphasis, toward making classification more of a tool and less of a restraint

---

* William E. Mosher, J. Donald Kingsley, and O. Glenn Stahl, *Public Personnel Administration* (New York: Harper & Row, Publishers, 1950), Third Edition, p. 210.

upon management and upon personnel development. This was reflected in two steps already noted: the Classification Act of 1949 which delegated classification authority to the agencies; and the various college entrance programs, which virtually ignore job content in initial recruitment and even in early assignments of junior personnel. The Civil Service Commission has encouraged the broadening of class specifications to make them less specifically confining. And, in 1960, it gave official recognition to the idea that a man may have an impact upon a job which could warrant its reclassification, a concept that would have been labeled heresy twenty-five years ago.

"EQUAL PAY FOR EQUAL WORK"

From the standpoint of those who are, or might be, federal employees, the most significant aspect of position classification is its impact upon levels of pay. In fact, initial classification legislation was designed primarily to eliminate flagrant variations in pay for comparable types of work within and between different government agencies. The fundamental and underlying principle of federal pay administration since 1923 has been that the pay range for each position was determined by the relative difficulty and responsibility of the work, and that comparable positions and comparable classes of positions warrant comparable remuneration. The pay system works about as follows: Congress by law establishes the grades of pay (now ranging from General Schedule (GS) one to eighteen) and different step rates in each grade. (There are now ten different steps in the lower grades, but their number diminishes at higher levels to a single step in grade 18.) The nature and difficulty of work determines to what class each position is allocated; and each class is assigned to one of the legally established grades. Employees are normally appointed to the bottom step of the appropriate grade. They receive periodic pay increases as they move from step to step. In order to advance from one grade to another they must assume a new position in a higher class or have their existing position reclassified upward.

The pay system, thus related to the work performed, is consistent with the ideology of the merit system; indeed, it is doubtful that the American ethic of justice and equal treatment would tolerate any substantial departures from it. Nonetheless, it gave rise to grave difficulties, difficulties which culminated in new pay legislation in 1962. One of these difficulties was that the principle of equal pay for equal work was not carried far enough. The pay scale for regular civil service employees applies to only a fraction of the federal service, and its relation to other federal pay rates was largely accidental. For example, the wages of manual workers have, for a long time, been determined by local wage boards on the basis of prevailing rates in each community. It was entirely possible for civil service supervisors of such manual workers to be paid at rates substantially below their own subordinates. The field employees of the Post Office, the Foreign Service, the military services, and others had their own independent pay legislation, often quite unrelated to that for regular civil service employees.

A second and more important difficulty has been the pay scale itself which has, quite expectably, been politically influenced. The greatest numbers of public employees—the postal workers, the unskilled, and the clerical groups—are at the lower end of the scale; and these also constitute the bulk of the membership of the influential employee unions. At the other end of the scale are a relatively small number of executives and professionals, largely unorganized. Furthermore, the salaries of federal administrators, scientists, and other professionals have bumped into a ceiling —a limit set by the salaries of congressmen themselves, itself relatively low because of congressional reluctance to vote themselves salaries higher than their constituents might approve. The result of these forces was a compression of the whole salary scale within relatively narrow limits. The pay of those at the lower end was equal to, or relatively higher than, compensation levels in the general labor market; at the upper end, pay was absurdly low; and in between, pay levels varied among different lines of work, from approximate equivalence to relative lowness. One effect of the low ceiling was, and is, the obstacle to bringing in and retaining well-qualified people for the crucially important professional and executive jobs. Many seasoned federal executives could, and did, greatly increase their earnings by departing for work of less scope and responsibility in the private sphere. Further, as salaries of professional and scientific personnel rose in the private economy, it became increasingly difficult to recruit and retain middle-level workers in many shortage fields. This put the government at a continuing disadvantage in competing for high caliber people in these areas. It also encouraged the skewing of the job classification system in varying degree through reclassifications upward which would not otherwise have been warranted.

A final problem in salary administration was its relative inflexibility in relation to both time and place. With the wide fluctuations in the price level in the first decade after World War II and the rapidly rising level of private incomes over the past quarter-century, it has been difficult for governmental pay levels to keep pace, primarily because the pay rates have depended upon congressional action. And as long as pay rates were set nation-wide on the basis of job content, it was impossible to adjust rates in accord with prevailing scales and costs of living in different parts of the country.

A frontal assault on most of these difficulties in the first year of the Kennedy Administration culminated in one of the most far-reaching pay acts in recent history—the Federal Salary Reform Act of 1962. This Act reaffirmed the principle of "equal pay for substantially equal work" and, in effect, extended it, declaring that "federal salary rates shall be comparable with private enterprise salary rates for the same levels of work." Henceforth, federal salaries were to be competitive with scales of other employers for "equal work." The Act required annual studies and reports to Congress of non-federal pay scales, accompanied by presidential recommendations, and authorized the President to make, on his own initiative, adjustments of steps in the salary scale to equate federal salaries with individual occupations and in particular sections of the country. Finally, the Act established relationships between the different civilian salary systems of the government and required that the principal of equal pay for equal work apply between salary systems as well as within each one.*

One of the most important objectives of the President's proposals, however—the raising of salaries at the upper end of the scale to more nearly competitive levels—was deleted from the bill in Congress, partly because its effect would have been to raise some civil service salaries above the level of their political chiefs. The Senate Committee on Post Office and Civil Service asked that the President recommend a rational salary plan for civil service executives, political executives, congressmen, and judges. Following another study conducted in 1963 by the President's Advisory Panel on Federal Salary Systems,† new proposals were submitted for congressional consideration in 1964. These comprehended all the high officials mentioned above. While the panel proposed substantially increased salaries for politically-appointed and elected officers,‡ it did not recommend comparability with private enterprise on the grounds that

---

* The 1962 bill established new and related pay scales for the classified civil service, the postal field service, the Foreign Service, and the Department of Medicine and Surgery in the Veterans Administration. It included a substantial number of other reforms not detailed here.

† A group of private citizens designated by President Kennedy, all of whom had had significant prior governmental experience.

‡ Up to $60,000 for Vice-President, Speaker, and Justices of the Supreme Court, $50,000 for cabinet secretaries, and $35,000 for congressmen.

such comparisons are hardly possible; that public service offers other compensation, notably prestige, besides money; and for other reasons. But it did recommend salaries high enough to permit executive civil service pay substantially comparable to private enterprise (up to $25,500 for GS 18), and it urged that the principle of comparability be maintained as far as possible for personnel in these top grades. Legislation to give effect to the Panel's recommendations, though considerably modified, was enacted in 1964.

CAREER DEVELOPMENT AND TRAINING

On a government-wide basis, progress toward career development systems has been somewhat sporadic, somewhat spotty, but in total quite promising. The college-entrance examining system, and particularly the Management Intern program, is a significant step at one end of the career view of public employment. The senior civil service would have been a significant step at the other end. A number of assaults have been made in recent years upon the important span between these two—the period during which the promising raw material is fitted and advanced toward the assumption of high level responsibilities in the future. The Civil Service Commission has encouraged all agencies to develop plans and programs, including inventory of their future needs as well as systems for the identification and planned development through assignment and training of promising personnel for meeting those needs. In 1960, it established an Office of Career Development to provide leadership and guidance in this field. The Commission has also promulgated a Federal Merit Promotion Program, providing guides and instructions for the establishment of promotion plans by each agency. Although the general features of the system are geared, as heretofore, upon position-to-position advancement, these regulations make possible exceptions under certain circumstances for what are termed "career promotions."

But perhaps the most significant development in the direction of a career-oriented civil service was the passage of the Government Employees Training Act in 1958. It is symbolic that 1958 was the year of the diamond anniversary of the Pendleton Act, since this was the first general legislation authorizing training programs for the federal civil service. For many years, rulings of the Comptroller General had prevented the allocation of federal funds for out-service training and education. The 1958 Act declared it government policy that ". . . self-education, self-improvement, and self-training by . . . employees be supplemented and extended by

Government-sponsored programs . . . for the training of employees. . . ."
In spite of a number of restrictions in the Act, its import was a nearly
revolutionary reversal of previous policy and attitudes toward systematic,
off-the-job training programs.

It is too early to assess the progress and effects of training since the
passage of the 1958 Act, but there is no doubt that the efforts and activities
undertaken pursuant to it have been considerable and that there has been
a real effort to correlate these undertakings with the development of
future top grade administrators. A number of agencies have now developed systematic training programs as integral parts of their plans for
career development. An impressive array of training courses, programs,
and institutes, mostly of short duration, has been established by various
departments and agencies on an interagency basis—i.e., operated by one
or more agencies but open to some employees from other agencies.* And
in 1963, the Civil Service Commission established an Executive Seminar
Center at Kings Point, New York, providing a series of two-week full-time
seminars (fifteen each year) for officials approaching the top of the career
ladder (mostly in grades GS 14 and 15). Each of these seminars is attended
by 35 to 40 executives assigned from various federal agencies.

Unions in Government

Public personnel administration contains few topics that are today as live, as controversial, and as intriguing as the role and activities of
labor unions. The concepts that gave rise to, and were built into, the merit
system were conceived without anticipation of large-scale organizations of
workers, and the emphasis of the civil service system upon individuals,
competition, and positions are in many ways opposite to the concepts of
collective organization, bargaining between labor and management, and
the employment of various kinds of weapons by one side or the other in
more or less legitimized warfare. The authors of the Pendleton Act can
hardly be blamed for failing to accommodate labor organizations within
their scheme of public personnel administration. Although there had been
some craft union activity in the Navy Department since early in the

* The mushrooming of interagency training is suggested by the fact that it had
grown from fewer than 100 courses in 1960 to almost 1,300 in 1963; those in Washington were attended by over 17,500 persons. They dealt with such topics as: Automatic Data Processing; Public Problems and Federal Programs; Hydraulics and Hy-
drology in Highway Design; International Labor Affairs; Effective Speaking; Com-
munist Strategy; Inventory Management; and Management Principles.

nineteenth century, among the white-collar workers with whom the Act was most concerned, there was virtually no labor organization in 1883. It was not until six years after the passage of the Pendleton Act, 1889, that the first national postal union, the National Association of Letter Carriers, was formed. Three decades later, in 1917, came the first national, non-postal and non-trade union for federal workers—the National Federation of Federal Employees (NFFE).

In spite of marked differences between governmental unions and those in private enterprise, their development has been surprisingly parallel. Both grew most rapidly during the New Deal period, and their size has been quite stable in recent years. In 1961, almost exactly one third of all federal employees, 762,000, were members of employee organizations (as compared with 32.4 per cent in non-agricultural private employment). Some of the federal unions are organized by trade or craft; some are industrial, at least in the sense that they comprehend a wide variety of employees. Some are affiliated with AFL-CIO, others are independent. The NFFE, for example, which had been affiliated with the AFL, split off in 1931 and has since operated as an independent union. It was succeeded as an AFL affiliate by the American Federation of Government Employees (AFGE), probably today the largest of general public unions. Unionization among public workers is strongest in those occupations most similar to private enterprises which are also organized. The blue-collar workers in government are highly organized; but membership is low among most white-collar workers. The Post Office is highly organized; its employees in 1961 accounted for 489,000 union members, 64 per cent of all organized federal employees. Among other agencies, union membership varies widely from virtually none in agencies such as the State Department to substantial proportions in the Tennessee Valley Authority and the Bureau of Reclamation. But aside from the Post Office and the industrial-type activities, union membership is infrequent as it is among professional, clerical, and administrative employees in private enterprise.

PROBLEMS OF ENDS AND MEANS

For a long time, it has appeared that unions in government could not operate in the same fashion as those in private enterprise. The practical problems attending the behavior of government unions largely derive from an apparent incompatibility if not collision of concepts between those governing organizations operating in the sphere of a capitalist economy on the one hand, and those governing the political and governmental institutions of an open democracy on the other. The first problem is the problem of sovereignty. Collective bargaining in the private sector rests in part on the recognition of two parties at contest, each equal before the law and equipped to exert its powers against the other. In government, such a position of equality cannot be acknowledged: the state is sovereign. This argument has frequently been used to inhibit the exercise of methods generally available to unions in the private sector, such as the strike. Not infrequently, sovereignty has been invoked against the right of public employees to organize at all. Many years ago, a U. S. Senator asserted that:

> . . . employees who work for the Federal Government are analogous to soldiers in the Army. They should owe their entire allegiance and loyalty to the Government for which they work. They should not enter into any movement of affiliation or association which might put them into an attitude of antagonism to the Government for which they work because the general welfare is at stake.*

The second problem arises from the separation of powers between legislature and executive. Who in government constitutes "management" as the term is understood in private business? The legislative body, particularly through its power over appropriations, has long been viewed as co-equal, if not supreme, with regard to employee wages, hours, working conditions, and like matters. It is hardly likely that formalized bargaining arrangements could be established between unions and the Congress of the United States. And the degree to which Congress can, should, or will delegate its powers over employment arrangements is problematic.

A third kind of dilemma for government unions stems from the nature of public employment, particularly when it operates under the rubric of the merit system. There is an apparent divergence of the collective bargaining approach from the underlying and largely implicit tenets and assumptions of the merit system. The principle of open and equal competition among different individuals in hiring, in advancement, and in retention is difficult to square with the collective principle of unionism. And the emphasis upon the content and responsibility of individual positions as the determining feature of compensation and some other rewards is not entirely consonant with collective negotiation.

A final issue of both theory and practice arises from the apparent con-

---

* Senator Henry L. Myers, quoted in Sterling D. Spero, *Government As Employer* (New York: Remsen Press, 1948), p. 9.

flict between unionism and the ideal of political neutrality of public servants. According to some, there is an inherent danger that public employee organizations may exercise their power and influence to modify and direct public policy in their own interests, which may not be to the advantage of the citizenry in general. The argument here has led to a variety of restraints upon the tools and channels which government unions can use as well as upon the subject areas in which their pressures can legitimately be exerted. There can be no doubt that governmental unions have influenced public policy in relation to employment. But that this influence has, on balance, been contrary to the public interest is arguable. And the danger that public employees, as a massive organized group, will exercise overpowering influence in this or any other field of interest is doubtful if only because the federal unions themselves are many, various, and not in collusion or even collaboration with each other. Pluralism in government unions, like pluralism in other aspects of American life, may prove one of our great protections.

The dilemmas of public unionism presented above seem to argue against conventional labor organization in the governmental sphere. Against these views are very much the same arguments that justify unions in private enterprise: effective employee participation in management decisions affecting employee welfare and sharing of responsibility therefor; elimination of abuses and discrimination; equitable sharing of economic advances; "economic" democracy. Over the years, these arguments have been effective. Employee unions in government have grown to about the same dimensions, on the average, as have those in private enterprise, and it is entirely possible that they have been just as successful in achieving their goals.

Public employee unions have developed effective *modi operandi,* considerably different from those utilized in private industry. As in other fields of American experience, the pragmatic development of means precedes rationalization in theory. Unions in the federal government are precluded from some of the principal weapons of those in private enterprise—notably the strike, the threat of the strike, and the closed shop. But they have effective political weapons: access to Congress and its committees and, through their membership and families of members, the constituents of congressmen. Over the years, they have influenced personnel legislation, particularly in the fields of wages and salaries, fringe benefits, classification, and employee protections of various kinds. By and large, like the veterans' organizations, they have supported and advanced the civil service system but have opposed decentralization of its administration. They have generally demonstrated greater confidence in the Civil Service Commission than in the President or the operating agencies.

FEDERAL POLICY CONCERNING UNIONS

Until the Kennedy Administration, national policy toward employee unions was usually silent or neutral when it was not hostile. Not infrequently the labor organizations appealed to Congress for redress against actions of the executive branch. Early in this century, President Theodore Roosevelt and, later, President Taft issued rules forbidding employees or organizations to lobby Congress. These rules grew out of activities of unions in the postal service to improve working conditions there. A consequence was the passage in 1912 of the Lloyd-LaFollette Act which affirmed the right of postal employees to organize and to petition Congress. This law came, by a kind of common law practice, to protect union activities for all public employees.

The administration of the second Roosevelt exhibited a surprising double standard in its approach to labor relations. Although encouraging legislation favorable to labor union organizations, FDR discouraged unions of public employees. In a letter to President Luther Steward of the NFFE in 1937, he wrote:

All government employees should realize that the process of collective bargaining, as usually understood, cannot be transplanted into the public service. It has its distinct and insurmountable limitations when applied to public personnel management. The very nature and purposes of government make it impossible for administrative officials to represent fully or to bind the employer in mutual discussions with government employee organizations.*

Possibly influenced by the 1937 report of the Committee on Administrative Management, the President in 1940 expressed his admiration for the "splendid new agreements between organized labor and the TVA" and declared that "collective bargaining and efficiency proceeded hand in hand." Although Roosevelt himself gave little impetus to collective bargaining in the federal government, some agencies developed comprehensive systems for formal recognition and bargaining with unions. Among these, the TVA remains today perhaps the outstanding example in the federal government.

*In Samuel Irving Rosenman, *The Public Papers and Addresses of Franklin D. Roosevelt, The Constitution Prevails* (New York: Random House, 1941), 1937 Vol., p. 325.

But labor relations programs within the government remained spotty and scattered. In fact, until 1962 the federal government had no general labor relations policy whatever, aside from the limited provisions of the Lloyd-LaFollette Act of 1912 and the prohibition against strikes of the Taft-Hartley Act. Representative George M. Rhodes of Pennsylvania undertook to correct this; starting in 1949, he introduced a bill in every congressional session from then until 1961 to provide statutory recognition of employee organizations. The bill would have guaranteed the right of unions to present grievances on behalf of members; required punitive action against administrative officials who violated this requirement; and required administrators to confer with union representatives on personnel matters and to bargain on terms and conditions of employment. The Eisenhower Administration opposed the Rhodes bills on the grounds that it was unnecessary and would reduce the needed flexibility of agency heads. The Rhodes bill was not enacted.

THE NEW FRONTIER FOR GOVERNMENTAL UNIONS

President Kennedy, long interested in and sympathetic with organized labor, gave attention early in his administration to labor relations in the federal government. On June 22, 1961, he issued a memorandum to the heads of federal agencies announcing the establishment of a cabinet-level Task Force "to review and advise me on employee-management relations in the federal service." The President's own inclinations on the matter were clearly indicated by his designation as Task Force Chairman Secretary of Labor Arthur J. Goldberg, who before his appointment to the Cabinet had for many years served as counsel to the CIO and to the United Steelworkers. Furthermore, in the preamble of his memorandum setting up the Task Force, Kennedy stated his position unequivocally:

> The right of all employees of the federal government to join and participate in the activities of employee organizations, and to seek to improve working conditions and the resolution of grievances should be recognized by management officials at all levels in all departments and agencies. The participation of federal employees in the formulation and implementation of employee policies and procedures affecting them contributes to the effective conduct of public business. I believe this participation should include consultation by responsible officials with representatives of employees and federal employee organizations.*

---

* President's Task Force on Employee-Management Relations in the Federal Service, *A Policy for Employee-Management Cooperation in the Federal Service* (Washington D. C., November 30, 1961), p. ix.

The Task Force reported to the President on November 30, 1961. Its findings, along with a set of specific recommendations for future federal policy, became the basis for two Executive Orders, No. 10987 and No. 10988, which were issued on January 17, 1962. The first of these set forth standards for employee appeals against adverse managerial actions. The second contained the bulk of the Task Force recommendations on labor-management relations. In brief and summary form, the Order did the following things:

It equalized employee appeal rights of veterans and non-veterans;

It affirmed the right of employees to join (or not to join) labor organizations, and the right of such organizations to affiliate with organizations outside the government;

It provided a decentralized system, each agency being required to set up and operate its own system of employee-management relations;

It differentiated three types of recognition of labor organizations: exclusive, where the union is chosen by a majority of employees; formal, where the union represents 10 per cent or more employees; and informal for others; and specified different rights and powers of unions under each category, up to the negotiation of written agreements on personnel policy and working conditions for those granted exclusive recognition;

It authorized the use of advisory, but not compulsory, arbitration in cases of unresolved disagreements.

In general, the new policy represented an effort to develop within the government institutions and regularized practices comparable to those used in private industry. But it did not authorize or contemplate the use of the strike, the union or closed shop, compulsory arbitration, or some other methods used in the private sphere. Furthermore, it specified that negotiations must be carried on within the framework of existing laws and regulations and the principles of the merit system. In effectuation of the program, both the Civil Service Commission and the Labor Department were given important roles. The inclusion of the latter agency was in itself significant, since historically its orientation had excluded governmental employees.

It is too early to assess the effects of the new policy, but it clearly has already brought about a considerable reorientation in much federal personnel activity. Most agencies have prepared and issued their own policy statements on employee-management cooperation. A large number of employee organizations have been granted exclusive recognition, and a few have already negotiated agreements. The Civil Service Commission and the Department of Labor completed two basic documents, one on "Standards of Conduct" for employee organizations, and the other a "Code of Fair Practices" governing employee-management relations. Both were placed in effect by presidential order in 1963. The Civil Service Commission took the leadership in developing and conducting training programs for personnel officers and supervisors on the new policy and on the conduct of collective bargaining, a practice previously unknown in large parts of the federal establishment.

In the past, labor organizations in the federal government have achieved many, perhaps most, of their great successes through actions of the Congress rather than through negotiative processes with administration officials. It is still true that many of the most important areas in which labor unions are normally concerned are controlled by legislation. President Kennedy's order was appropriately silent on union-congressional relationships. Whether the stimulus to management-employee cooperation on the executive side will ultimately modify, perhaps lessen, the congressional role in the oversight of personnel administration is an important question. Nevertheless, the practice of federal civil service administration, indeed the underlying concepts of the merit system, will almost certainly be greatly changed.

Preference for Veterans

The granting of special aid and benefits to war veterans is no new policy in the United States or in the world generally. Benefits of various types for veterans in our own country go back to colonial times and have been particularly evident following each of our major wars. The extent and nature of veterans' programs have fluctuated widely, as has the size and proportion of our veteran population. But at no period has our participation in wars been sufficiently infrequent to permit veterans' benefits to cease to have governmental significance.

But the ways in which the obligation should be fulfilled, the extent of the fulfillment, and the eligibility of the recipients have long been the objects of political debate and decision. In fact, in our own national experience with the veteran problem, the variety of means for aiding veterans and their families seems to be limited only by the boundaries of domestic government activity that are considered currently appropriate. Some might question whether even these boundaries have been respected. We have associated veteran benefits with our program for the disposition of public lands (forty acres and a mule); with our program for public education (the 1946 GI Bill); with aids to business, and stimulation of private housing. We have also developed programs not associated with other government objectives but rather for the veterans alone and *per se*—e.g., pension systems, cash gratuities or bonuses, GI Insurance, medical care, and others.

Foremost for purposes of this discussion, and certainly among the foremost in long-range significance, is the use of public jobs as a means of fulfilling the obligation to veterans. A permanent system of preference in public employment can perhaps best be understood in this deeply emotional and political context: that it is one of many compensations to veterans. It takes the form of an officially established advantage, ranging from slight to absolute, of the veteran over the non-veteran, and varying among different categories of veterans.

Quite obviously, the use of public jobs as compensation for war service is not easily made consistent with the objectives of the merit system. In a mild form of preference, the merit system may not be seriously affected; in extreme form, it may be mutilated. Collisions between the merit system supporters and veterans' organizations, long among the most influential of pressure groups, have been frequent. The potential of conflict rests unmistakably in their differing goals. As one critical student put it: "We know it [veterans' preference] as essentially the negation of merit." *

THE DEVELOPMENT OF VETERANS' PREFERENCE

Prior to the Civil War there was no legal recognition of veterans' preference, even though it probably had a considerable informal influence as early as Washington's administration. Near the close of the Civil War, President Lincoln said: "I shall at all times be ready to recognize the paramount claims of the soldiers of the nation in the disposition of public trusts. I shall be glad also to make these suggestions to the several heads of departments." Congress passed the first veterans' preference legislation in 1865. This early preference act provided only that disabled veterans have preference in appointment to offices for which they were qualified. This provision was later incorporated in the Civil Service Law of 1883 and stood as the basic preference legislation until the close of World War I.

The 1865 law was superseded in 1919 when Congress extended the

* John F. Miller, "Veteran Preference in the Public Service," in *Problems of the American Public Service* [Commission of Inquiry on Public Service Personnel] (New York: McGraw-Hill Book Company, 1935), p. 309.

principle of preference to all "honorably discharged" veterans, their widows, and the wives of injured veterans. The executive branch went beyond the letter of the law and provided for the addition of ten points to the examination scores of disabled veterans, their wives, and the widows of veterans, and the "absolute" preference of persons in these categories over all other eligibles. That is, if with the ten-point benefit they passed the examination, they went to the head of the list. Other veterans were given a five-point preference, but were placed on the list at the rank to which their score plus five points entitled them.

The latest, and still current, basic legislation was the Veterans' Preference Act of 1944. It had the effect, among other things, of incorporating into law many of the regulations already in force, including the five- and ten-point preference formulae. It gave absolute preference in certification to the ten-point veterans—disabled veterans, wives of disabled veterans, and widows of veterans—but it excluded from this grouping professional and scientific positions paying above $3,000. It excluded non-veterans from competing for certain categories of jobs—guards, elevator operators, messengers, and custodians—as long as veterans were available. This was the first major statutory provision of a veteran monopoly for jobs in our history. The 1944 act assured veterans protection against arbitrary dismissal and other disciplinary action, providing them an appeal in such cases to the Civil Service Commission. Finally, it provided that veteran status should be one of the factors to be considered in the retention of employees in the event of reduction in force.

There appears to be little pressure today that would lead to basic changes in the 1944 Veterans' Preference Act. In its two-decade existence it has weathered the greatest wave of returning veterans in our history and the largest reductions of force in the federal government's experience. Amendments have been fairly frequent. One of the most important was that of 1952 which extended its applicability to the ex-service men and women who had served in the Armed Forces at any time from the end of World War II (technically April 28, 1952, the date of the treaty with Japan) until July 1955. Those who served during the Korean action as well as others drafted or otherwise entering the services before or after are thus entitled to preference.

The three major laws of 1865, 1919, and 1944 were each occasioned by the conclusion or anticipated conclusion of a major war. Congress has passed no basic veterans preference legislation during the periods between the wars.

Finally, one must note the affinity that has developed between veterans' preference and the merit system—or at least the interlocking of their chief organizational expressions, the veteran organizations and the Civil Service Commission. Both have grown and flowered during the same period. Both have engaged a common enemy—political spoils. Veterans' preference could hardly be as effective without the formalized employment processes of civil service; and civil service could hardly have grown and expanded as it has without the support of the organized veterans. In fact, the Civil Service Commission has been perhaps the best friend the organized veterans have had within the government, other than the Veterans Administration. The Act of 1944 was prepared by the three major veteran organizations (The American Legion, the Veterans of Foreign Wars, and the Disabled American Veterans) over a period of seven or eight years, under the helpful and watchful eyes of the Civil Service Commission. The bill was vigorously supported by all of them. Furthermore, it was backed by President Roosevelt, even though one of its primary effects was to remove a large area of discretion from the executive to the Congress. The Commission itself stands in a dual position. In the words of a recent Chairman, Philip Young: "The Civil Service Commission is both the guardian of the career merit system and the watchdog of veteran preference in Government." *

THE SYSTEM TODAY

All those who served in any of the Armed Forces during a war or during certain peacetime campaigns (such as that in Nicaragua), and were honorably discharged, are entitled to some form of veterans' preference. Preference also applies to the wives of disabled veterans whose disability disqualifies them from civil service jobs; to the widows of veterans until they remarry; and, under certain circumstances, to the mothers of veterans who died in service or who have total disability.

Veterans' preference today has an important impact in only two areas of personnel activity: appointments and staff reductions, that is, the entrance and exit gates. For many years, veterans also had a distinct advantage over other employees in procedures and appeals against adverse personnel actions, including appeals to the Civil Service Commission. But these rights were extended to all employees in 1962 through Execu-

---

* From his talk before the National Executive Committee of the American Legion, Indianapolis, Indiana, May 4, 1954.

tive Order 10988 which was promulgated as part of the new program on employee management cooperation.

THE IMPACT: PRESENT AND POTENTIAL

There are today about 22 million war veterans in the United States. This number amounts to about 29 per cent of the labor force. That preference in federal employment has had considerable impact is indicated by the fact that of all federal civilian employees, war veterans and others entitled to preference comprise a little more than half—51 per cent in 1963. Most of the veterans are of course men, and of the male employees of the government, nearly two-thirds are veterans. These proportions are very high relative to earlier United States history. The year that the Veterans' Preference Act of 1944 passed, the number entitled to preference amounted to 13 per cent of the federal service. The proportion rose rapidly in the post-War years and then rose again after the Korean affair. Since that time, for nearly a decade, it has stayed at about the same level.

In the periods immediately following wars, veterans' preference has been defensible since it tapped the great reservoir of American young people drafted for military service. As Leonard D. White wrote in 1944, the millions of veterans then expected to return included "the best minds, the most indomitable energy, the needed aptitudes and skills, and the finest character of the American people." [*] But as wars recede into history, the disadvantages of preference grow in potential dimensions. The granting of preference to one group, to the extent that it is effective, means the restriction of opportunities to others. These others include the younger people, "denied" the opportunity to serve their country in time of war; they include those exempted from military service for physical reasons or because they were needed in other work toward the war effort. Perhaps most important of all, they include women, very few of whom enjoy veteran status.

Veterans' preference has its most biting effect in times of federal contraction like the years following World War II and in times of economic depression when there is widespread unemployment. Another depression would surely add to the impact of existing preference legislation, both in appointments and in retention; and it would probably inflame new

---

[*] Civil Service Assembly Pamphlet No. 17, "Veterans' Preference—A Challenge and an Opportunity" (Chicago: Civil Service Assembly, May 1944), p. 11.

pressures for more emphatic preference. But more important than such direct effects are the indirect ones—the effects upon administrative and supervisory officers, upon current employees, both veteran and non-veteran, and upon outsiders, the potential employment market. These effects are not the result of any single provision but of the cumulative impact of veterans' preference as a whole in appointment, in retention, in the discharge of incompetents. The best qualified non-veterans are deterred from seeking, or from staying in, an employment environment which offers them a continuous threat of being "bumped" by persons of equal or lower qualifications. The best qualified veterans may be deterred from jobs which offer more security than challenge and from work situations in which status is more important than performance. Veterans' preference is partly at least an attitude of mind. If the idea becomes prevalent that the public service is primarily a "refuge" for veterans, it will surely redound against the government's securing and keeping the best qualified people, veteran or non-veteran, in the federal service now or in the future.

National Security and the Merit System

Loyalty and security constitute one field of public employment practice that is quite immune to the historic safeguards set up to protect the applicant's equal opportunity and the employee's career. The security program knows no difference between a status and a nonstatus employee, a veteran and a non-veteran, an effective and an incompetent worker. It is uninterested in the vagaries of an appropriations subcommittee. A disabled veteran status employee working for an agency with an abundance of dollars can be dropped on security charges as readily as anyone else, and dropped under procedures that are in some cases virtually "summary."

Arising as it did in a period of war and cold war, generated by a widespread fear of subversion within the government, and fanned by some very strong political winds, the security system felled some of the most cherished protections and procedures, built up over the first 60 years of civil service. "Security" was a central theme during that long history, but, in the minds at least of the employees directly affected, the word had a quite opposite meaning to that commonly associated with it today.

Loyalty and security became factors in public employment quite recently. Until Congress attached an amendment introduced from the floor to the Hatch Act of 1939,* there was no federal provision against subversives in the government. The amendment prohibited the employment of any one who had membership in any "political party or organization which advocates the overthrow" of our form of government.

Thus modestly did it all begin. Prior to the Hatch Act, there had been no program, other than for handling espionage in wartime. The civil service law and its enforcement had, in effect, forbidden the consideration of what we would now call loyalty cases. The Civil Service Commission's Rule No. 1, issued in 1884, provided: "No question in any form or application in any examination shall be so framed as to elicit information concerning the political or religious opinions or affiliations of any applicant, nor shall any inquiry be made concerning such opinions or affiliations, and all disclosures thereof shall be discountenanced."

In 1941, funds were voted the FBI to investigate federal employees. A year later, Congress removed from Army, Navy, and Coast Guard civilians procedural protections against dismissal, when "warranted by the demands of national security"—the first instance of summary removal provision on charges of security as distinguished from loyalty. During the war, the functions associated with loyalty and security were performed in a variety of different ways with participation by the war agencies, the Justice Department, the Civil Service Commission, and various committees. Following the war, summary removal authority was extended, usually by riders on appropriation acts, to a few other agencies, such as the State Department.

Interest in the problem of loyalty and security was stirred to fever pitch in the late 1940s by the revelations about *Amerasia,* about espionage activities in Canada, and the charges made by Whittaker Chambers and Elizabeth Bentley. President Truman set up a commission to study the problem, and, on receipt of its report and recommendations, established a government-wide loyalty program on March 2, 1947.† This program involved, among many other things, the establishment of a great number of loyalty boards, headed up by a 22-man board in the Civil Service Commission, the last resort of administrative appeal of individual cases. Its decisions were virtually final. The program called for a variety of protective procedures, and for appeals within the Civil

---

* Hatch Act 9-A, 53 Stat. 1148, August 2, 1939.
† By Executive Order 9835.

Service Commission for new appointees and applicants and within the departments for incumbents. The program was directed at loyalty as vaguely distinguished from security. After the Korea affair started, Congress in 1950 authorized the head of each agency associated with the defense program, whom it specified by title, to suspend without pay any civilian employee "in his absolute discretion and when deemed necessary in the interest of national security." * Before such suspension could be converted into a dismissal, the employee was guaranteed the right of written charges, an opportunity to answer them, and a hearing. The decision of the agency head, following such procedures, was final and not subject to appeal to any outside body.

Under unceasing pressure and criticism during its six-year existence, the general trend of the Truman loyalty program was toward more rigorous standards and a broader definition of what constituted disloyalty. Truman amended his original order in 1951 to make "reasonable doubt as to the loyalty" grounds for dismissal rather than "reasonable grounds . . . for belief that the person involved is disloyal." † And the President's Loyalty Review Board became increasingly strict in its surveillance and guidance of the agencies and subsidiary boards.

One of the campaign pledges most stressed in the 1952 Eisenhower campaign was that he would rid the government of communists and subversives, and after his assumption of office this was one of the first domestic problems to which his administration gave attention. On April 27, 1953, Executive Order 10450 rescinded the earlier Truman order and abolished the elaborate structure which it had set up. This order remains the governing policy in this field. Among its effects were:

1. Abolition of the distinction between loyalty and security. To these terms has been added what the Civil Service Commission customarily calls "suitability"—i.e., personal habits, character, sexual and other immoral behavior, dishonesty, and so forth. All such behavior, as well as the traditional measures of loyalty and security, are now lumped in a single category which is associated with "the interests of national security."

2. Fixing of full authority and responsibility on the heads of the agencies. The President extended the applications of the security act of 1950, described above, to include all agencies of the government. Each is em-

---

* 64 Stat. 476, August 26, 1950.
† By Executive Order 10241, April 28, 1951.

powered to suspend anyone about whom doubt arises and, "following such investigation and review as he deems necessary," to terminate his employment.

3. Denial of any right of appeal or review outside the agency. Each department may set up appeals machinery within the agency, but no further appeal to the Commission or any outside board is provided. The Civil Service Commission's role in the activity is largely in providing investigating services to the other agencies, maintaining a central index of security investigations, and making studies and reports about the system.

4. Another complete "go-round" of investigation for incumbent employees. This had been done before in connection with the Truman order of 1947, and, with respect to some of the departments and agencies, has occurred a number of times in recent years. One prominent case in the State Department is said to have been brought up for reinvestigation and redetermination on nine occasions.

Few adult Americans need be reminded of the furor and the fury of the early and mid-1950s, often referred to as the "McCarthy Era." In retrospect, that period appears to have been the "sorriest hour" for the federal civil service and the merit system. The prestige of the service and morale within it sank to new lows. In spite of the efforts of reformers over seven decades to put the public service on a nonpolitical, nonpartisan basis, political considerations assumed a dominant role in many significant personnel activities. Indeed, the public service itself was a key political issue.

The storm over employee security gradually subsided during the late 1950s, and except for sporadic and usually short-lived explosions has not been a significant political issue in recent years. The prestige of the service and the morale of its members seem to have largely recovered from the attacks of a decade ago. The investigative process associated with security and loyalty has been routinized and largely absorbed into the normal, on-going fabric of federal personnel administration. A decade ago, the number of persons dismissed as "unsuitable" was front-page news; it is now next to impossible to find out how many are being dismissed.

Yet the security business has had, and continues to have, fundamental impact upon the public service and its administration; and the present situation is not a matter for complacency. As a political issue, alleged employee disloyalty, homosexuality, and unsavory associations have proved their potential effectiveness in attracting attention, support, and votes. It is not too unlikely that the smoldering coals could be fanned again into flames by new political winds.

Security activities have "moved in on" many of the basic personnel activities—new appointments, assignments, promotions, removals. And it has colored them with new and different approaches and orientations. A virtually new "profession" has developed in the last fifteen years—a profession of government sleuths into, and evaluators of, the most personal kinds of information about people who do, or who would like to, work for their government. In some agencies, this profession operates from a level very near the top. The main part of the investigation job today is done by the Civil Service Commission, and it is a big business indeed. In fiscal 1963 the Commission made 273,914 records checks on applicants for positions and 43,720 full-field investigations. The Civil Service Commission now spends two and one-half times as much on security investigations as it does on all its recruitment and examining activities. Its investigative functions account for about 45 per cent of the Commission payroll.

This relative dominance of the investigative function may be having important though unmeasurable effects upon the character of the merit system. In new recruiting, there appears to be a greater emphasis upon the negative factors and conformity than upon relative fitness for doing a job. Almost anyone who has talked with an investigator about a candidate could attest to this emphasis. Perhaps more important than this is the loss of some of the other features for which the merit system reformers have long been striving—objectivity, equal treatment, security for the career servant, protections against arbitrary action.

Equally unmeasurable and perhaps more serious over the long run are the effects upon candidates and potential candidates as well as upon those already in the service. How many individuals of initiative, imagination, and ability refuse to seek or to accept federal employment because they do not want to be investigated, because they are not social and political conformists, or because at some point in their past they have made a mistake? How many applicants are in fact rejected who might contribute notable service to the government? And to what extent has the atmosphere of "security" and suspicion within some federal agencies muffled free discussion, accurate reporting, imaginative recommendations, and frank confrontation with controversial issues? Those who have extensive contacts with actual and potential candidates for public office, and those familiar with federal agencies, particularly the ones deemed to be "sensitive," know of individual examples of all of these things. But the extent of their impact can only be guessed.

The Image of Federal Employment

The values and the handicaps of federal service as they are perceived by persons both inside and outside it, whether or not they are grounded in reality, have great significance for the quality of the service —a significance which has been increasingly appreciated in recent years. They are important in at least three respects: as a factor in recruitment and attraction to federal appointments and careers; as they affect the aspirations, the attitudes and the morale of those in the service; and as they encourage or discourage voluntary separation from the service for other employment. Of these undoubtedly the most important today is the impact upon recruitment, particularly upon the recruitment of professional, administrative, and potential executive personnel. In a society in which there is a great and growing demand for well-educated, professional personnel with high promise for future growth, government must attract its share of the best in a highly competitive market. The most important element in selection is not the competitive examination but rather the self-selection of the best qualified to opt for a governmental career.

The most recent and the most penetrating study of this subject was recently conducted by the Brookings Institution.* Based upon questionnaires and interviews of a broad sample of the public and the federal government itself, the study analyzed differing occupational, economic, and educational groupings of the population. The Brookings study warns against any "simple global evaluation" of its findings. There is surprising variation in opinions about occupational values and about the relative advantages and handicaps of federal employment among different educational, occupational, and income groups. But it is consistently true that federal employment is rated as less desirable among the higher level groups than among the lower. And near the top among scientists, professionals, and executives, it is rated lowest of all. These differential "images" probably explain the apparent absence of par-

* Kilpatrick, Cummings, and Jennings, *The Image of the Federal Service* (Washington, D. C.: The Brookings Institution, 1964).

ticular difficulty in recruiting for lower and middle level jobs—manual, custodial, clerical, and some technical. They also explain the current and probably growing difficulties in recruiting both junior and senior personnel for scientific, professional, and executive responsibilities; and they justify the current governmental emphasis upon these categories in recruitment.

The Brookings study and other evidence suggests that there is a considerable disparity between popular *opinions about* the federal service and the *realities of* the federal service. The wide differences of judgment about federal employment between the federal employees themselves and those outside are indicative of this, even though both groups could be expected to reflect some bias in their responses. The views of nonfederal people at higher educational and status levels that governmental work lacks challenge, stultifies initiative, and offers few rewards for individual achievement contrast sharply with those of the higher-level civil servants who cite very nearly the opposite features as advantages of federal service.

Yet behind the smoke of tradition and bias against federal employment, there is probably some smoldering flame. Certainly a good many have found federal employment unchallenging, unrewarding, and monotonous. The problems of the civil service are not alone to advertise and popularize its wares but also to make sure that it has a good product. In some occupational lines and in some agencies there is reason to believe that popular prejudices have justification.

In Conclusion

The civil service and the system by which it is employed and governed are in transition. The goals, the ideology, and the image of the civil service, as it developed and stabilized during the first half-century after the Pendleton Act, were severely shaken by the New Deal, reshaken by World War II, and have in the past one and one-half decades been largely replaced by a different, still emergent set of conceptions. No previous period in history has witnessed as many changes in as many diverse aspects of federal personnel administration as have the last fifteen years. The prime movers behind the changes, most of which are still at work, have been the increase in size of the service, in the grave importance and complexity of its responsibilities, and in the nature—size, complexity, education and aspirations—of the society which it services, which sustains it, and which provides its recruits. Although historical reflections in the middle of history-in-the-making are hazardous, a few simple generalizations on the directions to date seem warranted.

In the first place, civil service administration has moved far from the negative to the positive, from the passive to the aggressive, from the preventive to the causative. This is reflected in the changed stance of the Civil Service Commission but perhaps more significantly in the vitalization of personnel activities of the departments, bureaus, and agencies. It is further reflected in the changing emphases in the fields of recruitment and selection, in the developing interest in careers and training, in the tremendous concern in the past decade with executive and top-grade professionals. A corollary observation is that personnel administration, viewed in its large sense, is being increasingly recognized as important, even vital, in the conduct of the federal government. Personnel administration is less and less the prerogative of the Civil Service Commission and the personnel specialists in the agencies. In fact the gradual, though often reluctant, delegation of personnel responsibilities from the staff to the line managers has the long-run effect of enlarging the importance of personal functions. It is increasingly clear that the bringing in, the utilization, and the development of people comprise central elements in management responsibility for which personnel specialists ought to be primarily helpers and advisers.

Second, it appears that the federal civil service is becoming less and less different from other large employers, less and less *sui generis*. Increasingly, it has adjusted, and has been forced to adjust, to the general employment market and its practices. In a few respects, it remains unique, but in most areas its practices have come increasingly to resemble those of large private employers

in competition for recruitment and entrance;
in training and career development;
in de-emphasizing the position and re-emphasizing the man;
in union recognition and collective bargaining;
in increasing concern for developing generalist, as distinguished from purely specialist, competence.

Finally, with the decentralization of personnel authority and functions to the operating agencies, there is wide and probably growing disparity among them. It is becoming more difficult to generalize about the entire civil service. In fact, the staffs of the various governmental organizations and the methods and conditions under which they are employed vary widely. Their common denominators are some quite general laws, some rules, guidelines, statements of goals, and advice from the Civil Service Commission. The federal civil service is a "family of services" of extraordinary size and diversity, composed of "siblings" without common parents. Each service has considerable freedom of action and often does not communicate very effectively with the others. But the "family" analogy is a useful way to conceive of the direction of the future: a permissive arrangement in which a degree of unity is maintained amid diversity.

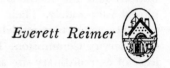

Everett Reimer

5

Modern Personnel Management
and the Federal Government Service

Modern personnel management is the task of reconciling the needs of individuals and the requirements of large organizations. Individuals need a dependable income, prospects of advancement, personal recognition, a feeling of accomplishment, and a sense of belonging. Different people need these things in differing degrees, but every job must provide opportunities for its incumbent to obtain at least the minimum satisfaction of his personal needs. Organizations in turn require at least part of the mental and physical energies of each job holder to be directed to the aims of the organization, regardless of personal needs. In varying degrees, large organizations require specialized services, predictable behavior, economy of resources, and centralized responsibility.

As the largest organization in the free world, the federal government of the United States has one of the most difficult tasks of reconciling its organizational requirements with the needs of the citizens it must em-

EVERETT REIMER, *now a consultant to the Department of Education of the Commonwealth of Puerto Rico, was formerly Secretary to the Committee on Human Resources of the Commonwealth. He has been Social Development Advisor to the Coordinator, Alliance for Progress; Director of Personnel of the Office of Price Administration; Consultant to the Survey Research Center, University of Michigan, in its comparative study of personnel policies and employee attitudes among major American corporations; staff member of the second Hoover Commission; and staff member of the recent Herter Committee, in its study of Foreign Affairs Personnel. He has contributed articles on personnel, manpower, and related subjects to many journals.*

ploy. Having had this task for some time, the federal government has been one of the pioneers of modern personnel management. If it seems, sometimes, to lag behind other large organizations, this is at least partly because a tremendous rate of progress is required merely to keep up with the growth of the task. The nature of this task and of the organization which creates and must cope with it are described in succeeding sections of this article. An appraisal follows of the progress of the race to date and, finally, an attempt is made not only to foresee the probable future course of this race but also to tamper with the odds.

THE FEDERAL CAREER SYSTEMS

It has become almost a cliché that the federal government is not *a* career system but many. A career system is a hierarchy of jobs which is entered in youth, ascended in the prime of life, and often left involuntarily (prematurely as the incumbent sees it but still not soon enough to suit others). Not all federal jobs belong to such hierarchies, and the majority, which do in some degree, are divided into a vast number of career system clusters, which have some important things in common but which constitute separate and distinct job hierarchies, almost as easy to enter from outside the federal government as from another cluster. The career systems contained within the federal service are, furthermore, as varied as they are independent. The Post Office, the Foreign Service, the Coast and Geodetic Survey, the Public Health Service, the regular Army, Navy, and Air Force, the Forest Service, the FBI and the TVA are merely a few examples of such diversity.

Of these, the regular military services come closest to being classic career systems. Young men compete for appointment to West Point, Annapolis, or Colorado Springs, take up active duty in their respective services at the junior officer level, and without too much competition from the ranks, the ROTC, and wartime recruits, go on to become the generals and the admirals of our fleets and forces. Some do, that is; those who do not retire after as little as 20 years service on enough to live in reasonable comfort. (Actually, many of those who retire early take up another career and frequently achieve a very adequate total income during their middle years.) The system seems, thus, to provide rather well, both for the needs of those who elect to retire early and of those who become generals and admirals. But what about the officers who would like to remain in the service and are not allowed to do so; or those who would like to leave but are induced to remain? There

must be quite a few of both kinds; for if self-selection could be relied upon
to satisfy the requirements of the services as well as the needs of individuals, there would be no need for such an elaborate system of selection-
up and selection-out as actually exists. It would be interesting to know
how many of the early retirements are really voluntary and how many
of the generals and admirals are actually frustrated civilians at heart.
It would be equally interesting, and perhaps even more important, to
know how many of those who retire early really ought to stay—for the
good of the services—and how many of those who are promoted the
services would be better off without.

Very few civilian employees of the federal government, and even fewer
administrators of civilian agencies, would shed a sympathetic tear, however, on behalf of their military counterparts. To be able to offer the
fringe benefits which go with being a general or an admiral to those
he wanted to keep in the service and, on the other hand, to be able
to offer early, and even forced, retirement to those whose room he preferred to their company would seem like heaven to the civilian administrator. And to the civilian employee the choices enjoyed by the
military do not seem so bad either, even if not worth the risk of being
shot at to enjoy. For the one thing that all the civilian services have
in common is the lack of one or more of the elements needed to provide at least a logical answer to the dilemmas which career systems
pose. Perhaps the most obvious of these dilemmas is created by the
scarcity of jobs at the top: by the fact that not all the individuals
needed at the lower and middle levels of the hierarchy can go on to become generals or ambassadors or bureau chiefs; and that those for whom
there isn't room at the top must either leave in midcareer or, if they
stay on, clog the promotional paths of those who at some later date
will be needed at the top of the ladder. This dilemma is solved, in terms
of human justice if not in terms of human needs, by the early entry
and early retirement which the military career systems are able to offer,
but which are only approximated in the civilian services.

The Foreign Service, for example, has many of the features of the
military services: competitive recruitment at the junior officer level,
regular promotion and involuntary selection-out of persons who fail
to be promoted, provisions for early retirement, and so forth. But the
average age of entry into the Foreign Service is about five years higher
than in the military and is creeping up, while retirement with less than
25 years service is not very attractive financially. As a result of these

and others factors, selection-out is a less dependable instrument in the Foreign Service than in the military, promotions are slower, and there are proportionally more Foreign Service than military officers who know that they have reached their peak, who would like to leave, and whom their juniors and seniors would also like to have out of the way, but who are nevertheless constrained to "serve out their time" until they can afford to retire. The same thing is true of the Public Health Service, the Secret Service and the other quasi-military services of the federal government.

In addition to these and other well-known federal career systems, almost every major bureau and minor agency of the federal government contains a career system of some sort usually lacking some of the elements which distinguish the better known ones, but in some cases lacking only time to become well known themselves. Besides being independent of each other and logically incomplete, these career systems all have at least one other common characteristic. They do not apply to everyone in their respective bureau or agency, and they do not apply equally to those to whom they do apply. For one thing, they usually apply only to professional, as opposed to clerical or manual jobs. This is not, of course, a distinguishing feature of the lesser-known systems or of those which deviate from the classic model. The military career systems do not include the ranks even though certain features of these systems extend to the ranks. The Foreign Service does not include clerical and, until recently, did not include administrative jobs. Furthermore, the Foreign Service was confined until late 1964 to the traditional bureaus of the Department of State when the United States Information Service was able to obtain entry into the Foreign Service system for its employees. The Agency for International Development has as yet none of the formal aspects of a career system. In general, career-system principles are reserved mainly for those jobs which characterize a bureau or an agency: agents in the FBI, foresters in the Forest Service, tax experts in the Bureau of Internal Revenue, and so on. Furthermore, most of these career systems favor persons who enter the service young and with especially approved credentials. The military academies, the foreign service examinations, and the forestry schools, are examples of preferred recruitment sources.

This is not to say, however, that people who do not come from the right schools and who do not fit the right jobs are without career status in the federal service. In the Post Office we have an example of a career system, of sorts, which does not recruit from an elite, and where most jobs belong to the system. There is no provision for early retirement at the option of the employee but neither can management require early retirement. The result is a low pressure system which provides security for all at the price of slow and uncertain prospects of promotion. The Post Office is, of course, unique in being the one large departmental career system. There are smaller departments and bureaus which approximate the Post Office system, but the more common pattern is the one previously described in which the career system includes only a core group of employees. Even here, however, the employees who do not belong are not without career status altogether. They are merely outside the "main" career ladder. They may have other career ladders and they may even be able to switch over to the "main" ladders under special circumstances.

Many of the principal Civil Service occupational series constitute career ladders, of a sort, which function not only within but also between bureaus and agencies. Secretarial jobs constitute such a series, as do accounting, engineering, and administrative jobs of certain kinds. The "career systems" constituted by these series leave much more to the initiative of the employee than do the more formal systems. The individual must seek promotion rather than be regularly evaluated for it. Furthermore, opportunities for promotion depend on turnover and agency growth and are not guaranteed by planned rates of recruitment and selection-out. Early retirement is not available to those who "get stuck" on the promotional ladder. There is, nevertheless, protection against arbitrary dismissal, some advantage in competition for higher jobs against outsiders, and eventual retirement at reasonable benefit levels.

More and more, the occupational career ladders of the federal service are extending outside the service, and in a greater variety of ways than even a few years ago. It is increasingly common for economists and political scientists, for example, to move back and forth between university and government, and for lawyers and accountants to shift intermittently from private to public employment. Military, research, and business careers have also become increasingly intertwined. Many kinds of government contracts, where the terms of employment are controlled by the federal government, tend to blur the distinction between government and private employment.

Despite recent efforts, there is nothing in our federal service like the

British Administrative Class. Rather, the civil servants who reach top rank in the federal service reach it by many routes. It would be difficult for an ambitious junior civil servant to justify the choice of one career ladder over another as a route to any position not on that ladder. It is rather a matter of all roads leading to Rome. The important thing, for the ambitious junior, is to get to the top of whatever ladder he may be on; the lightning is equally likely to strike any of them, or none of them for that matter. What distinguishes the United States from the British civil service, as much as anything, is the frequency with which the top positions in our federal service are filled from outside the civil service or any other federal career system. In addition to scores of assistant, deputy and undersecretary positions, there are large numbers of schedule C positions which are equally free of recruitment restrictions. At less august levels, there are literally thousands of consultant jobs and personal services contracts which permit at least the temporary employment of persons with no career status, as supplements and even substitutes for career employees. Some agencies have more flexibility than others in this respect but the trend is to extend such flexibility more widely. Frequently the incumbents of these temporary jobs belong to some other career system in private industry, in some university, in state or local government, and even occasionally in some other branch of the federal government. The career systems of the federal government are like the branches of a tree which, while separate, interlock with one another and with the branches of neighboring trees of different kinds.

Modern Personnel Management

Having briefly sketched the locus of federal personnel management, it seems desirable, before proceeding to an appraisal of it, to sketch the frame of reference which will guide this appraisal. A number of basic assumptions enter into any such frame of reference, which ought to be made explicit and plausible, even if they cannot be thoroughly justified. One such assumption is that neither the problems nor the major means of modern personnel administration are at all modern, in a restrictive sense. On the contrary, it is assumed that the pre-industrial era may be a more useful guide than recent history, for those problems of modern personnel management which will grow rather than diminish from now on. Put as briefly as possible, the thesis is that the problems of personnel management are products of the changing relationships of large or-

ganizations and their individual members and that, in the perspective
of history these relationships are returning to the kind of stability which
characterized the pre-industrial age. It may be objected that the following discussion tends to collapse the major problems of society into those
of personnel management. This tendency must be admitted, and defended on the grounds that the relationships of the individual and the
organization through which his major value exchanges with the society
are mediated cannot help but reflect the major social problems of his
time.

HISTORY AND PROPHECY

In terms of the definition previously given, the history of personnel
management must go back as far as the history of large organizations;
among the first of which were armies, the courts of kings, and temples.
It is interesting to speculate on the contribution each of these sources
may have made to the characteristics of modern organizations; hierarchy
may have come from the army, specialization from the court, indoctrination from the temple, for example. It is also instructive to note that,
from the beginning, serious compromises were involved in the relationships of men and organizations. Risk of life, subordination of status,
and celibacy are not among the most natural acts of men, but the advantages of belonging to these early institutions were so great that they
seldom lacked recruits. Throughout history large organizations have always had such an advantage in the levels of reward they could provide
their members as to give them a wide choice of whom they would admit
to membership.

The real mark of the modern age is that membership in large organizations is no longer a privilege of the few but is becoming so widely
available. It has not yet become universal, however, and essential aspects
of today's personnel management still depend upon this fact. Indeed, it
remains hard to imagine not being able to select from among those who
might want to join an organization; but as more of the work of the
world devolves on large organizations, this ability to select must, of
course, decline except insofar as organizations recruit from each other.
What happens to the "organization man," however, when he becomes
the regular object of recruitment by other organizations? And what happens to the relative efficiency of large organizations as they take in a
progressively higher proportion of the total population?

Many of the present characteristics of large organizations and their personnel policies are still rooted in the privileged minority status which these organizations have, in the past, enjoyed. Protection of privilege has been one of the functions even of labor unions and professional associations, and often the main function of the organizations which have ruled political and economic empires. As the masses, which in the past were ruled and exploited by political, economic and other organizations, have become absorbed into these organizations as more fully participant members the problems of personnel management have changed radically. If, today, we are still only dimly aware of the fundamental nature of these changes, this may be because large organizations still remain in a privileged position, still employ only a minority of the whole population, and still provide only marginal participation for most of those who do belong.

There can be little doubt, however, about the trends which are shaping the future. More and more people make their contributions as producers, and owe their claims as consumers, to large organizations. The very survival of independent organizations may depend upon their ability to provide employment and income, directly or indirectly, to everyone. As this occurs—or, alternatively, as people elect to depend upon socialist organizations, which include everyone by definition—the privilege which large organizations still enjoy, of choosing their members from among many applicants, will have to be recognized as the illusion which it is already becoming. Emphasis will then be focused, where it is already increasingly being placed, upon the position of the individual within the organization, rather than upon mere membership.

In a sense, this will be a return, by the industrial age, to some of the characteristics of the feudal order of a bygone agricultural age. We have been and still are in a transition stage which gives us false notions of what a stable society can be like. Almost by definition, a stable society cannot leave men's roles as indeterminate as they have been in the recent history of Europe and North America—in which thousands of peasants and peasants' sons and grandsons have become presidents of corporations, colleges, and nations, while millions have become professional and managerial workers. Already, the rate of major change of social role is slowing down, in the countries which are furthest along in the transition from an agricultural to an industrial society.

Most certainly the industrial society is not a static one; the second industrial revolution, brought on by automation, has only begun to be felt and already the space age is upon us. But the general patterns of social roles in an automated space age can be foreseen and they do not provide the opportunities for free-floating human molecules which have characterized the recent past. Even in countries which are still populated largely by peasants, the transition from peasant to professional is likely to be much more orderly than it was in the countries which pioneered the industrial revolution. Those who are still peasants are more likely to shift from one determinate social role to another without passing through those uncertainties which were the glorious opportunities of yesterday's European immigrants to the United States, but which are the plague of today's Indian peasants seeking opportunities in Indian cities.

It is not that the occupational patterns of the future can be foreseen in any detail, much less the transitional stages through which they will pass. What is predictable is the role of large organizations in these patterns. Steel is not going to be produced in backyards, even in China. Automobile manufacturers in India and Brazil are not, as they were in Detroit, the product of racing car drivers, mechanics, and wealthy sportsmen. The Flash Gordons who will pioneer the planets will not be Lone Eagles, nor even Diet Smiths.

Not only will pioneering as well as production fall progressively to large organizations in the future; as previously indicated, the time is rapidly approaching when these large organizations will have to provide, directly or indirectly, for the employment and income of everyone. Self-employment and small business may survive, but can only survive on a large scale by selling goods and services to large organizations as well as to each other. The policies of large organizations, private and public combined, will determine the roles which small organizations and individuals can play, whether these small organizations and individuals are contained or employed by the large ones, or whether they sell them goods and services on a contractual or other basis. Ultimate responsibility for the roles available to individuals will remain, therefore, with large organizations. In pluralistic societies some of this responsibility will be shared by all large organizations, while some of it will devolve upon particular organizations. In any case, the individual will not have, as he appears to have now, the ultimate responsibility for finding his place in the world. Even now this is largely a fiction; it would have been a fantasy in the pre-industrial world and it will survive only as a fantasy in the mature industrial world.

Reduced emphasis on selecting the membership of large organizations will, as previously indicated, lead to increased emphasis on the role of the individual within the organization. The fiction that when a president of Standard Oil retires an office boy is hired can be maintained only so long as the selection of office boys can be tightly controlled and, conversely, plenty of office-boy talent is available. Once the outer gates come down some inner distinctions have to be created, since it is obvious that not just anyone can be president of Standard Oil and, equally, that only a small proportion of all employees can be given access to the jobs which are a necessary prelude to the presidency.

When it becomes unfeasible, however, to extend the same system to all jobs, then hierarchies of systems become necessary and conflicts among them become almost inevitable. Finding a satisfactory role for everyone within the total complex of these systems without creating relatively impermeable hierarchies of privilege is probably the greatest problem of modern time, one in which personnel management obviously has a major role. The old feudal systems were able to provide a role for everyone only by creating permanent hierarchies of privilege, which are unacceptable in the modern world.

ETERNAL VERITIES

Differences among people, which in part create the need for different systems, also provide a way out of the resulting conflicts. People not only have different capacities but also different needs and, legitimately in some cases, different rights. A commitment to military or foreign service or to any danger, hardship, or sacrifice deserves certain commitments in return which cannot legitimately be claimed by everyone else. People cannot properly claim the same returns when they are young and inexperienced as later when they have made an investment representing effort on their part and potential value to their fellows. There is, furthermore, some correspondence between needs and claims. Among the people least likely to commit themselves to military or foreign service are those who would not want to be generals or ambassadors in any case. The income needs of young adults are not as great as when, later on, they have to put their own children through college.

Some recent research reveals striking differences among classes of jobs in the personality traits required of successful incumbents. Personality, as defined in these studies, consists, among other things, in characteristic ways of wielding power and dealing with power figures, characteristic ways of dealing with information and work content, and characteristic criteria for judging one's own success. Good stenographers, for example, try to anticipate and satisfy the needs of their bosses while good nurses try to live up to impersonal standards. Foreign service officers like work which combines the interpretation of data and influencing other people. Their style for analyzing information tends to be impressionistic and intuitive rather than formal, methodical, and statistical. Their preferred style of working within a formal organization is to do the work themselves rather than work through a hierarchy. They place great value on personal intellectual achievement and a moderate value on formal status, social service, and the approval of others.

According to this research,* the behavioral styles of individuals also show great variation. It should be possible, therefore, to fit people to jobs and career systems so as to minimize the strains imposed by organizational requirements and by the differential privileges associated with different jobs and career systems. There are limits, however, on what placement can achieve. The very fact that there are different groups and systems, the claims of each of which must receive minimum attention, means that no group can have its requirements fully satisfied. Flexible arrangements for time and place of work might be ideal for a group of creative problem solvers, for example; but they may depend on data files and systems operated by persons for whom such flexibility would be onerous and wasteful.

Priorities create another problem which cannot be resolved by judicious placement of people. No matter what they do or how, everybody likes to have high priorities assigned to the things they do. But priorities are, in part at least, influenced by uncontrollable factors and anyone can find himself and his priorities becalmed in an organizational eddy while the temporarily important tide of competitive events sweeps on around him. To the extent that priorities are under the control of organization members, they become items of contention among different organizational units and career groups and, because of the nature of priorities, one man's meat becomes another man's poison.

Priority conflicts have particular relevance to personnel policies on certain issues. One of these is the relative importance to be attached to program and administrative ends. Every organization has an outside job to do and also the task of maintaining itself in condition to do this job. An army must fight, at least on occasion, but must always eat, in order to be able to fight. In organizations with less primitive ends and needs the

---

* Initiated in the Department of State and now being continued at the Behavioral Sciences Center of George Washington University by psychologist Regis Walther.

issues which correspond in relative importance to fighting and eating may not be as easy to distinguish as they are in the case of armies—but they are always there, always important, and always tending to array people with different temperaments and organizational roles against one another.

Jobs in which power is concentrated tend to be filled by people who like to wield power, partly because these people are more likely to understand the organizational locations and mechanisms of power better than those who get less satisfaction out of its exercise. This knowledge also tends to make them more aware of the maintenance needs of organizations and more likely to be entrusted by others with responsibility for maintaining the viability of these organizations. The result is that the people who are most likely to want to use the power of an organization for the purposes it was created for, are among the least likely to possess this power, especially after an organization has been in operation long enough for its power positions to be filled on the basis of internal rather than external processes. The head of a large temporary agency of the federal government once said that every organization has three historic stages: an opening stage of buzzing, blooming confusion, a golden age, and the stage when the bureaucrats take over. By bureaucrats he clearly meant those to whom the program purposes of the agency were less important than its maintenance mechanics. The truth in this obviously oversimplified generalization may be responsible for the frequency with which new organizations are set up to deal with new tasks. The people running the existing agencies are just too busy running their agencies. Some organizations have recognized the tendencies cited above and have adjusted their personnel policies accordingly. A former oil company executive, contrasting the policies of Standard and Gulf Oil, says that while Standard continues to fill all of its key positions from within, Gulf now follows this policy only in technical jobs, choosing its policy making executives, more and more, from the outside.

Besides the minimum claims of every constituent group, which limit the accommodations which can ever be made to any one group, and the priority claims which, additionally, still further limit the accommodations which can be made to all groups except the one enjoying highest priority, there is one further important limiting factor on the degree to which personnel problems can be solved by assigning the right people to the right jobs. It is the restrictive aspect of those very factors which make an organization more effective than an uncoordinated collection of individuals. Coordination, which is the essence of organizational effectiveness, necessarily constrains the individual member and the constituent group in many ways. Timing, spatial relations, economy in the use of materials, subordination, and accountability, are merely a few of the ways in which organizations achieve effectiveness and, at the same time, limit the accommodations which can be made to their constituents. There is, further, the all-important fact that most of what goes on in an organization has to occur routinely, according to pre-established pattern. Unless individuals normally follow these patterns they can destroy the capacity of the organization even to maintain itself, let alone accomplish anything. In following organizational routines, however, individuals must frequently subordinate their own needs. Not always, since organizational routines can facilitate as well as thwart the satisfaction of individual needs, but when such facilitation becomes the rule, remarks about how well the individual in question has adjusted to his job cease to be flattering.

Neither the unconstrained individual nor the narrowly efficient organization are of course ideals. Insofar as organizational constraints help to shape and develop an individual who is socially productive as well as personally satisfied, they are an asset rather than a liability. The object of modern personnel administration is as much to foster these kinds of constraints as to minimize those which interfere with the development and satisfaction of the individual. Also, as long as men must spend a considerable portion of their time in organizational environments, the efficiency of organizations cannot be measured wholly on an input-output basis but must also be judged in terms of the quality of the environment they provide for human satisfaction and development.

ANCIENT MEANS AND MODERN TECHNIQUES

Most of the means on which modern personnel administration relies have a history as long as the problems with which they deal. Differential rewards, not only economic but of prestige and power, are as old as history. Punishment and the fear of it are equally old and actually declining over the long run, but there has probably been an increase in their use during the present century. This increase is associated with the growth of totalitarian systems but is not wholly confined to the countries which have succumbed to totalitarian regimes. Military organizations have never been able to abandon punishment as an incentive and the extension of national security systems into civilian affairs has brought the threat and, occasionally, the actuality of punishment with it. Indoctrination is, of course, nothing new, nor is training. The Ottoman Empire, in the case of the Janizaries, probably brought this combination to a degree of effectiveness which has never been exceeded, although the modern Roman Catholic Church achieves a fantastic degree of organizational decentralization on the basis of a highly developed indoctrination and training system. Selection on the basis of temperament as well as capacity, and for specialized roles as well as for initial membership, also has roots which go back into ancient history.

What is new in modern personnel administration is largely technical: the ability to measure with more precision, to record in greater volume, and to systematize on a larger scale. The ancients were less restricted in their use of means; they could be more selective in their choice of members, use a wider range of rewards and punishments, more easily bind people to organizations for life and thus add force to indoctrination and training. Modern management is forced to be, and is enabled by modern technical refinements to be, more subtle. Work measurements and piece rates were certainly not unknown in slave societies but did not have to be administered with precision. Without the movie camera and the metronome it might also have been difficult to make them precise. Depth psychology has probably added less insights into human motives than techniques for mass measurement and application. Freud found his basic themes in the ancient Greek dramatists; the representative sample, modern means of reproduction, and mass communication are new. Most of the hidden persuaders have been used before, in personal diplomacy and intrigue, and even in mass application, in the symbolisms of royal and religious pageantry. Today's scale is different because more people count, because of mass media, and because planning is becoming more systematic, in response to the opportunities of application on a larger scale.

The most recent trend in modern personnel management is an attempt to recapture the unity and humanity of older systems. The industrial revolution broke up many of the old social institutions and inaugurated a period of unusual dependence upon particular incentives and techniques. Money wages are still an almost exclusive reliance of many organizations. Scientific management, merit systems, paternalism, and other approaches have all had their recent vogues. But now that the new organizations of the industrial age are maturing, there is a tendency to return to a more complete theory of personnel administration; one which looks at the whole man and the whole organization. This is the present trend and it still has some way to go.

Personnel Management in the Federal Government Service

RECRUITMENT AND SELECTION

In the time of the first six presidents, the problems of deciding who should belong to the federal service were not very great. Not many people were needed and only a limited number of candidates had to be taken into account. Alternatives to government by an elite based on birth had not yet been seriously considered. There was no need even to think about the claims of those who did not belong to the "governing class." When Jackson and his successors broke through the class barrier, they first merely substituted party for class. There seemed to them, as to their predecessors, no reason to share the privileges of government with those to whom the government did not belong. It had previously belonged to a class; it now belonged to a party.

It may be instructive to view the history of recruitment and selection for the federal service as a struggle, which perhaps cannot be finally resolved, between these two principles. On the one side, we have merit motivated in the general interest of the existing social order and, on the other, power directed toward purposes authorized by the preponderant group of power holders. Just how merit is defined operationally may not make so much difference. In the pre-Jacksonian days it was assumed that merit could be recognized in those who had it by those who had acquired it in a similar manner. Later, with the recurrence of the merit principle in a more democratic garb, open competition and impersonal tests were relied upon. Today, with a strong labor-market demand for the best of the well-educated, a case can be made for a return to the old system of measuring merit. We send our best scientists as recruiters to our best schools, to personally persuade the best students to join the federal service. Few would argue that this is not the best way to get the cream of the college crop even in the subject matter area where merit is subject to the most objective test. The basic question then is not how merit should be defined and measured but whether merit should be the main principle of selection. No one thinks it should be in all cases. Thus, the President is allowed to choose his top executives freely because it is accepted that these men must share his convictions, have his confidence, and be able to speak for him, before the

Congress and elsewhere. No one believes, either, that routine jobs have to be filled on the basis of nationwide competition; nor that it pays to move people across the country and around the world in order to get the theoretically best person in every post. Most people believe that Negroes and other minority groups should have a reasonable proportion of federal jobs, that union membership is a legitimate consideration in selecting people for union jobs, that disabled veterans deserve preference —for certain kinds of posts at least—, and even that political parties and party workers have some legitimate claims on federal employment.

All the above, however, could be brushed off as exceptions or as necessary modifications of the merit principle. Program loyalties raise a somewhat more fundamental problem. Should people who are opposed to public housing, or to the regulation of stock exchanges, or to foreign aid, work for USHA, SEC, or AID, respectively? Another real exception to merit principle would seem to appear when there are competing claims by various agencies, whether these be competing federal agencies or a federal agency competing with outside organizations. Does the Department of State need the best people more than the Department of Defense, or can either claim to need them more than the universities or business firms with whom these agencies have major contracts? If the answer is that competition must decide which organization gets whom, then power rather than merit is the deciding principle. If the answer is that individuals must decide between organizations, then purpose rather than merit is the decisive factor.

Enough has been said to indicate why the merit principle has had a complex federal history. Merit is either a complex concept, which includes the principles of power, purpose and practicality; or else it must share the field with these other principles. Thus the success of federal personnel administration, in recruitment and selection for the federal service, cannot be appraised simply by asking whether the service has obtained the best possible recruits, unless "best possible" is qualified to take account of the needs of nonfederal organizations, the constraints of time and space, the motivation as well as the capability of recruits, and the general political and social health of the nation.

The actual history of federal recruitment reflects not so much the rearguard action of the patronage system as the growth of the government in variety of functions as well as in size, the growth of competition for scarce skills from private business and state and local government, and the growth in the number of geographic, ethnic, occupational, and po-

litical groups which can make legitimate claims upon federal employment.

In the pioneering days of the new merit system, beginning soon after
the Civil War, the simple competitive tests, applied at first to a small
number of simple jobs, worked pretty well. The essential skill requirements of the jobs in question were few; there wasn't much competition
from other employers; there were plenty of remaining jobs available
for political patronage; and policy positions and highly technical jobs
were not often involved. Gradual extension of merit selection to a gradually growing number and variety of jobs also worked well; so long as
there was plenty of time for recruitment, there were plenty of candidates,
and plenty of federal posts remained outside the merit system. Complications, on a large scale, ensued in World War I, when lots of people had to be hired quickly for a variety of new jobs and in the face
of stiff competition from other employers. To merit system purists World
War I was a hiatus in the development of modern personnel administration, but actually the federal service learned, during World War I, how
to fill many new kinds of jobs, rapidly, in the face of competition, and
without as much irregularity and inefficiency as characterized the Civil
War. It was, of course, necessary to modify sharply the peacetime competitive selection practices. After the war, competitive selection was resumed and gradual progress continued in bringing more jobs under the
merit system and in devising an ever expanding variety of tests and
recruitment procedures. During the depression and the New Deal the
"merit system" had its golden age. For the first, and hopefully the last,
time in the nation's history the cream of the country was readily available to the federal service. An excellent job was done of skimming a
small part of this cream, which still enriches the federal service, but the
number of jobs which could be filled was low.

World War II produced a new hiatus in competitive recruitment, but
more than that, World War II appears to have marked a permanent
change in the competitive situation. Not only during but ever since the
war there has been more competition among employers than among applicants for jobs; and, despite rising unemployment among the currently swollen stream of new entrants to the labor force, this will continue to be the case for the jobs that count—including secretarial, clerical and technical as well as scientific and professional jobs.

With no more lag than must be expected, considering the size and
public character of the federal service, federal recruitment and selection

practices have been adapted to the new labor market and to the vastly increased federal responsibilities of the post-war world. Considering the increased importance and variety of its present functions, the federal government is probably doing as well as it ever has, except during the depression of the 1930s, in recruiting the talent needed to carry out these functions. On the whole, the federal service has always found people pretty well qualified to do its jobs, since it must be remembered that in the earlier eras the tasks performed by most federal servants were not of crucial importance to the national welfare. Today's problems of federal personnel administration are not mainly in the area of recruitment. The federal service has a harder time keeping and utilizing the people it needs than it has in getting them originally.

RETENTION AND MOTIVATION

Every year the federal service hires one-sixth as many persons as are employed in total and loses a comparable number. Some of this turnover is accounted for by retirement, Christmas-season postal workers, short-term construction jobs, new and declining programs, and so forth, but not very much. By far the bulk of it represents the replacement of one person by another, and by far the majority of the people replaced leave voluntarily for other jobs. No one can really be sure why they leave and it might be both useful and interesting to try to find out. Meanwhile, it would seem from the turnover figures that the much publicized problems of recruiting people for and removing them from the federal service have been over-emphasized, at least in relation to the problem of retention. The turnover is so large that if the service were retaining either the better or the worse employees, to a significantly different degree, there would quickly be either an obvious improvement or deterioration in the quality of the federal service. Absence of any such obvious change means that turnover is either screening out rejects and rejectors indifferently or that quality does not distinguish those who reject—from those who are rejected by—the service. It cannot, of course, be assumed that those who leave voluntarily are not rejects; there is no better reason for leaving, voluntarily, than the perception of not being wanted. It seems highly likely, in fact, that most cases are mixed; that people who tend to reject significant aspects of the federal service tend also to be less highly valued, especially by those who wield power in the federal service, as well as vice versa. But, even though it may not be possible to classify people according to the motives for which they leave the federal service, it is important to classify the motives themselves; to distinguish things which lead the individual to be dissatisfied with the service from those which lead the service to be dissatisfied with him.

Money appears to deserve first place on the list of personal motives, especially in a society in which so many relationships are mediated by money. Although it might appear that the money motive affects recruitment more than retention, the two are closely related. The argument for higher salaries is not only that it would permit the recruitment of better talent but also that it would reduce turnover, first, by giving people more reason to stay, and second, by reducing the number of inadequate recruits who have to be pushed out. Federal salaries, have, of course, frequently lagged behind at least part of the competition, especially in the jobs which are growing most rapidly in number and importance. There have also been times, however, when federal salaries have run ahead even of private industry, excepting the jobs which are probably peculiar to private industry. Furthermore, federal salaries have usually been higher than those of most universities and state and local governments. The pay bill enacted in 1964 by the Congress put the federal service, for a time at least, in a fair competitive position, even considering the importance and difficulty of many of the technical and managerial jobs to be done. For the basic fact is that no amount of money, in higher salaries, would help very much to satisfy the most critical needs of the federal service. The President could undoubtedly get some mileage out of a few hundred jobs for which he could personally set the salary, but the results would be fairly temporary. As soon as the hypothetical incumbents began to try to earn their super-salaries, they would find themselves in a self-defeating competition for talent, program funds, the time of key people including the President himself, and other priorities for more basically inelastic production factors than salary levels. It is these factors which determine how long men stay in federal service and how much they accomplish. This comes to the same thing for it is lack of achievement which drives men out of the federal government, whether they drive themselves or are driven.

Achievement is, of course, defined by each person for himself. For some men achievement is measured by money, but since money is tied to promotion and promotion to achievement as evaluated by others, even money motives can be satisfied only by getting things done which contribute to the purpose of the federal government, as seen by others. Thus, even most of those who leave for money reasons leave not because some jobs do not pay enough but because they cannot get the jobs they want when they want them.

If large numbers of people leave the federal service because they are not able to get enough done to satisfy themselves, or others, this implies either a great waste of human talent or a continuing frustration of the aims of federal programs by outside forces. Neither implication can be rejected. Our present military effort, for example, is a defensive one, and while maintaining our defensive power is a vital goal it does not provide the widespread opportunities for satisfying personal achievement that many much smaller military ventures have done. Much the same could be said of our veterans' programs, many of our agricultural programs, and so forth. At the present stage of our history most federal programs are devoted more to holding than to gaining ground.

It is equally true, however, that much human talent is being wasted in the federal service, at least theoretically. Under better conditions less people could do what is now being done or, alternatively, more could be achieved with the number there are. There are some who say that more could be done with less, under present conditions; and even some who claim that more would be done if only there were fewer federal employees.

None of these critics have a practical program, however. Nor are the laws which protect the rights of employees the principal obstacle, as is so often claimed. Anyone who has actually tried to streamline an organization discovers immediately that the protection of other people, in one kind of power position or another, is a much more potent obstacle than the law. And while the law provides a convenient rationale for the protectors, it is obvious that the abolition of legal rights would lead merely to the strengthening of personal political ties. Streamlining the service was surely no easier in the Jacksonian era than it is now, and while an old-fashioned political-party patronage system would not necessarily replace the present system of procedural restraints on the removal of federal employees, some reasonable facsimile thereof almost certainly would.

Removing people from the federal service has, at bottom, the same obstacles as retaining them; namely, the conflicts of motives which multiply as an organization grows in size—and which reach an apogee in the federal service. This conflict of motives limits the success which any system for motivating federal employees can have whether the system be based on pay, fear of dismissal, work quotas, career incentives, personal loyalties, or devotion to program objectives. It is fairly clear, for example, that not one of these systems of motivation could be carried to its logical conclusion in the federal service, as it might in a smaller independent organization. For one thing, the government cannot do entirely without any of these principles of motivation which, in some respects, contradict each other. Conflicts among programs also limit what can be accomplished in establishing optimum motivational conditions. Thus, U. S. help for Israel hurts her Arab neighbors, by Arab definition. Higher prices to farmers must be paid by people who live in cities. Protection of the western range and forests limits the profit potential of ranchers. Each of these conflicts is reflected in the work situation of federal servants.

There is also one further kind of motivational conflict, previously discussed, which is most sharply illustrated in the formal career system. For maximum efficiency such a system must select a relatively small number of recruits from among the general population. It must also be confined to a relatively small part of the total work force needed to achieve its work objectives. Finally it must shunt off those who fail to be promoted and thus can offer only half a normal work life to its average member; more of course, to some, but correspondingly less to others. This career system model represents, nevertheless, the best way we now know of organizing a highly efficient work force for the achievement of continuing nonroutine program objectives. A highly competitive piece work system, which wears people out and then dismisses them, is the most efficient way to get routine work done. The motivational contradictions implicit in the career system are not much harder to see than those in the piece work model. Basic questions arise concerning the people who never get in as well as those who are cast off. Such questions might not be very relevant to independent, special-purpose organizations, but the federal government of the United States cannot so easily ignore the implications of personnel systems which leave most people out in the cold and which cast out others after they get in.

Considering the problems cited above, it may be that the motivation to work and the motivation to remain in the federal service are as high as can be expected. It is not easy to say, since few organizations are comparable. Since the turnover is not increasing and there is no evidence of a decline in motivation, it would seem that, in sum, the various incentives systems are keeping pace with the growing complexity and difficulty of the federal task. Furthermore, most people who move between the federal service and other large organizations do not make comparisons unfavorable to the federal service, at least not without qualification. One cannot work in the federal service, however, without becoming acutely aware of the large numbers of frustrated people and frustated projects it contains. Perhaps these are not more numerous than elsewhere; but there would seem to be great opportunities, at least theoretically, to increase both output and job satisfaction.

INDOCTRINATION AND TRAINING

Indoctrination seems unAmerican, somehow, although usually only when the other fellow's doctrine is in question. Company loyalty seems a legitimate goal to company executives and union loyalty to union leaders. Most people would agree that federal employees ought to be instructed in their obligation to the federal service, but they might not agree on what these obligations are. Defining indoctrination as communication aimed at insuring loyalty helps define the problem. In these terms, loyalty to the United States in conflict with its enemies is clearly a legitimate objective, to be pursued by all legitimate means. But what about loyalty to the United States government in conflict with a corporation or a labor union, also of this country? Or loyalty to the Navy in conflict with the Office of the Secretary of Defense? Or loyalty to the executive branch in conflict with the Congress? Or loyalty to one's boss in conflict with his peers? Within proper limits, each of these kinds of loyalty is indispensable to the proper functioning of the federal service and, furthermore, cannot be taken for granted but must be the subject of indoctrination. It is easy to see, however, how such loyalties get out of hand and come into conflict with others.

The typical federal employee is a member of many hierarchical work groups, stacked on top of one another, and also, frequently, of several functional work groups, ranged alongside or interpenetrating one another. His relative loyalty to each of these groups is a matter of delicate balance, which can change with even subtle changes in circumstance. Learning how to balance his loyalties, in varying circumstances, is a continuing and difficult task for the federal servant, one of the most difficult he has and one on which he frequently founders; his own career interests, as well as the interests of the federal service, are frequently at stake. Most of the indoctrination which occurs in the federal service— and there is a lot of it—occurs informally as an integral part of the work situation. This is, in many respects, desirable and inevitable, but one dubious advantage of doing it in this way is that the delicate issues of conflicting loyalties do not have to be faced in open discussion.

Indoctrination and training are, of course, as hard to disentangle as the values and facts which are their respective currencies, and this may be an important reason why formal training plays so small and sterile a role in most federal activities. The military services are an exception to this rule, possibly because indoctrination is more respectable in the military services. Interservice rivalries among the Army, Navy, and Air Force are more acceptable, somehow, than similar rivalries among the Bureaus of Agriculture or Commerce. Whatever the reason, this greater acceptability seems to bring indoctrination in the military services out into formal materials and sessions and into more intimate relationships with technical training materials. In the past there has often seemed to be no need, for example, to distinguish the technically correct from the Army, Navy, or Air Force way of doing things, even though the three might differ. Perhaps those days are over, however.

There are, of course, other adequate and well known reasons why both indoctrination and training have been much more prominent features of the military than of the civilian federal service. What needs to be explained is not this difference but how little of both indoctrination and training can be identified in the budgets and programs of most civilian federal agencies and how gradual the trend of increase is, despite an enormous growth in the size and complexity of programs and, in many cases, of technological change which rivals the rate of change in military technology. Congressional restrictions on training funds is too easy an answer. Many agencies do not use what they now have to much advantage.

Part of the answer may be that there is a meager training tradition in civilian government activities. Up to the time of the Civil War, the jobs to be done were fairly simple, although in the era of patronage, indoctrination and training would have been labeled as, and probably would have been, party propaganda.

Since the Civil War, training has increased in the civilian as well as the military services. Particularly during the two World Wars, training activities expanded; budgetary precedent and training technique spilled over from military to civilian activities. But most of the civilian agencies, for one reason or another, have not proved to be very fertile ground and have made remarkably few original contributions to training technique. The need, on the other hand, is great. The federal civil servant has to learn how one of the worlds most complicated systems works, before his own work can have more than a mechanical impact on the outside world. And yet the devices for teaching new employees how the system works are primitive, except in the military. In some parts of the service the mystique of the "unknowable system" is actually fostered. There is some excuse for this, since many procedures are not only complex but, quite properly, flexible and forever in flux. One result, however, is that the average federal employee leaves the service long before his potential for achievement has reached its maximum. Another result is to create a great dependence upon and to leave a correspondingly large amount of power in the hands of service veterans. The widely known congressional seniority system thus has its counterpart in the executive.

It could, of course, be argued that if most rather than just a few federal employees understood the federal service well enough to make it responsive to their ideas and purposes, this would make it more difficult to achieve consistent and disciplined action. Concentration of procedural expertise in the hands of veteran federal servants probably does make it easier to obtain working consensus. Both the strength and weakness of this argument are illustrated in the rationale for the British system of government, where the permanent senior civil servant is assumed to be a necessary counterfoil to the temporary political minister. In our system, however, there is probably less insurance that the most senior civil servant is also the most fully competent and the most worthy to exercise greater power. Furthermore, the British system, making better provision along this line, does not have to depend upon the relative ignorance of the majority of civil servants for the achievement of program continuity and leadership.

Building more effective formal training into the civilian services and bringing the indoctrination process out into the open would, undoubtedly, temporarily disrupt some of the informal processes which are now depended upon to make the service run smoothly. But the game might be worth the candle.

WORK AND CAREER MANAGEMENT

The above heading is not a standard subdivision of personnel administration and is not intended as an organizational suggestion. It is rather a convenient frame in which some of the policies and practices of federal work management and career management can be examined together. Job classification is one example of a standard element of personnel administration which vitally affects both the management of work and of careers. Promotion systems, where they exist, are another. Organization planning is an example of an element, sometimes not included in personnel administration, which, nevertheless, vitally influences supervisory practice, career management, and other major aspects of personnel administration, broadly conceived. Work measurement programs provide another such example. Another reason for joining the discussion of career and work management is that the two are intimately related. A formal career system decides who does what, which is also one of the central decisions in the management of work. Further evidence for the close relationship of work and career management is found in the fact that most formal career systems cannot adapt themselves to the typical position classification system, but usually introduce some notion of rank inhering in the individual, regardless of the nature of the work currently assigned to him. The importance of considering work and career management together is underscored by such developments as automation, which radically affect the nature of work, the kinds and numbers of people required for it, and many aspects of the relationship of individuals to large organizations.

In the early days of the Republic, no elaborate provisions were needed for managing the civilian work of the federal service, and careers, if any existed, just happened. Jobs were sufficiently differentiated by such titles as postmaster, customs collector, clerk, and custodian. Problems of work and career management probably began when chief clerks began to do the work of assistant collectors and when constituents, having moved their households to the federal district, lost their jobs in the change of parties and appealed to their congressmen for help in finding new ones. At some point the number of individual titles, salaries, qualifications, and job conditions got to be too long and irksome to deal with, so grades, categories, standards, and rules were invented; or, more probably, these were borrowed from the military services, which had for a long time categorized military roles and must have found it natural to treat civilian jobs in the same way. Work and career management took a long step toward independence of each other the day some bright and lazy bureaucrat, tired of dealing with a host of individual, stubborn, human problems was asked to prepare a plan for future operations—thus permitting him, temporarily, to indulge himself in pushing people around on paper.

So long as the key decisions affecting federal work and federal careers were made by people directly responsible for the work, work management, and career management could scarcely be separated. But, as the increasing scale of federal operations led to centralized decisions on organization, workloads, schedules, and budgets on the one hand, and on salaries, promotions, and recruitment on the other, work and career management began to be pulled apart. The last century has seen the progressive specialization and development of organization planning, work measurement, work scheduling, cost accounting, budgeting, job analysis and classification, wage and salary administration, retirement planning, scientific selection, and so on, without mentioning any of the more recent and esoteric innovations at all. Many of these management tools have not only been widely adopted but, to a considerable extent, were developed within the federal service. During the same hundred years, most of the specialized civilian and quasi-military career services, previously mentioned, have also had their birth and growth.

It is hard to see how the work of the federal service could get done today without the help of these management tools and career services. On the foreign front, we are now dealing with a hundred nations. We collect weather information from all over the world and from outer space. We test more new chemicals every year than were known at the beginning of our history. But while the new management tools have made this vast expansion of work and careers possible, they have also themselves created problems in the management of work and careers. Some of the newest developments in personnel management are attempts to cope with the problems created by earlier developments.

New Themes

A common theme of the latest developments in personnel administration is the rediscovery of the warm, living, breathing person—with feelings, prejudices, self-protective mechanisms, pride, and all the rest of a full assortment of psychological attributes. To some discoverers this has opened up new opportunities for getting people to work harder, be more loyal, and make less trouble. Others have become concerned about the brutalizing effects of machines and mechanical systems on tender people. The action programs stemming from the new insights run the gamut from employee welfare programs and sensitivity training for supervisors to schemes for democratic or participative management, which try to give everybody a voice in decisions which concern them and with which they are concerned. These more recent developments in personnel administration have not yet been fully adopted into the federal service.

Another recent trend is a renewed emphasis on career systems. One example is the ill-fated attempt of a decade ago to launch a senior civil service. Another is the recommendation, repeated by a series of distinguished study groups, to extend the Foreign Service system to persons engaged in foreign economic assistance and other foreign affairs.

The current emphasis on employee-centered programs and on career systems indicates a common concern with the inadequacy of the arsenal of management tools elaborated over the past century. Individually valid as these tools are in rationalizing what was previously done on a personal and highly variable basis, and indispensable as they are to the operation of large organizations, they do, nevertheless, break up the individual person and the concrete work situation into a bewildering number of pieces which, like Humpty Dumpty, never succeed in getting put together again. The feeling of unreality and irrelevance aroused by many aspects of personnel administration, a feeling which has been experienced by everyone who has ever worked in the federal government or in any other large organization, is the best testimony to this fact. And this is in spite of the fact that the acts which give rise to this feeling can usually be fully justified in terms of the specialized logic of the system to which they pertain.

Be this as it may, there is widespread recognition of the need for *systems* of personnel administration, as opposed to mere collections of management tools. This is why career systems, particularly, arouse so much current professional interest; they provide a logic which subordinates the use of the various techniques of management to a more general system, one which can accommodate most of them and which has a history of proven effectiveness, both in getting work done and in satisfying the people who get it done.

Evidence of how great is the felt need is provided by the continued interest in career systems despite a fairly general awareness of the serious problems they raise. These problems are, to repeat what has already been said several times, that career systems, in their fully developed and more effective state, can accommodate only the cream of the required work force, and that even half of that must be discarded during the span of the normal work life.

Participative management, perhaps the best term to describe a comprehensive version of the new employee-centered personnel management, is free of some of the defects of the career system, but it is also free of most of its virtues. Career systems, having adapted themselves to the changes of thousands of years, can find a definite place and function for almost everything—except all of the people. Participative management has not yet reached the point, in any widely known application at any rate, of having a settled philosophy and procedure for recruitment, job-classification, salary administration, work assignment, efficiency measurement, and so forth. Participative management, so far, is mainly a gleam in some people's eye, lacking specific form and content. There is, on the other hand, no doubt that the management of modern organizations requires above all a solution to two problems: first, to find a role for every member of the society who needs to be included, for his own well being and that of the society, in the work life of the society; and second, to tailor each individual role both to the needs, capacities, and potential of the individual and also to the requirements of the organization. This is, of course, both a statement of an ideal and a tall order, but it is not a goal which can be ignored. Solutions which appear to move away from this goal, as career systems do, may, nevertheless, be the appropriate short-run choice. Few goals can be so directly pursued as to remain at all times in sight. But if the career system route is pursued, there must be a concurrent search either for a solution to the basic inadequacies of career systems or for a long-term alternative. At the moment there is no better candidate for the long-term alternative than participative management which, even if it never succeeds in filling the whole bill, can be counted on to make significant contributions to personnel administration, in the federal service and elsewhere.

FUTURE HORIZONS FOR FEDERAL MANAGEMENT

None of the traditional problems of federal personnel administration seem to retain much urgency. Even more, it appears that most of these problems have been pretty well solved, at least in the terms in which they have traditionally been posed. There is no general lack of talent within the service to meet the current work demands. Salaries are on the way to becoming as comparable as, probably, they should be. Federal employees are as competent and well satisfied as the employees of comparable organizations; recruitment, promotion, job and salary administration, retirement systems, and so on, are being conducted with a reasonable mixture of efficiency, flexibility, and justice. Training may leave quite a bit to be desired and a lot could be done to improve the placement of present employees, especially between agencies and geographic areas; but not many other organizations do much better in these matters. Staff reductions are being carried on in several parts of the service without either excessive delay or injustice.

And yet, a reasonable solution of most of the old problems, as attested by the absence of even any loud murmurs of discontent, has led not to a happy situation but to a sort of quiet resignation in which some depart, others wait for retirement, some wait for promotion and the achievement of personal ends, but very few go to work with the hope of achieving deeply felt goals, or leave work with the sense of having accomplished something worthwhile, or live in the hope or expectation of being called upon to give of their best in a cause which appears worthy of their best.

It would be possible to cite, in apparent refutation of the above statement, a minority of federal servants who work very hard, and with an even deeper satisfaction than many of them like to admit. Among this minority are many heads of agencies and their immediate subordinates, and to this minority it must seem that the fate of the majority is of their own choosing; that, if only they were properly motivated, the members of this majority could also find more urgent tasks than hours in which to perform them. If the underworked people and overworked people were stable categories, this impression would be hard to challenge but, with a few exceptions, they are not. Program priorities rather than personalities determine who the busy people are.

Political hot-spots, economic crises, catastrophes, occasionally inventions, or scientific breakthroughs, determine priorities—that is, which programs and policies get the center of the stage and which are shunted to the wings. Heads of major agencies and those who hold power within these agencies have a good chance of staying on stage much of the time, and people who are personally known to the President and his most responsible aides may even be shifted from one hot-spot to another; but these make up only a tiny fraction of the minority who at any time are working to capacity. The rest of this minority are plucked out of the underemployed mass by the temporary exigencies of fate, and returned to the mass as the finger of fate moves on to other acts of the drama.

Their response in emergencies, to which every experienced federal official can testify, shows that there is no lack, in the vast majority of federal servants, either of idealism or of realism, of vigor or of sophistication. Most of them recognize a phony call to arms before it has left the bugle, but they also respond to a genuine call with an energy that could double or triple the output of the federal service if the response were universal. The analogy is both misleading and instructive. One of our basic problems as a nation is our failure to find a moral equivalent for war, capable of touching off a unified response in the American people. And when the people are without goals that unite them in a common cause, it is scarcely to be expected that their servants will be in a better state.

While the above statement may appear to remove the basic problem from the realm of personnel management to that of broader public policy, it does not do so entirely. For apathy and disunity are no more desired and deserved by the American public than are the apathy and disunity from which they suffer desired or deserved by federal servants. Both groups, as well as the elected leadership which forms the link between them, are enmeshed in inherited problems of the most basic and difficult character. One thing seems certain, however: If these problems can be solved at all, much of the concrete formulation of solutions must occur within the federal service. Very few of today's problems can be solved by inspiration or personal leadership alone. Almost all of them, the, political, economic, and social, as well as the scientific and engineering problems of our day, are too complex and interdependent to yield to individual genius, unaided by inspired organizational support. A creative federal service is, therefore, an indispensable part of the solution to the nation's problems and its own.

This is not to say that the federal service must look to itself alone for the solution of its problems; or to say that the nation must look mainly to the federal service for the solution of the nation's problems. It is rather to say that the major challenge to federal personnel administration today is the creation of conditions which will foster creative work in the federal service. First, because organized creative work is a necessary if not sufficient condition for the solution of the nation's problems. Second, because creative work is what federal servants need most, both to satisfy themselves and to justify their employment. Third, because creative work is also what all other Americans need most, to make their lives worthwhile to themselves and others. And, finally, because the federal service may be in the best situation to show how, in America at any rate, the large organization can be made the locus of creative, satisfying work.

These would be utopian goals if other urgent goals were in competition with them. But there are no current, urgent, competing demands on federal personnel administration, and any future crisis which brings such demands will at the same time increase the urgency of the demand for creative work.

It is harder to refute the charge of utopianism when it takes the form of asking how creative work is to be built into the federal service. It is obviously not necessary to start from scratch to build creative work into the federal service. This has been done in many places, in many ways, and for a long time. Success has nowhere been complete or permanent but neither has it been totally absent anywhere nor completely ephemeral. Besides, there is as much to be learned from failure as from success. A disturbing recent development, however, has been the acceptance of failure, as illustrated in the trend toward contracting creative work to universities and other agencies outside the federal service. It is not that all the decisions to do this have been wrong, but many of them have been made on the false assumption that creative work cannot successfully be carried on within the federal service. This is the wrong way to learn from failure; unfortunately it has been a characteristic reaction of recent years. During the war there was a placard in almost every federal office that read, "the difficult we do immediately; the impossible takes a little longer." Today we are more realistic: what cannot be done immediately we suspect of being impractical; if it takes very long it must be utopian. There are exceptions, of course, such as the projected moon shot, but most exceptions are in the physical sciences field.

It is undoubtedly impossible, at this time, for the President and Congress to commit the nation fully to really thoroughgoing, long-range programs: to eliminate poverty in the United States, to achieve equal rights for Negroes, to effectively help other nations make the transition to the industrial age, and to pursue other similar objectives. It is impossible first because the American people are not united in support of these objectives; but a second and equally valid reason is that no effective means have been outlined for their achievement—means which can be relied upon for results, of which the cost and benefits can be assessed, and which are spelled out in a series of feasible procedural steps.

It is admittedly very difficult for the federal service to work concretely and realistically on programs which have not been specifically authorized by the President and Congress. If it were impossible, however, no new programs would ever be authorized. Since there is no alternative, the difficulties involved in large-scale, concrete planning prior to political commitment must be faced. Facing them is first of all a challenge for political leadership, but political leadership cannot do enough to meet this challenge, without inspired help from experts in personnel management.

The American Assembly

The American Assembly holds meetings of national leaders and publishes books to illuminate issues of United States policy. The Assembly is a national, nonpartisan educational institution, incorporated in the State of New York.

The Trustees of the Assembly approve a topic for presentation in a background book, authoritatively designed and written to aid deliberations at national Assembly sessions at Arden House, the Harriman (N. Y.)

Campus of Columbia University. These books are also used to support discussion at regional Assembly sessions and to evoke consideration by the general public.

All sessions of the Assembly, whether international, national, or local, issue and publicize independent reports of conclusions and recommendations on the topic at hand. Since its establishment in 1950, The American Assembly has joined with over 75 educational institutions in holding these sessions. Participants constitute a wide range of experience and competence.

American Assembly books are purchased and put to use by individuals, libraries, businesses, public agencies, nongovernmental organizations, educational institutions, discussion meetings, and service groups. The subjects of Assembly studies to date are:

1951——United States—Western Europe Relations
1952——Inflation
1953——Economic Security for Americans
1954——The United States' Stake in the United Nations
——The Federal Government Service
1955——United States Agriculture
——The Forty-Eight States
1956——The Representation of the United States Abroad
——The United States and the Far East
1957——International Stability and Progress
——Atoms for Power
1958——The United States and Africa
——United States Monetary Policy
1959——Wages, Prices, Profits, and Productivity
——The United States and Latin America
1960——The Federal Government and Higher Education
——The Secretary of State
——Goals for Americans
1961——Arms Control: Issues for the Public
——Outer Space: Prospects for Man and Society
1962——Automation and Technological Change
——Cultural Affairs and Foreign Relations
1963——The Population Dilemma
——The United States and the Middle East
1964——The United States and Canada
——The Congress and America's Future
1965——The Courts, The Public and the Law Explosion
——The United States and Japan

American Assembly Books in the Spectrum Series